PINDAR.

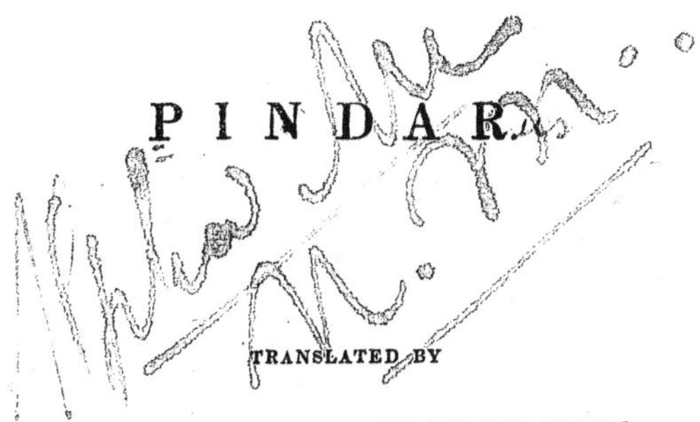

TRANSLATED BY

THE REV. C. A. WHEELWRIGHT,

PREBENDARY OF LINCOLN

AND

ANACREON.

TRANSLATED BY THOMAS BOURNE.

NEW YORK:
HARPER & BROTHERS, PUBLISHERS,
329 & 331 PEARL STREET,
FRANKLIN SQUARE.
1864.

CONTENTS.

THE NEMEAN ODES.

THE ISTHMIAN ODES

PREFACE.

THE version of Pindar's Odes which is here offered to the public was first undertaken in compliance with a suggestion contained in a critique written some years ago in the Quarterly Review; to which was annexed, by way of illustrating the plan, a metrical translation of the first two Olympic odes, in which the usual division into strophe, antistrophe, and epode was neglected, after it had been exposed in a strain of playful irony, and that into corresponding paragraphs made use of in its stead.

The versions of these two odes were afterward republished at the end of a small volume of poems by the late Bishop Heber; and this plan appeared to the author of the present translation to be so worthy of adoption, that he has been induced to go regularly through the odes in the same manner; and now submits his effort to the ordeal of public opinion.

If the sentiment of Denham, in his fine panegyric on Sir R. Fanshaw, translator of Il Paster Fido, expressed in the following lines, be well founded,

> "Nor ought a genius less than his that writ,
> Attempt translation; for transplanted wit
> All the defects of air and soil doth share,
> And colder brains like colder climates are,"

few would be sufficiently bold to grapple in verse with a poet of so sublime a genius as the Theban bard; the difficulty of transfusing whose peculiar beauties into another language can be appreciated by those alone who have attempted to preserve this poet's sublimity without soaring into empty loftiness; and to adopt his occasional free tone of diction, without degenerating into the language of colloquial familiarity: so high a degree of caution is required in the translator always to be on his guard, lest

> "Migret in obscuras humili sermone tabernas;
> Aut dum vitat humum, nubes et inania captet."
> HORAT. AD PISON. 229.

But whatever fate may attend the present version, I shall scarcely know how to repent of the temerity which urged me to the undertaking, and induced me to persevere in a labour that has furnished an agreeable occupation for many a vacant hour.

It has been my wish to give throughout my version some idea of the energetic, but rather abrupt, style and manner of an author whose language is exalted by sentiments of piety and genuine patriotism—deserved encomiums to the virtuous and brave, as well as heartfelt gratitude to his generous benefactors; whose various compositions are appealed to as authority in doubtful cases by Cicero, Pausanias, and other ancient writers quoted by the scholiast on different passages; whom Plato distinguishes by the epithets *most wise* and *divine;* who was considered by one of the early Christian fathers, Clement of Alexandria, to have been well versed in the Scriptures of the Old Testament, and to have borrowed many passages from that treasury of sacred wisdom and sublime eloquence, particularly from the Book of Proverbs; to whom, while living, honours all but divine were paid; and whose dwelling was spared, many ages after his death, in the general sack of his native city.

I have annexed a brief account of the four most celebrated games of Greece, as well as an analysis of each ode; sufficient, I trust, to show the connection of idea that often binds together the most apparently digressive of Pindar's compositions; and added occasional illustrative notes, which may be found useful in explaining historical and mythological allusions: nor shall I, perhaps, be thought too presuming in expressing a hope that the English reader may now be enabled to form a more accurate idea of the poetical character of Pindar than he has hitherto been enabled to effect.

BIOGRAPHICAL SKETCH

OF

PINDAR.

PINDAR was a native of Thebes in Bœotia, or, as some authors, among whom is the geographical writer Stephanus Byzantinus, affirm, of the town of Cynocephali, which was under the Theban jurisdiction. He was the son of the musician Scopelinus, or, according to Suidas, of Deiphantus and Myrto : his birth is stated by the same author to have taken place in the sixty-fifth Olympiad, corresponding nearly with the year 520, A.C. His parents were probably of obscure situations in life, although of illustrious descent; as he asserts in his fifth Pythian ode that they were of the same origin with Arcesilaus, king of Cyrene. It is said of Pindar when verging to manhood, that a presage of his future lyrical eminence was drawn from the circumstance of a swarm of bees having settled on his lips. For his early skill in musical and poetical composition he is said to have been chiefly indebted to the instructions of Corinna; against whom, however, when a competitor for the prize, it was his fate to be adjudged inferior in no fewer than five contests: but this perhaps is as much to be attributed to the personal charms of his fair rival as to her poetical superiority; since in the other Grecian assemblies, which did not allow of female competitors, he was almost invariably declared victorious. He also received instruction from Simonides of Ceos, at that time the most celebrated lyric poet in Greece. He was contemporary with Æschylus, and senior to Bacchylides, having flourished one hundred and fifty years later than Alcman, one hundred after Alcæus, and fifty after Stesichorus, and surpassed them all in lyrical excellence. Of his numerous compositions, consisting of hymns in honour of the gods, pæans to Apollo, dithyrambics to Bacchus, funeral songs, and odes to the victors at the four great festivals of Greece, the latter only have been preserved to us, with the exception of some considerable fragments, one especially of great poetical beauty on the solar eclipse, cited by Dionysius of Halicarnassus, and the opening verses of a fine dithyrambic hymn.

One slight effort of Pindar's juvenile muse has also escaped the ravages of time, but not sufficiently considerable to have served, like Pope's Ode on Solitude, or Cowley's Constantia and Philetus, as a presage of that future excellence which placed him, when he had attained his fortieth year, in the first rank of the lyric poets of Greece.

The encomiums which our poet often lavishes on the wealthy have sometimes been mentioned as a subject of reproach; but if Pindar's chaste and decorous muse delighted to panegyrize kings, demigods, and heroes, in common with the poets of his time, we shall not be able to find throughout his odes any instance of vice in high station flattered, or prosperous wickedness enriched by the golden dews of poetical adulation. In the sincere and judicious advice which he fearlessly bestows on Hiero or Arcesilaus, the reader will be reminded of our own Chaucer, who, in the independent spirit of true genius, concludes his "Ballade sent to King Richard" by this grave admonition to the reigning monarch:—

"Prince, desire to be honourable,
Cherish thy folk, and hate extortion," &c.

It is to the bold and animated language of the Theban bard that we are in a great measure indebted for the feeling and interest that accompany the contemplation of those magnificent festivals which, being interwoven with the structure of the popular religion, hailed by the hopes of the religious and the aspirations of the devout, have no parallel in the history of modern solemnities.

His hymns and pæans in honour of Apollo were frequently chanted in the temples of Greece by the poet, seated in his iron chair, which was afterward placed as a venerable relic in the temple at Delphi; and the priestess herself declared it to be the will of the presiding deity that Pindar should be rewarded with one half of the first fruits which were offered at his shrine.*

We are not acquainted with many particulars of his early life, but may collect from the accounts of various authors that the character of the living bard was held in the highest degree of estimation, especially by King Hiero, and his memory after death contemplated with the deepest reverence. It is related of him that he had a particular devotion for the god Pan, and therefore took up his abode near the temple of that deity. He was appointed to compose the hymns which were sung by the Theban virgins in honour of that mystic emblem of universal nature. It also appears from Pyth. iii., 139, that near the dwelling of Pindar stood a shrine or chapel dedicated to the great goddess Rhea, where the nymphs were wont to assem-

* See the note on the tenth Olympic ode, line 61.

ble at the close of day for the purpose of performing their vows to her and to Pan. We further learn from Aristodemus, quoted by the scholiast on this passage, that Pindar himself raised this shrine to the venerable Mother of the Gods. He likewise cites a fragment of an ode or choral hymn addressed to Pan by our poet, invoking that deity, as president of Arcadia, and companion of the nymphs in their dances, to smile propitiously on his songs. Indeed, the piety of the Theban bard is everywhere conspicuous, and worthy of admiration. It is related by Plutarch, in his Life of Alexander, that when, after a most determined and vigorous defence, the city of Thebes was levelled to the ground by that conqueror, the posterity of Pindar were exempted from the hard fate which attended his captive fellow-townsmen.

The same honour had on a former occasion been paid to the habitation of his descendants by the Lacedæmonians; and Pausanias, the Grecian traveller, relates that he had seen the ruins of this house near the fountain Dirce.

The manner of Pindar's death has been variously related by different authors. Pausanias gravely records as authentic the traditionary tale, that while our poet was living in the height of honour and glory, Proserpine appeared to him in a dream, and complained that she alone of all the deities had been neglected in his poems: this defect he promised to supply as soon as he should arrive in the kingdom of Pluto, when he would consecrate a hymn to her honour; and that he died either in the theatre or the gymnasium on the tenth day after his dream.

Another account, by Valerius Maximus, (b. ix., c. 12,) is so far removed from all recorded instances of the departure of illustrious men from the world, as naturally to excite the skepticism of the reader —although it is mentioned by that author as a sign of the favourable regard of the gods, no less than the excellence of his poetic faculty. This event is said to have taken place when the poet had attained the advanced age of eighty-six years. A monument was erected to his memory in the hippodrome at Thebes, near the Prœtæan Gate, at the distance of a furlong from the city, and an inscription engraved on it, recording his candid and agreeable manners both to his fellow-townsmen and to strangers.

The reader will perhaps not be displeased if to this short biographical sketch is added, from Heyne's excellent edition, a life of Pindar digested according to the order of years, together with a notice of the victors who are celebrated in his odes.

Olymp. 65,1, A.C. 520, Pindar born.

[Suidas says that he was forty years of age at the battle of Salamis, which account agrees with this.]

Æt.	Olymp.	Pyth.	A C.	
22	70,3	22	498	Hippocleas victor—Pyth. x.
30	72,3	24	490	Xenocrates—Pyth. vi. Battle of Marathon. In the same, or in the 25th Pythiad, Midas gains the prize on the flute—Pyth. xii.
32	73,1		488	Epharmostus—Ol. ix.
36	74,1		484	Agesidamus—Ol. x. and xi.
40	75,1		480	Battle of Salamis.
42	75,3	27	478	Hiero conquers in racing—Pyth. iii.
44	76,1		476	Asopichus—Ol. xiv.
46	76,3	28	474	Megacles—Pyth. vii.—Telesicrates—Pyth. ix.
48	77,1		472	Theron—Ol. ii. and Ergoteles—Ol. xii.
50	77,3	29	470	Hiero in the chariot race—Pyth. i.
54	78,3	30	466	Telesicrates—Pyth. ix.
56	79,1		464	Xenophon in the stadic course—Ol. xiii.
58	79,3	31	462	Arcesilaus—Pyth. iv. and v.
60	80,1		460	Alcimedon—Ol. viii.
66	81,3	33	454	Thrasydæus—Pyth. xi.
68	82,1		452	Psaumis—Ol. iv. and v.
74	83.3	35	446	Aristomenes—Pyth. viii.

This, according to Corsini, (Fast. Att.) is the year of Pindar's death, which however is by different authors assigned to various years between the 79th and 87th Olympiad.*

* The various themes on which his prolific muse was employed are thus enumerated by Horace, in his ode beginning "Pindarum quisquis," &c.; which it may not displease the English reader to peruse in the paraphrase of our excellent Cowley:—

"Whether th' immortal gods he sings
In a no less immortal strain,
Or the great acts of god-descended kings,
Who in his numbers still survive and reign;
Whether in Pisa's race he please
To carve in polish'd verse the conqueror's images;
Whether some brave man's untimely fate
In words worth dying for he celebrate;
Such mournful and such pleasing words,
As joy to his mother's and his mistress' grief affords."

THE OLYMPIC ODES.

OF THE OLYMPIC GAMES.

THE Olympic Games, the most illustrious of all in Greece, take their name from Olympia, a city of Elis, the place of their celebration; or from having been instituted by Hercules in honour of Jupiter Olympius, after a victory obtained over Augeas, tyrant of Elis, B. C. 1222. They were held at the full moon on the first month of every fifth year, and lasted five days, as appears from Ol. v., 15. *πεμπταμεροις εν ἁμιλλαις.*

According to some authors the date of their institution was B.C. 1453. After a long interval of neglect they were reinstituted B.C. 776, in which year Chorœbus obtained the victory; and from this time the era of the Olympiads is usually dated.

The exercises at these games consisted of running, wrestling, leaping, throwing the discus, and boxing with the cæstus; which were altogether called by the name *πενταθλον*, or quinquertium, and comprehended in the well-known Greek verse:

ἁλμα, ποδωκειην, δισκον, ακοντα, παλην.

The reward of the victor was a crown of the wild olive-tree, called (Ol. iv., 19,) *ελαια Πισατις*: which, according to the mythological story, had been transplanted at Olympia by Hercules from the hyperborean regions; which fable is related at large in the third Olympic ode. Besides the five contests mentioned above, there were at these games horse and chariot races, and contentions in poetry, eloquence, and the fine arts. They were celebrated with every mark of solemnity: the preparations for the festival were very great: none but persons of unblemished character were allowed to present themselves as combatants; and they were attended by spectators from every part of Greece. Near the goal of the stadium was placed the semicircular seat of the Olympic judges, who were called *hellanodici*; and behind them was the large tract of land known by the name of Altis: for a description of which see the note on Ol. x., 62.

THE FIRST OLYMPIC ODE.

TO HIERO, KING OF SYRACUSE, VICTOR IN THE SINGLE-HORSE RACE IN THE SEVENTY-THIRD OLYMPIAD.

ARGUMENT.

In this ode Pindar, who, together with other bards, was probably at this time a guest at the royal table, sets forth in a beautiful strain of poetry the glory and superiority of the Olympic contest, in which Hiero has been victorious, to all other games; he then digresses to the history of Pelops, son of Tantalus, who formerly possessed Pisa and Olympia, and is now honoured as a hero within the sacred grove Altis. Returning to his principal subject, he concludes the ode with good wishes for the continued prosperity of the victor.

Note.—The inner number, placed at the end of the several paragraphs, shows the corresponding line of the original.

Water with purest virtue flows;
And as the fire's resplendent light
Dispels the murky gloom of night,
The meaner treasures of the mine
With undistinguish'd lustre shine
    Where gold irradiate glows.

1 In the Thalesian philosophy water was considered the most excellent of all the elements, as that to which all other things owed their origin. This opinion Plutarch (de Iside et Osiride) considers that Homer as well as Thales borrowed from the Egyptians. Juno, in the Iliad, b. xiv., v. 200, tells Venus, and afterward repeats it to Jupiter, that she came to visit the extremities of the earth, and *Ocean, the progenitor of the gods, and their mother Tethys.*

Thus too when flames the orb of day
The anxious eye in vain would soar
Along the desert air,
Intently gazing to explore
Another star whose lustre fair
Shines with a warmer ray.
And we will sing in loftiest strain
The contest of Olympia's plain;
Whence, Saturn's mighty son to praise,
Poets the hymn of triumph raise,
To Hiero's festal dome who bend their way. 17

The monarch whose supreme command
In Sicily's prolific land
The righteous sceptre sways,
Culling the pride of every flower
That blooms in Virtue's hallow'd bower;
A wreath of highest praise.
While music adds a brighter gem
To gild the regal diadem,
When poets' sportive songs around
His hospitable board resound. 26

Then from its lofty station freed
Quickly seize the Dorian lyre,
If Pisa or the victor steed,
Ne'er doom'd beneath the scourge to bleed
The mind with sweetest cares inspire.
When by Alpheus urged, his flight
Exalts his lord with conquering might,
In Syracuse who holds his reign,
And loves the generous horse to train. 36
Such too his fame and lustre high
From Lydian Pelops' colony;

38 A temple was erected to Pelops in the Altis, or sacred grove, which had been fenced from profane tread by Hercules, (see Ol. x, 62.) near to that of Jupiter at Olympia. Hence the

Whom earth-encircling Neptune loved,
When from the glowing caldron's round,
His arm with ivory shoulder crown'd,
Clotho the newborn youth removed.
So much to fabled lore we trace—
For wrapp'd in varied falsehood's veil
Full oft the legendary tale
Can win to faith the mortal mind,
While truth's unvarnish'd maxims fail
To leave her stamp behind.

When from poetic tongue
The honey'd accents fall,
Howe'er from monstrous fiction sprung,
They win their unsuspected way,
And grace disguises all,
Till some far-distant day
Render the dark illusion plain.
Yet not to mortal lips be given
By tales unworthy to profane
The majesty of Heaven.

Offspring of Tantalus! my strain
A different story shall record;
How to the genial board
Thy father call'd each heavenly guest,
To share the blameless feast,
With grateful hands upon the head
Of his dear Sipylus outspread.

'Twas then, by fond desire subdued,
Thy form the trident bearer view'd,

story of Pelops is less episodical, and has a closer connection with the poet's subject than might at first appear.

Within the precincts of the Altis was planted the sacred olive tree, called callistephanos, from which victors in the Olympic games were crowned.

65 It was on the top of this mountain that, in a later age,

And whirl'd thee on his golden steeds above
To the high palace of immortal Jove;
Where Ganymede in days of yore
The same illustrious office bore. 71

But when the long inquiring train
Had sought their absent charge in vain
To his fond mother to restore,
The slanderous whisper circled round
That in the fervid wave profound,
Hewn by the sword, his limbs were cast,
And to the lords of heaven supplied a sweet repast!

But far the impious thought from me
To tax the bless'd with gluttony;
For well I know that pains await
The lips that slanderous tales relate.
If the great gods who on Olympus dwell
High favour e'er on man bestow'd
Above the undistinguish'd crowd,
To Tantalus the lot of honour fell.
But ah! too feeble to digest
The raptures of the heavenly feast,
His haughty soul incensed to ire
The might of his immortal sire;
Who o'er his head a massy rock
Suspended, that with direful shock

Niobe, the daughter of Tantalus, melted away into her shower of snowy tears. See the exquisite description of Sophocles—(Antig. 824—833.;) also that of Ovid—(Met. vi. 301—312.)

87 Hesiod (Theog. 638, et seq.) declares that the same effects of pride and insolence were wrought on the minds of the Titans after they had been allowed to partake of the divine aliments:—

"Their spirits nectar and ambrosia raise."
Cooke's Version.

Might not this fable, which is also related, almost in the words of Pindar, by the scholiast on the Odyssey, (iv. 58.,) owe its origin to some obscure tradition of the gathering of manna by the Israelites in the wilderness, when *man did eat angels' food?*

92 Lucretius, in his magnificent description of infernal pun

Threatens to crush him from on high,
And scare his proud felicity. 94

Thus still in unavailing strife
He drags a weary load of life,
The fourth sad instance of destructive pride
Whose hand th' ambrosial food convey'd
(Which had himself immortal made)
To earthly guests beside.
Then hope not, mortal, e'er to shun
The penetrating eye of Heaven;
For lo! the rash offender's son
Far from the happy haunts is driven
To join his kindred shortlived train,
And wander o'er the earth again. 108

But when the thick and manly down
His black'ning chin began to crown,
From Pisa's lord he seeks to prove
Highborn Hippodamia's love.
Full often near the hoary flood
The solitary lover stray'd,
And shrouded in nocturnal shade,
Invoked the trident-bearing god;
Who, ready the loud call to greet,
Stood near the youthful suppliant's feet—

ishments (iii. 991, seq.,) appears to have had this passage in his mind, when he says,

"Nec miser impendens magnum timet, aëre, saxum
Tantalus, ut fama est, cassa formidine torpens;
Sed magis in vita Divom metus urguet."

Our own Spenser, too, has the same allusion, speaking of old Malbeceo, who lives

"In drery darkenes, and continuall feare
Of that rock's fall; which ever and anon
Threates with huge ruine him to fall upon,
That he dare never slepee."

Faery Queene.

97 The other three being Sisiphus, Tityus, and Ixion.

When thus he spoke: "If fond desire,
Neptune, could e'er thy bosom fire,
Œnomaus' brazen spear restrain,
And whirl me on thy swiftest car
Victorious to th' Elean plain,
Since conquer'd in the rival war
Thirteen ill-fated suitors lie,
And still the sire delays his daughter's nuptial tie.

Nor think I bear a coward soul
Which every danger can control;
Since all the common path must tread
That leads each mortal to the dead,
Say wherefore should inglorious age
Creep slow o'er youth's inactive bloom,
And sinking in untimely gloom,
Should man desert life's busy stage
To lie unhonour'd in the tomb?
This strife be mine: and thou, whose might
Can bless the issue of the fight,
Oh! grant me thy propitious aid."
'Twas thus the ardent lover pray'd;
Nor sued with supplication vain
The mighty ruler of the main;
Who, mounted on his golden car,
And steeds' unwearied wing
Gave him to conquer in the war
The force of Pisa's king.
Obtaining thus the virgin fair,
Her valiant hero's couch to share;
From whom six noble chieftains born,
With warlike fame their stem adorn:
Now by Alpheus' stream he lies,
Bless'd with funereal obsequies,

123 The same number of Trojans are related by Homer to have been slain by Diomed in his celebrated night expedition, (Il. x. 493, &c.,) the last of whom is Rhesus himself.

The scholiast on this passage gives us two catalogues of their names.

And every rite divine;
Where strangers' feet innumerous tread
The precincts of the mighty dead,
Is rear'd his hallow'd shrine.
At distance beams his glory's ray
Conspicuous in Olympia's fray,
Where strength and swiftness join in arduous strife:
And round the victor's honour'd head
The verdant wreath of conquest spread,
Heightens with bliss the sweet remains of life. 159

Such bliss as mortals call supreme,
Which with its mild, perpetual beam
Cheers every future day:
And such my happy lot to grace
His triumphs in the equestrian race
With soft Æolian lay.
Nor will the muse another find
Among the bless'd of human kind
More potent or in regal fame,
Or arts that raise a monarch's name,
For whom she rather would prolong
The rich varieties of song.
The god who makes thy cares his own,
Thee, Hiero, still with favour crown.
And soon, if his protecting love
Not vain and transitory prove,
I hope to find on Cronium's sunny height
A sweeter vehicle of song
To publish, as it rolls along,
Thy rapid chariot's flight.
For me the muse with vigorous art
Prepares her most puissant dart. 179

165 I. e. Dorian; for the Dorians and Æolians were descended from a common origin: see v. 30.

176 Pausanias (1. vi.) informs us that the Cronian or Saturnian hill at Olympia rose above the Altis, so as to command a full view of the course.

While men in various paths their efforts bend
The steep of glory to ascend,
Sublime above the rest on high
Glitters the orb of majesty.
No further then thy wishes raise,
Supreme in glory as in praise,
Long be it thine to tread:
Meanwhile my hymn's triumphant strain,
That celebrates the victor train,
Exalts through Greece thy bard's illustrious head.

THE SECOND OLYMPIC ODE.

TO THERON OF AGRIGENTUM, (IN GREEK ACRAGAS,) ON HIS VICTORY IN THE CHARIOT RACE, GAINED IN THE SEVENTY-SEVENTH OLYMPIAD.

ARGUMENT.

THE poet congratulates Theron, sprung from ancestors who had experienced much adversity, though sometimes attended with better fortune—extols him for his skill in the contests, his unsparing expense in bringing them to a happy issue, and the right use to which he applies his great wealth, assuring him that the recompense of his virtuous dispositions will attend him after death: this leads to a most noble description of the infernal and Elysian abodes. Returning from this digression, which he defends from the carping malignity of his detractors, Pindar concludes with the praises of Theron

---

Ye hymns that rule the vocal lyre,
What god, what hero shall we sing?
What mortal shall the strain inspire?
Jove is fair Pisa's guardian king;
And Hercules Olympia's glorious toil
Ordain'd the first fruits of the battle spoil.
Theron too demands my strain,
Whose four-yoked steeds in triumph sweep the plain. 9

The hospitable, just, and great,
Bulwark of Agrigentum's state,
Of his high stem the flower of fairest pride. 14
Who by their long afflictions toss'd,
Regain'd their sacred mansion lost,
Upon the kindred tide.

14 The river Acragas, on which the city of Agrigentum situated. (See the opening of the twelfth Pythian ode.)

Of every care they found at last
    A sweet and tranquil close,
A balm for every danger past,
    A haven of repose.
And hence to fair Sicilia springs
Her long illustrious line of kings,
Whose happy life and wealth their native virtues wait.

Oh Rhea's son, Saturnian Jove,
Lord of th' Olympic seats above,
Whose favouring power the victor gave
To triumph by Alpheus' wave,
Still to their latest offspring bear
These gifts of thy paternal care.
Not Time himself, the sire of all,
By mortal or immortal power
The deed perform'd can e'er recall:
But sweet oblivion of the gloomy hour
Succeeds when joy's enlivening train
Scatt'ring the melancholy gloom,
Bid the light heart its wonted ease resume,
And Heaven's o'erruling lord emits his bliss again.

Cadmus, thy daughters' wayward fate 36
    This moral truth can prove,
Who changed their suffering mortal state
    For happy thrones above.
Fair Semele, of flowing tresses vain,
By the loud blast of thunder slain,
Her joyful recompense can boast,
And lives among th' Olympic host.

36 Cadmus was an ancestor of Theron, and therefore his daughters, Ino, who was married to Athamas, king of Thebes, and whose story is finely told by Ovid, in the fourth book of the Metamorphoses, and Semele, the concubine of Jove, are judiciously selected by the poet to illustrate the mutability of human fortune, while at the same time they show the antiquity and regal splendour of the monarch's descent.

Now Pallas sooths the happy fair
With everlasting love,
The ivy-circled stripling's care,
And fond delight of Jove.

Bless'd too, as ancient tales agree,
Is Ino's alter'd destiny.
Their forms where sister Nereids lave
With them at large to stray,
And sport amid the ocean wave
Her happy hours away.

Then let not vain presumptuous man
Seek with unhallow'd eye to scan
Th' irrevocable doom;
If clouds invest his final day,
Or Heaven shall gild with cheerful ray
The darkness of the tomb.
For bliss and sorrow with alternate flow,
Sway the uncertain tide of life below.

'Twas thus the fates' supreme command
Which bless'd old Laius' regal line
With power and happiness divine,
In after times decreed the blow
That plunged their hapless race in wo.
Impell'd the parricidal hand
Which struck the Theban monarch's breast,
Perfecting the decree in Pythian gloom express'd.

With sharpen'd eye's avenging speed
Erinnys view'd the murderous deed,
And soon by mutual slaughter gave
The warlike brothers to the grave.
Surviving Polynices' doom,
Thersander bade in times to come
Adrastus' house revive again,
First in each youthful sport, and in the strife of men.

Then justly, noble king, to thee,
Ænesidemus' progeny,
Thy willing poet's lyre shall raise
The tributary song of praise. 86

Alone in the Olympic sand
    The victor's crown he wore;
But when upon the Pythian strand,
    As on the Isthmian shore,
Twelve times his steeds the destined bound
The car triumphant whirl'd around,
The social Graces who decree
Each high reward of victory,
To his loved brother's head the wreath of conquest
        bore. 93

This honour'd guerdon to obtain
Has power to free from mental pain.
Such bliss the envied wealth of kings,
When crown'd by patient labour brings,
    And emulation's flame.
True star of glory! given to cheer
The clouds that hang on life's career,
    And gild the path to fame.
But let the proud oppressor know
What torments in the world below

79 Ænesidemus, the father of Theron, was the seventh in lineal descent from Thersander.

100 These are concisely enumerated by the learned Propertius: (l. III., v. 39, sqq.:)—

" Sub terris si jura Deum, et tormenta gigantum,
    Tisiphones atro si furit angue caput;
Aut Alcmæoniæ furiæ, aut jejunia Phinei;
    Num rota, num scopuli, num sitis inter aquas," &c.

Tibullus also (Eleg. I. iii. 58.) poetically contrasts the joys of Elysium with the pains of Tartarus:—

" Ipsa Venus campos ducet ad Elysios.
Hic choreæ cantusque vigent;—
At scelerata jacet sedes in nocte profunda

The harden'd soul await.
By Jove's command what judges there
From stern necessity declare
The fix'd decrees of fate. 108

Where beams of everlasting day
Through night's unclouded season play,
Free from mortality's alloy,
The good shall perfect bliss enjoy.
They nor with daring hands molest
Earth's torn and violated breast,
Nor search the caverns of the main
An empty being to sustain;
But with the honour'd gods, whose ear
The faithful vow delights to hear,
Shall be their tearless age of rest;
While pangs of aspect dire distract the impious train. 122

But they whose spirit thrice refined
Each arduous contest could endure,
And keep the firm and perfect mind
From all contagion pure;

Abdita, quam circum flumina nigra sonant.
Tisiphoneque impexa feros pro crinibus angues
Sævit, et huc illuc impia turba fugit," &c.

105 One might almost imagine that Pindar had taken this sentiment from a passage in the book of Proverbs (iv. 18, 19)—

"The path of the just is as the shining light, that shineth more and more unto the perfect day.
"The way of the wicked is as darkness."

117 According to the scholiast, Pindar in this passage follows the Pythagorean doctrine of the metempsychosis, and reserves the beautiful Elysium of the blessed islands to those who have passed with the divine approbation through the two conditions of mortality, on and beneath the earth. With this whole description of the Elysian and Tartarian abodes, compare Hesiod; (Op. et Dies. 225.;) where, however, the paradise of the just, as well as the opposite residence of those who delight in violence and wrong, is terrestrial.

Along the stated path of Jove
To Saturn's royal courts above
Have trod their heavenly way,
Where round the island of the bless'd
The ocean breezes play;
There golden flow'rets ever blow,
Some springing from earth's verdant breast,
These on the lonely branches glow,
While those are nurtured by the waves below.
From them the inmates of these seats divine
Around their hands and hair the woven garlands
twine.

Such Rhadamanthus' just decree,
Who sits by Father Saturn's side,
Where with his all-possessing bride
Rhea, supreme he holds his court.
In those high ranks Peleus and Cadmus shine,
And to the blissful seats above
The prayer of Thetis won the breast of Jove
To waft the scion of her line,
Achilles, whose resistless might
The pride and hope of Troy o'erthrew,
Hector, till then unconquer'd, slew;
Till then th' unshaken pillar of the fight.
Cycnus the hero gave to death,
Aurora's Æthiop son to him resign'd his breath.

Full many a sharp and potent dart
That shows unspent the poet's art,
And to the wise sounds clear and shrill,
Rests in my well-stored quiver still.
But minds untaught some guide will need
Safe through the mystic paths to lead;

143 So Catullus, addressing Peleus, says,
"Thessaliæ columen Peleu."—*De Nupt. Pel. et Thet.* 26.
145 Memnon

While witlings learn'd with empty sound
Like crows pursue their ceaseless round,
That through the airy plains above
Track the majestic bird of Jove. 158
Then take, my soul, thy fearless aim—
Drawn from the quiet storehouse say
To whom thine arrows wing their way
Along the path of fame?
Far as proud Agrigentum's height
Should they direct their devious flight,
If sworn to truth, I will declare
That in the hundred years whose course hath fled
O'er her imperial head,
No heart more friendly, no more liberal hand
Than Theron's, who now sways the subject land,
Hath held dominion there. 173

Yet Insolence her voice will raise
Unjust to thwart the monarch's praise,
And Envy's rancorous tongue invade,
Casting his merits into shade.
Howe'er the base malignant crew
His name with violence pursue,
If thou wouldst all his generous deeds explore,
As soon the sandy grains thy tongue shall number o'er. 180

175 So Catullus: (ad Lesbiam:)—

"Quam magnus numerus Libyssæ arenæ
Laserpiciferis jacet Cyrenis,
Oraclum Jovis inter æstuosi,
Et Batti veteris sacrum sepulchrum:
* * * * * * *
Quæ nec pernumerare curiosi
Possint."

THE THIRD OLYMPIC ODE.

TO THE SAME THERON, ON OCCASION OF A VICTORY OBTAINED BY HIM IN THE CHARIOT RACE: THE DATE IS NOT RECORDED.

ARGUMENT.

This ode was addressed to the King of Agrigentum, to whom the victory was announced as he was celebrating the Theoxenia: (a festival in honour of all the gods, instituted by the inhabitants of Pallene, or, according to the mythological story, by Castor and Pollux.) Pindar therefore begins by invoking the aid and approbation of the Dioscuræ and their sister Helen—thence on the mention of the olive wreath he digresses to the fable of Hercules transplanting the wild olive tree from the Hyperborean regions to Olympia He concludes by congratulating Theron, who had attained the highest point of human glory, and attributes his success to the favour of the twin deities, influenced by his piety and the regularity with which he celebrated the festival of the gods: the attempt to proceed farther would be as vain as the endeavour to sail beyond the Pillars of Hercules, the supposed boundary of the old world.

To please the hospitable pair
From godlike Tyndarus who spring,
And Helen, nymph of lovely hair,
I would awake th' Olympic string,
And raise the lyric song, to crown
Bright Agrigentum with renown,
And Theron's glories sing,
Whose steeds' unwearied feet achieve the guerdon fair.

1 This epithet, as West observes, is very appropriately bestowed on the Dioscuri, Castor and Pollux, on account of the establishment, by them, of the Theoxenia, a feast to which the

Then may the muse her bard inspire,
Who first upon the Dorian lyre
Raised the melodious strain on high
To swell the pomp of victory. 10

The verdant wreaths that proudly glow
Round the triumphant courser's mane,
Call on the shrill-toned flute to flow,
The varied lyre and well-connected strain.
Which may a due encomium raise
Ænesidamus' son to praise. 16

And Pisa joins the general claim—
From her proceeds the song of fame,
To whom the umpire's just decree
Awards the meed of victory.
Prompt to fulfil Alcides' high command,
Who bade the verdant olive glow
Twined by th' Ætolian judge's hand
Around the conqueror's brow. 22
Which erst Amphitryo's godlike son
From Ister's shady fountains bore.
The fairest mark of triumph won
By victor on Olympia's shore.
Gift of the Hyperborean race,
Who worship in Apollo's fane,

gods were invited. With the opening of this ode compare Euripides, Orestes, sub fin.

Ἑλενην Ζηνος μελαθροις πελασω, κ. τ. λ.

We may observe that the praises of Agrigentum are a favourite theme of Pindar's grateful muse.

18 Thomson, in his Castle of Indolence, (ii. 13.,) says of his Knight of Arts and Industry, that

With varied fire
He roused the trumpet and the martial fife,
Or bade the lute sweet tenderness inspire,
Or verses framed that well might wake Apollo's lyre.

31 It would be tedious and not very edifying to the reader to detail the various opinions of the ancients respecting the geo

The plant which shades that hallow'd place
His voice persuasive could obtain;
Where Jupiter's tall grove a shelter gave
Common to all mankind, and chaplets to the brave.

For now to his great father's name
Perform'd was every sacred rite;
And when the full-orb'd lamp of night
Pour'd from her golden car the severing flame,
He gave each fifth revolving year,
Where falls Alpheus' high career,
To judge the well-earn'd meed of fame. [39]

But in Saturnian Pelops' vale
No trees waved beauteous to the gale—
No verdant grove, no depth of shade
The raging solar beam allay'd;
His mind impell'd him then to go
Where Ister's streams through Scythian regions flow;
Latona's huntress daughter there
Received the hero as he came
From Arcady's deep glens and summits fair.

graphical position of the Hyperboreans: some placing them in Europe and others in Asia; nay, they have been said to dwell within the polar circle, in a fruitful and temperate clime, free from all *skyey influences* of an adverse and malignant nature. In Olymp. viii. 70, Pindar says that the Ister flows through the land of Scythia. Hence this northern El Dorado would be situated in a latitude above the equator, as high as that of the modern Siberia. But nothing can be more vague and undefined than the notions of antiquity respecting the limits of the Ister and the territories of the Scythians. In the sixth Isthmian ode, v. 36, Pindar appears to consider the Nile and the Hyperborean regions as the northern and southern extremities of the habitable globe. It appears that the sacred olive which the Theban Hercules is fabled to have transplanted from their regions grew somewhere above the fountains of the Ister or Danube. The tenth Pythian ode contains a poetical description of the fertility and blessedness of these Utopian regions.

39 The Olympic games were celebrated on the day nearest to

When, as Eurystheus' will was told,
Necessity from Father Jove
To bring the hind with horns of gold
His persecuted offspring drove:
Which erst, in sacred pomp array'd,
Taygeta had given to please th' Orthosian maid. 54

This as he urged in warm pursuit,
His eyes survey'd the region there
Which chilling Boreas render'd bare,
Admiring the tall olive's shoot;
Then sweet desire possess'd his soul
To plant the consecrated root
Around the twelve-times circled goal.
And now to crown the solemn feast,
The hero comes, propitious guest,
With deep-zoned Leda's twinborn pair.
To them the glorious charge he gave,
Ascending to Olympus' height,
To fix the contest's laws, and crown the brave
Who sped his victor car, or won the palm of might. 67

Then justly noble Theron's fame
My mind exhorts me to proclaim;
And sing th' Emmenidæs' high race,
Whom Jove's equestrian offspring grace
With honours and rewards divine,
So bright their virtuous actions shine.
By them the sacred rites are paid,
By them the liberal banquet laid
With more abundant plenty stored
Than often crowns a mortal board. 74

the full moon of that month, the new moon of which immediately followed the summer solstice.

58 I. e. Diana: so named from her salutary obstetrical influence, or from a mountain of Arcadia.

The younger scholiast gives a long account of the reason why this stag with gilded horns was offered to Diana, who had benevolently metamorphosed into the form of that animal Taygeta, the daughter of Atlas.

If water then and shining gold
The rank of highest glory hold,
Even thus has virtuous Theron gain'd
The farthest point by man attain'd.
His fame has reach'd that distant land
Where the Herculean pillars stand.
Beyond this point who strives to sail,
Wise or unwise, can ne'er prevail—
No farther I pursue—my course is here restrain'd. 81

THE FOURTH OLYMPIC ODE.

TO PSAUMIS OF CAMARINA, ON HIS VICTORY WITH THE QUADRIGÆ, OR CHARIOT WITH FOUR HORSES, GAINED IN THE EIGHTY-SECOND OLYMPIAD.

ARGUMENT.

THIS ode opens with a sublime invocation to Jupiter, and a prayer for Psaumis.—The poet then proceeds to the praise of the victor, on account of his hospitality, love of peace, patriotism, and the care he bestows on the training of his horses.—Subjoins the story of Erginus, the son of Clymenus, as an excuse for the premature whiteness of his hair.

THY circling hours, immortal Jove,
Who mak'st th' unwearied lightnings move,
With song and lyre's accordant string
Rouse me the victor's praise to sing.
When friends succeed, the good rejoice,
And hail the sweet-toned herald's voice.

Oh son of Saturn!—thou who rul'st above
Where Ætna with his burning load impress'd
Weighs down the hundred-handed Typhon's breast,
Deign with thy favour to approve
This hymn which to the victor's praise address'd,
Aspires to crown th' Olympic strife,
That gilds with glory's beam the latest hour of life.

High on his car triumphant placed,
His brows with Pisa's olive graced,
Lo! Psaumis brings the meed of fame
To raise his Camarina's name.

The god who joys to bless thee now,
Propitious hear each future vow! 22

Him shall my constant praise await,
Who skill'd to train the generous steed,
To every guest unfolds his gate,
And tranquil aids his native state
Nurtured to each pacific deed.
No falsehood e'er shall stain my lay,
Experience proves the man, and will his worth display. 30

From taunts by Lemnian women made,
This Clymenus' brave offspring freed.
The course, in brazen arms array'd,
He left to take the victor's meed,
And thus Hypsipyle address'd :—
" 'Tis I who gain the palm of speed,
Mine the firm hand, th' undaunted breast—
Howe'er upon my youthful brow
Are shed untimely hues of snow." 42

28 Erginus, one of the Argonauts, who, on their departure for the golden fleece, contended at Lemnos in the funeral games instituted by Hypsipyle in memory of her father Thaos, king of the island. He is mentioned by Statius (Theb. ix. 305.) among the heroes killed by Hippomedon, who, in imitation of Achilles, rushes into the Ismenus, and dies its waves with slaughter. Erginus's complaint of his premature gray hairs may be parodied by Boethius (de Consol. Philos. i. 11.) Intempestivi funduntur vertice cani. Hesiod (Op. et Dies, 181.) mentions as a mark of the iron race that they are gray headed from their birth.

THE FIFTH OLYMPIC ODE.

TO THE SAME PSAUMIS, ON HIS THREE VICTORIES, ONE IN THE CHARIOT DRAWN BY FOUR HORSES; ANOTHER IN THE APENE, OR CHARIOT DRAWN BY MULES; AND THE THIRD IN THE SINGLE-HORSE RACE—ALL GAINED IN THE EIGHTY-SECOND OLYMPIAD.

ARGUMENT.

The poet in this ode invocates Camarina, a sea nymph, from whom the town and lake in Sicily were fabled to have taken their name; to bespeak her favourable acceptance of the hymn in which are celebrated the three victories of Psaumis; whom he also commends for his liberality and patriotism.—Concludes by supplicating Jupiter to grant continued prosperity to the victor, and expressing his own good wishes towards him.

Daughter of Ocean! this sweet strain,
Which Psaumis' lofty virtues wake,
Whose mules untired glide o'er Olympia's plain,
And victory's fairest chaplet gain,
With mind propitious take. 7

Eager to grace with high renown,
Oh Camarina! thy well-peopled town;
To the bright rulers of the skies
He bade the six twin altars rise,
And spread to each celestial guest
Of oxen slain the liberal feast;
Five times the sun's diurnal blaze
Each well-contested strife surveys,
The strong-yoked chariot's conquering speed,
Drawn by fleet mule or generous steed;

Or where impatient of control
The courser presses to the goal.
Thy mighty combatant to thee
Conveys the meed of victory,
That bids the herald's loud acclaim
Ioin with thy new-built walls his father Acron's name. 19

From Pelops' and Œnomaus' pleasant seat,
Oh Pallas! our loved city's guardian pride,
The victor comes with festal hymn to greet
Thy solemn grove and fair Oanus' tide,
The native lake, the sacred source
Whence Hipparis directs his course,
And pours, the thirsting host to lave,
Through long canals his fruitful wave,
Transported down whose rapid tide
Beams for the stable fabrics glide,
When Psaumis rears the wondrous pile,
Lightens his country's woes, and renovates her smile.
But labour still and cost his steps attend,
Whose virtue strives to gain this glorious end,
Around his path uncertain hazards wait, 36
And clouds obscure the mighty combat's fate—
Yet when his persevering toils succeed,
A nation's voice confirms the wisdom of the deed. 38

Hear, earth's protecting sovereign, Jove,
Who dwell'st enthron'd in clouds above,
And on the Cronian mount—whose care
Alpheus' widely flowing wave,
And Ida's venerable cave
Protects, oh hear thy suppliant's prayer!—
Who, breathing on his Lydian reed,
Implores thee still to crown this state with valour's meed.
Oh Psaumis! victor in th' Olympic strife,
Who mak'st Neptunian steeds thy joy and pride,

May placid age attend thy closing life,
Thy children standing round to grace a father's side!

Of fortune's ample stores possess'd,
And with fair reputation bless'd,
No higher let thy wishes rise,
  Since all that mortals gain is thine,
Nor madly try to reach the skies,
  Ambitious of a lot divine.

THE SIXTH OLYMPIC ODE.

TO AGESIAS OF SYRACUSE, ON HIS VICTORY IN THE CHARIOT DRAWN BY MULES.

ARGUMENT.

The scholiast informs us that this ode, according to some, was inscribed to Stymphelius, son of Sostratus, and that his victory was achieved in the eighty-sixth or eighty-seventh Olympiad. —The poem opens with a noble simile drawn from the frontispiece of a building, to which he compares the opening of his ode, expatiating on the glory of the Olympic contest.—He then proceeds to mention the praises and regret expressed by Adrastus on Amphiaraus, occasioned by the death of the latter; instituting a comparison between Agesias and the Theban seer.—The birth of Iamus, one of the ancestors of the victor, who are thence called Iamidæ, is then related at great length, together with the story of Evadne, daughter of Æpytus.—Agesias derived his lineage on the mother's side from Arcadia; and as there was a connection between the inhabitants of that country and the Thebans, the poet includes them in his praises.—He then addresses Æneas, the master of the chorus, whom he compliments on his musical skill, and exhorts to wipe away by his exertions the proverbial disgrace attached to his countrymen by the appellation of *Bœotian swine.*—Renews his praise of Agesias, and concludes with a prayer to Neptune, still to keep the victor under his propitious guidance, and to render the poet's hymns agreeable to those in whose honour they are written and sung.

Oft as the architect's creative hand
  Bids the fair porch on golden columns rise,
And all the dome's magnificence expand,
  To strike the gazing eye with mute surprise—

1 Gwillim, in a quaint epigram placed after the title page to his book on heraldry, thus alludes to the opening of this ode:—

"The noble Pindar doth compare somewhere,
Writing with building, and instructs us there

Thus splendid from afar should gleam
A noble deed's incipient beam—
The guard of Jove's prophetic shrine,
If he thy wreath, Olympia, bear,
Sprung from that old and noble line
Who founded Syracusa fair,
A grateful city hymns the hero's name,
While her unenvying sons unite in glad acclaim

In this exalted station placed,
The son of Sostratus is found
With no inglorious chaplet graced,
But with his well-earn'd honours crown'd.
The warrior on the battle plain,
The sailor on the trackless main,
Through paths of peril and dismay
Wins to renown his arduous way,
And when his toils achieve some glorious deed,
The memory of the good shall be his meed.

Agesias, may such ready praise be thine,
As to Oiclides, seer of Theban line,
Adrastus gave, when in an earthly tomb
Himself and noble steeds were hurried to their doom.

But when the seven funeral pyres
Raised to the dead their sacred fires,
In sorrow thus his Theban host
The son of Talaus address'd:
"The pride of all my army lost
Fills with regret this aching breast.
Quench'd is the augur's prescient light,
Nerveless the warrior's arm of fight."

That every great and goodly edifice
Doth ask to have a comely frontispiece.

23 Amphiaraus, son of Oicleus. I have here followed the ingenious emendation of Dr. Bloomfield, *εν Διρκᾳ*, instead of the common flat reading *εν δικᾳ*.

The triumphs which these hymns afford
Wait on my Syracusan lord. 32

No lover of contention, I
Respect my oath's compulsive tie—
And while this honest suffrage crowns my lays,
The sweet-toned muses' choir will ratify his praise

Oh, Phintis! spurn each dull delay,
And haste the vigorous mules to join—
Pursue thy clear and open way
To reach his ancestors' remotest line. 41

No other guide our steps will need
Safe through these lofty paths to lead.
Since upon their victorious brow
Olympia's verdant chaplets glow—
Then to their flight expanding wide
Let us unbar the gates of song—
Where Pitane in towering pride
O'erlooks Eurotas' sacred tide,
This day the bard must pass along. 47

To Neptune of Saturnian race
She the black-hair'd Evadne bore—

40 The commonly received interpretation of the word *Phintis* or *Philtis*, given by the elder scholiast, is doubtless the true one, viz., the poet's own soul, considered as the directing charioteer of the body. With this passage compare Cowley (to his muse :)—

" Go, the rich chariot instantly prepare,
The queen, my muse, will take the air.
The wheels of thy bold coach pass quick and free,
And all's an open road to thee—
Whatever god did say,
Is all thy plain and smooth, uninterrupted way."

50 The metaphor here is strikingly similar to that in Psalm cxviii. 23.

" Open me the gates of righteousness, that I may go into them, and give thanks unto the Lord."

This tale to rumour's voice we trace—
But when the circling moons reveal'd
What virgin throes her bosom long conceal'd,
To brave Eitatides her high command
Bade the attendant damsels bear
The nursling to the hero's care,
Whose sceptre ruled Arcadia's land
In fair Phæsana by Alphéus' shore.
Apollo taught her there to prove
The fond solicitudes of love. 57

When time to Æpytus confess'd
The stolen caresses' fruit divine,
The hero in his manly breast
Unutterable rage repress'd,
And humbly sought the Pythian shrine,
With mind intent the end to know
Of this intolerable wo.
Her virgin zone with saffron died,
And urn of silver laid aside,
In the thick grove conceal'd from sight
She brought the heavenly babe to light.
Meanwhile the god with golden hair
Propitious fate invoked, and kind Eleutho's care. 72

Her pleasing pains without delay
Produced young Iamus to day.
While there upon the verdant glade
By his afflicted parent laid,
Two dragons of cærulean eye
Commission'd by the will divine,
With bees' innoxious produce hie
To feed the youth of heavenly line.
But when from Pytho's rocky height
The monarch urged his chariot's flight,
He sought of all the menial train
Evadne's infant to regain,

77 I. e. Apollo: this epithet is applied by Alcæus to Zephyrus. (Frag. v. ap. Blomf.) χρυσοκομᾳ Ζεφυρῳ μιγεισα.

Whom erst from his prophetic throne
Phœbus, he said, had call'd his own. 84

That he, o'er all of mortal birth,
His sire's prophetic power might claim,
Nor should his race e'er fail on earth
To keep alive their deathless name.
Thus spoke the god—but they averr'd
No eye had seen, no ear had heard;
Though since his natal day
The fifth revolving sun had shed
Its lustre o'er the infant's head. 89
Meanwhile within the rushy glade,
And tangled bushes' thickest shade,
His tender frame all wet with dew,
And gemm'd with violet's purple hue,
Conceal'd from human sight he lay 93
And hence his mother bade the prophet's name
To each succeeding age his birth proclaim.

Soon as he gain'd from opening time
The golden flower of youthful prime,
Shrouded in night his steps he bore
Down to Alphéus' middle shore,
Invoking from the depths below
His great forefather Neptune's might,
And potent sire, whose silver bow
Defends the heaven-built Delos' height.
That public honour and renown
His brows might with their chaplet crown.

When thus in accents of eternal truth
His father's voice approved the suppliant's prayer,
"To Pisa's crowded plain, adventurous youth,
Follow my call, and strive for glory there." 108

104 The exquisite periphrasis of the original may be illustrated by a passage in Lord Byron, (*Childe Harold*, iv. cxvii.)

"The sweetness of the violet's deep-blue dies,
Kiss'd by the breath of heaven, seems colour'd by its skies."

To lofty Cronium's sun-crown'd hill they came;
Where great Apollo bade his son receive
A twofold portion of prophetic fame;
To hear the voice that knows not to deceive—
But when the glory of Amphitryo's line
Alcides prosperous in each bold design
Appear'd to crown his sire's immortal feast,
From every clime to call the frequent guest,
And fix the laws of each heroic game,
He placed the augur's seat near Jove's exalted
shrine. 119

New glories hence through Hellas grace
Th' Iamidæ's illustrious race—
And wealth attends to crown their state—
For those who seek with high emprise
The steep where virtue's guerdon lies,
The brightest walks of life await.
In his own path each seeks renown,
But carping Envy most his course attends,
Who first to win Olympia's crown
Twelve times around the goal his chariot bends—
On him sweet Grace distils a lustre all her own. 128

Agesias! if thy brave maternal line,
Who dwelt beneath Cyllene's hallow'd shade,
Duly their suppliant vows and rites divine
To Mercury, the god's swift herald, paid;
Whose favouring power the contest's law maintains,
And guards Arcadia's richly peopled plains;
By him and by his thundering sire decreed,
Oh son of Sostratus! expect the victor's meed.

Another motive prompts my tongue—
Which as the stone that whets the blade
Upon its sharpening surface laid,
Impels me down the flowing tide of song. 143

153 Pindar uses the same metaphor—(Pyth. i. 172.) Hence

From the Stymphalian nymph, Metopa fair,
My mother drew the vital air—
Within equestrian Thebes, whose fame
Salutes her with a founder's name.
At her pure wave my thirst I slake, and raise
The varied hymn that chants the warriors' praise.

Now, Æneas, urge thy tuneful band,
Parthenian Juno first demands the strain.
Then let clear truth the old disgrace
That loads Bœotia's sons efface;
Thou, like the general's trusty wand,
Art charged the faithful embassy to bear,
From the sweet muses with the lovely hair,
Who bade thy cup the sounding lays retain.

Command them in their grateful verse
The praise of Hiero to rehearse,
That monarch whose unblemish'd sway
Ortygia's isle and Syracuse obey.

probably Horace borrowed the idea in his well-known lines, (ad Pis. 304:)—

"Fungar vice cotis, acutum
Reddere quæ ferrum valet, exsors ipsa secandi."

166 The scholiast on this passage gives a long explanation of the *scytale*, or staff, which was used in battle to convey orders from the Lacedæmonian general that were to be unintelligible to all but the person to whom they were sent.—(Corn. Nepos. in vit. Pausan. cap. 3.) Aulus Gellius is still more minute in his account of this enigmatical wand. (Lib. XVII., cap. ix. 1.) His description is too long to be transcribed, and will not easily admit of abbreviation. Pindar calls Æneas the scytale of the muses, as being the faithful messenger in conveying his poetical strains to those in whose honour they were addressed.

172 The reader will be reminded by this passage, especially in the original, in which Hiero is spoken of as *governing with a clear sceptre*, of Macbeth's commendation of the royal Duncan:—

"Besides, this Duncan
Hath borne his faculties so meek, hath been
So clear in his great office."

To Ceres and her daughter fair
Whose milk-white steeds the goddess bear,
Duly he pays each sacred rite,
Adoring Jove's Ætnæan might.
His name the song and sweet-toned lyre resound,
Oh! may no future age his happy state confound!

With willing mind may he receive
The hymn which in Agesias' praise I weave.
Since Fortune now the hero calls
To kindred Syracuse again,
Far from his own Stymphalian walls
That crown Arcadia's fleecy plain.
E'en thus amid the wintry tides,
Secure the rapid vessel rides,
If two firm anchors' grasp her bulk maintain. 173

Still may the god exalt thy state
With either nation's prosperous fate;
And sceptred Amphitrite's lord,
Whose trident rules the stormy sea,
Through his own realm a path afford
From adverse winds and troubles free.
Adorning with sweet flowers my song,
To hail thy vessel as it speeds along. 180

188 Compare Casimir, (Lyric. iv. 36, 27.)

"*Fortius proram gemino revincit*
Anchora morsu."

THE SEVENTH OLYMPIC ODE.

TO DIAGORAS, THE RHODIAN, ON HIS VICTORY WITH THE CÆSTUS, GAINED IN THE SEVENTY-NINTH OLYMPIAD.

ARGUMENT.

PINDAR begins this beautiful ode (which, as the younger scholiast informs us, was said to have been written in letters of gold, and suspended in the temple of Minerva) with a highly poetical simile drawn from domestic life, which introduces the praise of the Rhodian victor and his race.—He then proceeds to the story of Tlepolemus, an ancestor of Diagoras, who, after having murdered Licymnius, departed for Rhodes by the command of Apollo; the shower of gold which Jupiter caused to descend there.—Then follow the fables respecting the origin of Rhodes, the birth of Pallas, her most ancient sacrifices instituted without the aid of fire, and the gifts imparted by her to the favoured Rhodians, especially their skill in statuary.—Then follows a digression explaining the reason for consecrating the island to the sun—(Hyperionides;) his intrigue with the nymph Rhodos, from which sprang seven sons, one of whom gave birth to Camirus, Lindus, and Ialysus, who built the three cities of the island of Rhodes, which were named after them.

The poet then proceeds to panegyrize Tlepolemus and Diagoras, enumerating the several victories of the latter.

The ode concludes with an invocation to Jupiter, to whom divine honours were paid on Atabyrius, a mountain of Rhodes, propitiating his continued favour both for the poet and the victor, and a moral reflection on the mutability of human fortune

---

As when a sire the golden bowl
All foaming with the dew of wine,
Takes with a liberal hand and soul,
Chief gem where all his treasures shine—
Then tends the beverage (hallow'd first
By prayers to all the powers above)

To slake the youthful bridegroom's thirst,
In honour of connubial love.
The social pledge he bears on high,
And homeward as his course he bends,
Blesses the fond connubial tie,
Admired by all his circling friends.

E'en thus I bring the nectar'd strain,
The muses' gift, to those who gain
The Pythian and Olympic crown;
Thrice bless'd, to whom 'tis giv'n to share
The arduous fruit of mental care,
Cheer'd by the voice of high renown!
Full many a victor in the fray
My life-inspiring strains survey—
Which bids the sweet-toned lyre its music raise,
And wake the sounding flutes through all their notes of praise.

And now, Diagoras, to thee
They breathe united melody.
When Rhodes the warlike isle is sung,
Apollo's bride from Venus sprung;
He too, the hero brave and bold,
With hardy frame of giant mould,
Who by Alphéus' sacred tide,
And where Castalia's waters glide,
First in the cæstus' manly fray
Bore the triumphant prize away.
Let Damagetus next, his sire,
To justice dear, the strain inspire.
Fix'd on that isle which three fair cities grace,
Where Embolus protects wide Asia's coast,
They dwell united with the Argive host.

36 "Lycia," says the younger scholiast, "is opposite to Rhodes, and in Lycia is a place called Embolus, sharp and narrow, and jutting into the sea, so named from its resemblance to the prow of a ship."

Now to Tlepolemus my song would trace
As its first source Alcides' potent race.
From Jove their sire's high lineage springs;
While to Astydameia's line
Amyntor, born of race divine,
An equal lustre brings. 42

But ah! what crimes round erring mortals wait,
Unnumber'd torments in their happiest state—
Who, ere the checker'd scene of life be past,
Can tell if weal or wo shall mark his lot at last? 48

Since the high founder of the Rhodian state,
Impell'd by fierce ungovernable hate,
Laid with his olive sceptre's deadly blow
On earth Alcmena's bastard brother low.
Licymnius, whom his hand to Pluto sent,
From Midea's chamber as his steps he bent.
'Tis thus the maddening tumults of the mind
Have oft seduced the wisest of mankind. 56

He sought the god who could unfold
The purpose of the will divine,
When thus the power with locks of gold
Spoke from his perfume-breathing shrine:
"Go, launch your fleet from Lerne's strand,
To gain the sea-encircled land,
Where the great monarch of the skies
Sent from his golden clouds a shower
With flames commission'd to devour
Th' accepted sacrifice.
What time by aid of Vulcan's art
And brazen axe, Minerva sprang

38 Homer relates the history of Tlepolemus, son of Hercules and Astydameia, and the Rhodians at great length, (Il. ii. 653.)

Τληπολεμος δ' Ἡρακλειδης, ηΰς τε μεγας τε,
Εκ Ῥοδου εννεα νηας αγεν, κ. τ. λ.

Astydameia was the daughter of Amyntor, son of Jupiter.

From Jove's head with impetuous start,
With long-continued warlike clang:
While heaven's high dome and mother earth
Shuddering beheld the wondrous birth.

Then too the god whose splendour bright
Glads mortals with his radiant light,
Bade his loved sons the high behest obey.
Them first he urged to rear the splendid shrine,
And to the goddess every rite divine
With prompt submissive reverence pay.
This their immortal sire with joy would cheer,
And please the maid who wields her sounding spear.

Yet oft oblivion's shadowy veil
O'erclouds the well-intending mind;
Then wise Prometheus' counsels fail,
And reason's path is left behind.
So they, obedient to their heavenly sire,
Bade in th' acropolis an altar rise,
But carried to the shrine no spark of fire
To waft from earth the pious sacrifice.
On them the supplicated power
Rained from his yellow cloud a golden shower.

87 This was a clear manifestation of the divine presence. The same portent attended the birth of Apollo, according to Callimachus, (in. Del. 260:)—

> Χρυσεα τοι τοτε παντα θεμειλια γεινετο Δηλε,
> Χρυσῳ δε τροχοεσσα πανημερος ἐῤῥεε λιμνη, κ. τ. λ.

Thus, too, at the birth of Hercules, Bromia relates to the astonished Amphitryo, (Act. v., sc. i. 44:)—

> "Ædes totæ confulgebant tuæ, *quasi essent aureæ.*"

So Theocritus, (Idyl. 24:)—

> "And see what light o'er all the chamber falls!
> Though yet not morn, how visible the walls!
> Some strange event!"—*Polwhele's version.*

Compare also Homer, (Od. xix. 37—40.)

Meanwhile the maid with azure eye
Her favour'd Rhodians deign'd to grace
Above all else of mortal race,
With arts of manual industry.
Hence framed by the laborious hand,
The animated figures stand,
Adorning every public street,
And seem to breathe in stone, or move their marble feet. 98

Wisdom true glory can impart
Without the aid of magic art.
As ancient fame reports, when Jove
And all th' immortal powers above
Held upon earth divided sway;
Not yet had Rhodes in glittering pride
On Ocean's breast appear'd to ride,
But hid beneath his briny caverns lay.

Then while the absent god of light
Delay'd to claim his equal share,
No friendly voice maintain'd his right
Of all the bless'd assembly there.
Jove, to repair the wrong, in vain
Wish'd to adjudge the lots again.
Since in his course the sun had found
Retired within the hoary deep
A fertile land with heroes crown'd,
Prolific nurse of fleecy sheep. 116

Then straight he gave the high command
To Lachesis, whose locks of jet

97 Pindar probably alludes to the Telchines, an ancient people of Rhodes, much addicted to magical fascination, from which probably they derive their name: (Ov. Met. vii. 365:)—

"Phœbeamque Rhodon, et Ialysios Telchinas,
Quorum oculos ipso vitiantes omnia visu
Jupiter exosus, *fraternis abdiait undis*."

117 This ratifying power, which distinguishes Lachesis above

Are gather'd in a golden net,
To fix with her extended hand
The oath that binds the powers above,
And stamp with fate the nod of Jove,
Which the bright isle emerging from the wave,
To Phœbus and his latest offspring gave.

Hence o'er the land extends his sway
Who darts the piercing beams of day;
The charioteer whose guiding rein
Wide over the celestial plain
His fire-exhaling steeds obey.

With Rhodos there in amorous embrace
Conjoin'd, the god begat a valiant race;
Seven noble sons, with wisdom's gifts endow'd
By their great sire above the vulgar crowd.
Cameirus from this root with Lindus came,
And Ialysus, venerable name:
Three chiefs who over the divided land
In equal portions held supreme command.
Apart they reign'd, and bade each city bear
The monarch's name who sway'd the sceptre there.

In that bless'd isle secure at last
'Twas thine, Tlepolemus, to meet
For each afflictive trial past
A recompense and respite sweet.
Chief of Tirynthian hosts, to thee
As to a present deity,
The fumes of slaughter'd sheep arise
In all the pomp of sacrifice:
Awarded by thy just decree
The victor gains his verdant prize.

her sister Destinies, is also asserted by Plutarch: (De Facie in Orbe Lunæ, sub finem.)

129 Their names, according to the scholiast, were Cercaphus, Ochimus, Actis, Macaresas, Tenages, Triopes, Phaethon.

That crown whose double honours glow,
Diagoras, around thy brow:
On which four times the Isthmian pine,
And twice the Nemean olive shine:
While Athens on her rocky throne
Made her illustrious wreath his own. [151]

Trophies of many a well-fought field
He won in glory's sacred cause,
The Theban tripod, brazen shield
At Argos, and Arcadia's vase.
Her palms Bœotia's genuine contests yield;
Six times Ægina's prize he gain'd,
As oft Pellene's robe obtain'd,
And graved in characters of fame,
Thy column, Megara, records his name. [159]

Great sire of all, immortal Jove,
On Atabyrius' mount enshrined,
Oh! still may thy propitious mind
Th' encomiastic hymn approve,
Which celebrates in lawful strain
The victor on Olympia's plain,
Whose valorous arm the cæstus knows to wield.

Protected by thy constant care,
In citizens' and strangers' eyes
Still more exalted shall he rise
Whose virtuous deeds thy favour share:

151 Athens is here put synecdochically for the whole of Attica. Pindar, as the younger scholiast observes, leaves it doubtful in what Attic contest Diagoras came off victorious: whether in the Panathenaic, the Heraclean, the Eleusinian, or the Panhellenic; or whether he obtained the prize in all these. The same epithet is applied by Homer to Ithaca: (Il. ii. 201.)

165 A mountain in Rhodes, on which was erected a temple to Jupiter, containing brazen bulls, that, according to the scholiast, had the property of lowing whenever any unseemly action was about to be committed there.

Since he to violence and fraud unknown,
Treads the straight paths of equity alone:
His fathers' counsels mindful to pursue,
And keep their bright example still in view.
Then let not inactivity disgrace
The well-earn'd fame of thine illustrious race,
Who sprang from great Callianax, and crown
Th' Eratidæ with splendour all their own.
With joy and festal hymns the streets resound—
But soon, as shifts the ever varying gale,
The storms of adverse fortune may assail—
Then, Rhodians, be your mirth with sober temperance crown'd. **175**

THE EIGHTH OLYMPIC ODE.

TO THE YOUTH ALCIMEDON, ON HIS VICTORY IN THE PALÆSTRA, GAINED IN THE EIGHTEENTH OLYMPIAD; HIS BROTHER TIMOSTHENES, VICTOR IN THE NEMEAN GAMES; AND TO THEIR PRÆCEPTOR, OR ALIPTA,* MELESIAS.

ARGUMENT.

THIS ode begins with an address to Olympia; after which Pindar proceeds to congratulate Alcimedon and Timosthenes, the former on his Olympic, and the latter on his recent Nemean victory.—Then follow the praises of the victor's native island Ægina, from its founder Æacus, a theme which appears to be always grateful to our poet, who relates the fables connected with its origin; as well as the assistance of that hero, which was engaged by Apollo and Neptune when building the walls of Troy.—The praises of Melesias are then sung and the Blepsiadæ, a tribe of Æginetans, is recorded, as well as the memory of the victor's departed relatives, Iphion and Callimachus.—The ode concludes with the expression of good wishes.

OLYMPIA, mother of heroic games,
Whose golden wreath the victor's might proclaims,
Great queen of truth!—thou whose prophetic band
From victims blazing in the sacred fire
Jove's sovereign will, the lightning's guide, inquire,
What favour'd mortal shall the crown command 6
Which bids the anxious hour of contest close,
And gives to virtuous toil the guerdon and repose. 9

The gods above with favouring ear
The prayers of pious mortals hear. 10

* Who anointed the combatants, and prepared them for the ing.

Ye woody shades of Pisa's grove,
That o'er Alphéus' waters bend,
From you the wreath which victory wove,
And the triumphant hymn descend;
Receive the pomp and festal song
Which justly to your fame belong. 14

The deeds of glory and renown
Mankind with well-earn'd chaplets crown;
And by th' indulgent powers of heaven
Success in various paths is given.
Timosthenes, the influence shed
By Jove around thy youthful head,
In Nemea's plain effulgent shone;
While Cronium's hill return'd the sound,
What time Olympia's chaplet crown'd
Thy victor brow, Alcimedon.
On that fair form and lovely face
His glorious deeds shed no disgrace.
Triumphant from the wrestler's toil
By glory fired and filial pride,
His loved Ægina's naval isle
With high renown he dignified.
Where Themis, the lorn stranger's shield,
Assessor of protecting Jove,
Her righteous sceptre joys to wield,
Adored by more than mortal love. 30

Where nations meet and various laws prevail,
'Tis hard with even poise to hold the scale.
But the immortal gods' behest
Ordain'd this ocean-girded land,
Sure refuge of each wandering guest,
Firm as the column's shaft to stand.
(And oh! may future ages join
Unwearied to assist their great design!) 38

Hence ruled by chiefs of Doric race,
Who from great Æacus their empire trace.

On him, to raise the towers of Ilium's wall,
Wide-ruling Neptune and Latona's son
Deign'd in the mighty work for aid to call.
Those towers which, when her destined course was run,
Tremendous war's depopulating sway
Should on the ground in smoky ruin lay. 47

When now complete the stately pile appear'd,
Their hostile forms three azure dragons rear'd;
But from the threaten'd wall with gasping breath
Two fell exhausted in the pangs of death.
One with terrific shout advancing still,
Apollo thus pronounced the boded ill:
  " Uprear'd, great hero, by thy hand,
  Prostrate shall Pergamus be laid;
  (For true will future ages prove
  The omen sent from thundering Jove;)
  But not without thy children's aid—
  What by the fathers is begun,
Shall in the fourth succeeding age be done." 59

  Thus having clear'd the fatal sign,
  Sure presage of the will divine,
To Xanthus and the Amazonian band,
Whose guiding rein the generous steeds obey,
And where flows Ister through the Scythian land,
His flaming chariot urged its rapid way.
  But he who wields the trident's might,
  His course to sea-beat Isthmus bent,
  And with his golden coursers' flight
  Hither great Æacus he sent
  To view from Corinth's lofty brow
  His solemn festival below. 69

  But no delight to men secure
  Shall in this earthly state endure.

65 Telamon and Neoptolemus.

If of the beardless train I raise
The hymn that sings Melesias' praise,
Let not the tongue of Envy rail,
Nor with sharp stone my fame assail.
His valiant deeds in Nemea's plain
Alike inspire the poet's strain—
And next the great pancratium's meed,
Which to the strife of heroes is decreed. 77

His triumph is our surest guide,
Whose feet the arduous paths have tried;
But light their mind and counsel vain
Whose skill could ne'er the palm obtain.
Who tells his own victorious deeds
To others points the path of fame,
And shows what glorious lot succeeds
His conquest in each sacred game.
So thine the thirtieth garland won
Adds to thy teacher's fame, Alcimedon. 87

With fortune and his manly arm to aid,
He sent four vanquish'd striplings back in shame,
Darken'd their homeward path with sorrow's shade,
And gave to slandering infamy their name. 101
'Twas this his grandsire's age inspired
With vigorous youth's returning breath;
For by the victor's glory fired
His mind forgot the hour of death. 96

Be mine the task, Blepsiadæ, to raise
A record worthy of your deathless praise.

101 Statius appears to have had this highly poetical passage in his mind when, speaking of the return of the worsted and dejected Pelasgi from the field, he says—(Theb. xi. 759 :)—

" Eunt taciti passim, et pro funere pulchro
Dedecorem amplexi vitam reditusque pudendos.
Nox favet, et grata profugos amplectitur umbra."

Ye whom the verdant wreath six times decreed,
Again encircles with the victor's meed.
And even the dead will joy to share
This tribute of the poet's care:
Since the bright actions of the just
Survive unburied in the kindred dust.

There let Iphion's tongue proclaim
Callimachus, to charm thine ear,
The tale which Hermes' daughter, Fame,
Gave him, while yet on earth, to hear.
That Jove once more had deign'd to grace
With Pisa's crown their favour'd race.
His blessings may he still impart,
And ward disease's bitter dart!
Forbear amid the happy state
Discordant Nemesis to throw,
But give secure their life to flow,
And crown their country's prosperous fate.

THE NINTH OLYMPIC ODE.

TO EPHARMOSTUS, THE OPUNTIAN, ON HIS VICTORY IN THE PALÆSTRA, GAINED IN THE SEVENTY-THIRD OLYMPIAD.

ARGUMENT.

Beginning with the praises of the victor, Pindar digresses to those of his native city Opus.—Then, being led by the mention of the propitious power of the Graces, to speak of Hercules' contest with Neptune, Apollo, and Pluto, which was carried on by their assistance, he checks himself, considering it an act of impiety to relate tales that may be disparaging to any of the gods.—Then follows a digression relating to Deucalion's flood, and the reparation of the human race after the waters had subsided.—The poet addressing Epharmostus and the citizens of Opus, as being descended from Deucalion and Pyrrha, through their daughter Protogeneia, who had by Jupiter a son called Opus, from whom the city was named.—His hospitality is celebrated, and his reception, among his other guests, of Menætius, whose son Patroclus is mentioned with high commendation as having assisted Achilles in his attack on Telephus, who had put to flight the Grecian band.—He then aspires to the car of the muses, who would enable him to frame a song that might do justice to the several triumphs of Lampromachus and Epharmostus, which he enumerates; attributing the victor's excellence and various graces to the favour of the gods, and concluding with a compliment to his hero, who, after his victory in the Oilean games, offered sacrifices and funeral rites at the tomb of Ajax.

Archilochus' Olympic strain
With triple harmony combined,
Might have sufficed the friendly train,
And gratified the victor's mind.

1 It appears to have been customary to sing at the Olympic

What time, as Epharmostus leads,
By Saturn's hill the pomp proceeds.
But haste the sounding shafts to throw
From the far-darting muses' bow;
The first to heaven's eternal king,
Who guides the lightning's lurid wing;
The next to Elis' sacred tower,
Uprear'd the rocky heights above,
Which Lydian Pelops gain'd, fair dower
Of chaste Hippodameia's love. 16

Towards Pytho next thine efforts bend,
A sweet and winged shaft to send.
Nor shalt thou raise a feeble strain,
Earth sprung, that falls to earth again.
When in fair Opus' praise you shake the string,
And her brave hero of the wrestler's ring;
Whose sons, preserved by equal laws, obey
Bright Themis and her glorious daughter's sway.
There now the virtues flourish wide,
And with transplanted radiance glow,
Blooming as by Alphéus' tide,
Or where Castalia's waters flow.
Hence from her verdant grove the frequent crown
His Locrian city's fame exalts with fair renown. 32

But I, who joy my much-loved state
With festal hymns to celebrate,
Swift as the courser sweeps the plain,
Or winged vessel ploughs the main,
To all the listening world around
Will send the conquest's joyful sound.

games a hymn of Archilochus, consisting of three strophes, and composed in honour of Hercules; which began thus:

Καλλινικε χαιρ' αναξ
'Ηρακλεις.

To this Pindar here alludes.
7 Addressed to the chorus.
22 Eunomia, the genius of good government.

Since, aided by a hand divine,
Within the Graces' choicest bower,
I make their blooming treasures mine,
And cull the sweets of every flower.
For they the charms of life bestow,
While all the brave and wise to them their virtues owe. 43

How else could great Alcides' hand
With shaken club provoke to fight
The god who wields the trident's might,
At Pylos when he took his stand,
To drive the hero from the land?
How dare to challenge as a foe
The monarch of the silver bow?
Nor could stern Pluto's grasp retain
Unmoved the sceptre of his reign,
Which drives the forms devoid of breath
Within the hollow vale of death.

No more, unhallow'd lips, assail
The mighty gods with slanderous tale.
It sounds of madness thus to rise
In impious vaunts against the skies.
Be contests banish'd from the strain
That celebrates th' immortal train;
And rather by the poet's tongue
Protogeneia's city sung.

50 The office which is here attributed to the sceptre of Pluto, is by the poets usually described as characterizing the caduceus of Mercury.—See Homer, Il. xxiv. 243; Virg., Æn. iv. 242; Horat., Od. i. 24.—The last of which passages is thus translated by Francis :—

"Yet ne'er returns the vital heat,
The shadowy form to animate.
Soon as the ghost-compelling god
Forms his black troops with horrid rod,
He will not, lenient to the breath
Of prayer, unbar the gates of death."

Where, as ordain'd by heaven's eternal king,
Whose power directs the lightning's varied wing,
Descending from Parnassus' lofty height,
Pyrrha and her Deucalion sought the plain,
Rear'd the first dome, and call'd that race to light,
Whose stony birth they bade the name retain.

Then wake for them the tuneful string—
Though wine improved by mellowing age
The palate's suffrage more engage,
Yet choose a newer lay the victor's praise to sing.

In tales of ancient lore 'tis said
O'er earth the whelming waters spread
Urged all their congregated force.
But Jove's high will his headlong course
Bade the usurping foe restrain,
And sink absorb'd the refluent main.
From them your sires, the warlike race
Of old Iapetus, descend;
Whose glorious deeds the brightest grace
To Saturn their forefather lend;

63 Λαος, a people, from λαας, a stone. So Ovid, speaking of Deucalion's Deluge, (Met. i. 411,) says:—

"Superorum munere, saxa
Missa viri manibus faciem traxere virilem;
Et de fœmineo reparata est fœmina jactu.
Inde genus durum sumus, experiensque laborum,
Et documenta damus, qua simus origine nati."

Pindar, by deducing the origin of the Locrians from a daughter or daughters of Jupiter, gives another proof of his anxiety to assign to the cities in honour of whose townsmen his odes are composed, as ancient and illustrious a source as history or mythology will permit. It would be a futile attempt to supply the defective links in the genealogical chain between Deucalion and Locrus, from whom the people derive their appellation; but this perplexity involves the origin of many ancient nations, who have recourse to mythological fiction for that which the integrity of truth will not supply.

And hence a line of native kings
In regular succession springs. 84

Ere yet th' Olympic ruler's hand
Had ravish'd from th' Epean land
The daughter of fair Opus' lord,
And on the dark Mænalian heights
Mingled with her in love's delights;
To Locrus then his bride restored,
Lest age, death's harbinger, should doom
The childless monarch to the tomb. 92

Soon as the heavenly scion came,
The raptured hero gazed with joy
On the supposititious boy,
And call'd him by his uncle's name—
In manly deeds and outward grace
Above the sons of mortal race—
Permitting to his sceptred hand
Dominion o'er the subject land. 100

From Argos some, from Thebes, and Pisa's plain,
And fair Arcadia, throng the frequent train.
But most his love and admiration won
Menætius, Actor and Ægina's son:
Whose offspring, when brave Atreus' host
Invaded Teuthras' Mysian land,
Alone could with Achilles boast
The adverse army to withstand:
When Telephus the Grecian train
Drove seaward to their ships again.
Hence might the wise and prudent find
The strength of great Patroclus' mind. 115

Hence might the tender love appear
By Thetis' warlike offspring shown;
" Quit not," he said, " my conquering spear,
Nor join the war's array alone."

Oh! could I in the muses' car
Soar, eloquent of speech, afar—
Since bold emprise and power belong
To the high-favour'd child of song.
Inspired with hospitable aim
I come the virtues to proclaim,
Which round thy honour'd temples twine,
Lampromachus, the Isthmian pine;
When both in one triumphant day
The victor's chaplet bore away.
Two other joys at Corinth's gate
His brow in after times await;
And victory twice in Nemea's grove
The wreath for Epharmostus wove.
In Argos' strife of men renown'd,
While yet a boy at Athens crown'd;
When in the Marathonian field,
Departing from the beardless train,
He made the veteran warriors yield,
The cup of silver to obtain.
Oh! with what matchless swiftness there
He ran the circus' destined round,
While shouting myriads rend the air
With admiration's joyful sound.
His lonely form and deeds of might
Bursting upon the raptured sight.
Wondrous in the Parrhasian plain
Before contending hosts he strove,
When all the congregated train
Hallowed thy feast, Lycæan Jove.

And when Pallene's robe he bears,
Warm refuge from the chilling airs.

132 I. e., in the Isthmus, where the games were celebrated So Æschylus, describing the Cimmerian Bosphorus, says, (P V. 754, :)—

Ισθμον δ' επ' αυτις στενοπορους λιμνης πυλαις
Κιμμερικον ἥξεις.

Full oft has Iolaus' shrine
Upon Eleusis' sea-girt strand
Witness'd the splendid acts which shine
To crown the efforts of his hand.
In his own path each labours well,
As nature grants him to excel.
While many with laborious aim
Toil up the rugged steep of fame,
If the kind god forbear to bless
Their vain endeavour with success,
Let silence hide th' unfinish'd tale
Within oblivion's dusky veil.
Far different are the ways which tend
To glory as their common end. 158

Not all mankind are prone to feel
In the same care an equal zeal.
But arduous paths must they explore
Who to the heights of wisdom soar.
While I this lay triumphant bring,
With voice sonorous let me sing
The hero's praise whose spirit bold
Join'd to a frame of hardy mould,
Urged him upon th' Oilean plain
The palm of glory to obtain.
Then round the Æantean shrine
In festal pomp the wreath entwine. 168

171 It was the custom for the victors on their return from Olympia to institute sacred rites in honour of the indigenous hero Ajax, son of Oileus, and to crown his shrine with a chaplet. The Æantean games were particularly celebrated at Opus.

THE TENTH OLYMPIC ODE.

TO AGESIDAMUS, SON OF ARCHESTRATUS, THE EPIZEPHYRIAN, OR WESTERN LOCRIAN, ON HIS VICTORY WITH THE CÆSTUS GAINED IN THE SEVENTY-THIRD OLYMPIAD.

ARGUMENT.

This ode opens with an address to the muse and to Truth, whom he wishes to remind him of his long-forgotten promise to celebrate the son of Archestratus and the city of the Locrians; as well as his alipta Ilas, who encouraged him by the example of Hercules and Patroclus to persevere in the contest notwithstanding its unfavourable commencement.—Then follows a digression concerning the institution of the Olympic games by Hercules, with an enumeration of his conquests over the Molionidæ, and Augeas, king of Elis: the victors in these games are likewise recorded.—The poet then sings the praises of Jupiter, and concludes with complimenting Agesidamus on his prowess and personal beauty, comparing him in this respect to Ganymedes.

Inscribed upon the poet's mind
Archestratus' illustrious son,
Who late th' Olympic wreath has won,
Thou know'st, celestial muse, to find:
For dull oblivion swept away
All record of the promised lay.
And thou, oh Truth! fair child of Jove,
With thine unerring hand efface
The tale that speaks his foul disgrace,
Who slights a claim, and wrongs the stranger's love.

For when time's rapid course had flown,
I felt the glowing tinge of shame,

To think how large the debt became.
But ample interest now shall close
The sharp reproach of envious foes,
And all the guilty past atone.
Now whelm'd beneath the flowing tide,
Where is the pebble seen to glide?
And to confound the slanderous tongue,
How shall the friendly strain be sung? 16

For Truth her Locrians' favour'd land,
Refresh'd by Zephyr's breath, defends:
Calliope her guardian hand
O'er them with brazen Mars extends.
E'en Hercules' superior might
Fainted in the Cycnean fight.
And as Patroclus, safe from harm,
Bowed grateful to Achilles' arm,
So should Agesidamus pay
His thanks to Ilas in the fray.
Who gave him on Olympia's plain
The wrestler's chaplet to obtain.
For by the favouring god inspired,
To glorious deeds the breast is fired,
Where emulation points the way. 25

But few to eminence can rise,
And without labour seize the prize,

17 The metaphor in the original is similar to that in Joshua, v., 9: "*I have rolled away the reproach of Egypt.*" I understand the words of Pindar interrogatively with the Oxford editors, although against the opinion of Heyne.

21 One of the scholiasts, instead of Ατρεκεια, here reads ἁ τραχεια πολις, as if the poet was alluding to the rocky situation of the town; but the common reading appears far preferable.

36 This passage is rather obscure, and the construction not very clear. From the words as they stand, I have endeavoured to elicit the most obvious and natural meaning. By the Themites, daughters of Jupiter, the poet probably means nothing more than the righteous eye of the heavenly king, surveying with especial interest his own Olympic contests. The younger

The light and joy of fleeting life.
Daughters of heaven's eternal king,
Urged by your high command, I sing,
Ye Themites, the glorious strife,
Which Hercules at Pelops' ancient shrine
Ordain'd, when from unwilling Augeas' hand,
That he the promised guerdon might demand,
Neptune's proud sons he slew, who scorn'd his might divine.

Within Cleonæ's thickest wood
Alcides in dark ambush lay,
When blameless Cteatus pursued
With Eurytus his deadly way.
Thus was avenged his brave Tirynthian host,
By Molion's haughty race in pass of Elis lost. 42

Ere long the fraudulent Epean king
Saw potent fire and the devouring blade
Destruction to his rich dominions bring,
Deep in the lowest gulf of misery laid.
'Tis hard a mightier foe's assault to quell.
Thus the devoted Augeas, seized at last
By vengeful fate, bereft of counsel, fell,
And death atoned for all his treachery past. 50

His whole array the warlike son of Jove
On Pisa's plain assembling with the spoil,
Raised to his mighty father Altis' grove,
And fenced from tread profane the hallow'd soil.

scholiast says: *αἱ Θεμιτες, ηγουν αἱ νομοθεσιαι του Διος, αἱ κατα νομους συνηθειαι.*

51 This story is related at great length to Patroclus by old Nestor, (Il., xi. 670, et seq.,) whose unseasonable garrulity on the occasion is justly reprehended by Pope.

61 An early instance of the consecration of a tenth part of the spoils taken in battle to the service of the gods is given by Xenophon, (Anab., v., 3. ;) *και την δεκατην, ἥν τῳ Απολλωνι εξειλον και τῃ Εφεσιᾳ Αρτεμιδι, διελαβον οἱ στρατηγοι, το μερος εκαστος, φυλαττειν τοις θεοις·* at the end of the chapter the planting of a large grove

Shrines to th' immortal twelve he placed,
Who the celestial banquet graced,
Ranking with these Alphéus' wave,
To Saturn's hill the name he gave.
(For erst, while old Œnomaus' hand
Possess'd the sceptre of the land,
Upon the nameless mountain's head
Their snows unnumber'd ages shed.)
On the first rites with aspect mild
The destinies assistant smiled;
And hoary Time, whose steady ray
Oft brings undoubted truth to day. 67

He in his onward course reveal'd
What time Alcides' conquering might
Bestow'd, to found Olympia's field,
The earliest offerings of the fight.
And on each fifth returning year
Bade victory's sons the chaplet wear.
Tell, muse, in that illustrious day
Who first the glorious prize obtain'd;
Who bore the wrestler's palm away;
Who the high meed of swiftness gain'd:
Or urged his chariot to the goal,
Curbing by deeds the pride of boastful rivals' soul. 75

around the temple of Jupiter is mentioned. Thus Ovid, addressing Bacchus, says, (Fast. iii., 729)—

"Te memorant, Gange, totoque Oriente subacto,
Primitias magno seposuisse Jovi."

And Callimachus, addressing Apollo, (in Del. 278)—

Αλλα τοι αμφιετεις δεκατηφοροι αιεν απαρχαι
Πεμπονται.

On which passage see the learned dissertation of Spanheim, who mentions the same custom to have prevailed among the Jews, who were wont to convey to their holy metropolis the first fruits and tenths of the produce of the soil for the maintenance of the temple and its service. Spencer (de Legg. Heb. 1161, &c.) shows at great length that many of the rites observed in bringing the first fruits to Jerusalem were borrowed from heathen nations.

First in the stadium's level course
Œonus, brave Licymnius' son,
Who brought from Midea's walls his force,
The chaplet's glorious honours won:
And Echemus his Tegea's name
Raised in the wrestler's ring to fame.
Doryclus bade the manly cæstus crown
His lovely Tirynthian city with renown. 82

And Semus' steeds unwearied in the race,
Mantinea with the hymn of triumph grace.
Phrastor with certain aim the javelin threw;
While from Eniceus' hand the discus flew,
And as the circling orb ascended high
Above the rest, what clamours rent the sky!
The full-orb'd moon, with her nocturnal ray
Shed o'er the scene a lovely flood of day. 91

And all the grove with festal chorus rang,
Oft as the crowd the victor's praises sang.
Now shall the muse prepare her loftiest verse,
Obedient to the rites of ancient days,
The lurid bolts and shafts of light rehearse,
And sing the mighty Thunderer's deathless praise
Symphonious with the song shall wake the reed,
By Dirce's sacred fount—a tardy note indeed!

Grateful as comes th' expected heir
To bless his age—enfeebled sire,
The source of sweetly anxious care,
And object of his fond desire.
Since wealth, if foreign hands must seize the hoard,
Is view'd with hatred by its dying lord.
E'en thus, arrived at Pluto's dark domain,
The hero, nameless in the poet's lay,
By glorious acts and aspirations vain
Will not have soothed life's brief and anxious day.

The dulcet flute and lyre's accordant string
Thy happier deeds, Agesidamus, sing,

While the Pierian maids, Jove's tuneful race,
On thy fair deeds bestow illustrious grace! 116

And I, the muses' faithful friend,
With ardent zeal my efforts bend
To hymn the mighty Locrians' name:
Shedding o'er their well-peopled town
The honey'd dews of fair renown,
Archestratus' loved stripling I proclaim.
Victorious near th' Olympic shrine,
With strength of arm I saw him shine
In bloom of youth and beauty's flower,
Incipient manhood's golden hour,
Which with the Cyprian queen of love
Disgraceful fate from Ganymedes drove. 125

THE ELEVENTH OLYMPIC ODE.*

TO THE SAME AGESIDAMUS, A SUPPLEMENTARY ODE, KNOWN BY THE GREEK TITLE Τοκος, OR INTEREST

ARGUMENT.

The poet addresses this short ode to Agesidamus, as a kind of amends for his delay in sending him the preceding.—It contains the praises of the Locri and of Agesidamus: the latter on account of his victory with the cæstus; the other for wisdom, hospitality, and fortitude.

As men, o'er ocean's paths who sail,
Implore from Heaven a favouring gale,
And others joy when, at their call,
Showers, the clouds' humid daughters, fall;
Thus too when some laborious deed
Is crown'd with victory's well-earn'd meed,
The hero's virtues soft-toned hymns proclaim,
Sure pledge that after times shall celebrate his name.

Praises like these unenvied yield
The conquests of Olympia's field;
And such my tongue aspired to gain.
But human wishes all are vain,
Unless the god his aid bestow,
From whom success and genius flow.
Son of Archestratus! I raise
In thy triumphant cæstus' praise
The hymn whose melody around
The golden olive's wreath shall sound;

* The Greek title of this ode was Τοκος, or *Interest*, as it was sent to Agesidamus with the preceding, in order to compensate for the poet's tardiness in sending him the preceding.

While the melodious numbers grace
The western Locrians' honour'd race.

Thither, ye muses, lead the festal train,
If to that land your hallow'd footsteps stray,
Ye find no rude, inhospitable swain,
Who drives the stranger from his door away.
But one, in wisdom's ample treasures bless'd,
Whose veins with all his father's valour glow;
For time but steels the rugged lion's breast,
Nor can the tawny fox his wiles forego.

THE TWELFTH OLYMPIC ODE.

TO ERGOTELES OF HIMERA, ON HIS VICTORY IN THE FOOT RACE, CALLED Δολιχοδρομος,* OR THE LONG COURSE, GAINED IN THE SEVENTY-SEVENTH OLYMPIAD.

ARGUMENT.

This ode, almost as short as the preceding, begins with an invocation to Fortune, the supreme arbitress of events, the issue of which is always uncertain, to be propitious to the Himeræans. The victor would have remained in ignoble obscurity, passing his life in domestic broils, had he not removed from Crete, his native land, to Himera: in which town, being favourably received, he cultivated those faculties of strength and swiftness which enabled him to obtain the Olympic, Pythian, and Isthmian crowns.

Oh Fortune, saviour of the state,
Daughter of Eleutherian Jove,
For Himera thy constant love
And guardian care I supplicate.
Toss'd on the rough and stormy sea,
The rapid ships are sway'd by thee;
And marshall'd in its long array
Uncertain war allows thy sway.

Since, or in council or in field,
All to thy sovereign fiat yield.
While flattering hope's delusive dream
Cheats men with visions false and vain;

* This course, according to some, consisted of six, according to others, of twenty-four stadia. It was longer than the diaulos, which was a course from the starting post to the goal and back again without intermission.

Now glads the heart with transport's beam,
Now whirls them in despair again. 9

But not to any son of earth
Has ever yet a sign been given
By the immortal powers of heaven
To know th' event before it come to birth.
Full oft the wishes of mankind
An unexpected issue find,
When joy's bright promise ends in wo.
Oft too the beams of bliss arise
To him whose shatter'd vessel lies
Whelm'd in the stormy gulf below. 18

Son of Philanor!—like the bird
Whose shouts within are only heard,
Ne'er had thy speed, unknown to fame,
Exalted an inglorious name.
Driven by sedition's broils to roam
Far from thy native Cretan home,
Olympia's verdant chaplet now
Encircles thine illustrious brow.
For thee their twofold chaplets twine
The Delphic palm and Isthmian pine,
Now fix'd in Himera's adopted plain,
The tepid fountains of the nymphs you crown,
Ergoteles, with your own high renown,
And bid their springs unwonted honour gain. 28

25 I. e., the cock, sacred to Mars. By this simile Pindar intimates that had not Ergoteles been expelled by domestic sedition from his native land, he would still have remained inglorious at home, like a cock enclosed within a coop. Heyne remarks that this image is the more obvious, as the coins of Himera were usually distinguished by the image of that bird. The Himeræans experienced in a remarkable manner the instability of human fortune, as their city was destroyed by the Carthaginians in little more than two hundred years from its foundation.

38 This allusion to the celebrated warm springs of Himera is understood by some commentators in an allegorical sense.

THE THIRTEENTH OLYMPIC ODE.

TO XENOPHON, THE CORINTHIAN, ON HIS VICTORY IN THE STADIC COURSE AND THE PANTATHLON, GAINED IN THE SEVENTY-NINTH OLYMPIAD.

ARGUMENT.

The poet begins this ode with celebrating the praises of Xenophon, conjointly with those of his native town.—He then proceeds to enumerate the different conquests of the victor and his father Ptæodorus.—Then returns to Corinth, and digresses to the story of Bellerophon, thrown to earth by Pegasus, who was afterward received into the celestial stalls.—Then follow encomiums of the Oligæthidæ of the tribe Xenophon, who had been victorious at Thebes, Argos, and various other cities where games, inferior to the four great contests, were celebrated.—Concludes with a prayer to Jupiter that he may bless them with continued prosperity.

While to the house of Xenophon I raise
The grateful tribute of poetic praise,
Who, thrice victorious in Olympia's field,
With equal care the friend and stranger shield,
Well-peopled Corinth, Isthmian Neptune's gate,
In this triumphant strain I celebrate.
    Ennomia with her sisters fair,
    The state's firm guard, inhabit there—
    Concord and Justice, who dispense
    To man unbounded affluence.
    They, prudent Themis' golden train,
    Impetuous arrogance control;
    And foul-mouth'd insolence restrain,
    Which breeds satiety of soul. 12

12 The oracle of Bacis, mentioned by Herodotus, (Uran. lxxvii.,) ascribes the same birth to satiety:—

Κρατερον Κορον, Ὑβριος υἱον.

But truth and upright confidence prevail
O'er my bold tongue to speak its pleasing tale.
Sons of Aletes! vainly would you hide
The native valour stamp'd upon the mind.
To you full often in triumphant pride
Victory's high palm the blooming hours assign'd;
And oft they bade your skilful art explore
The secret mysteries of ancient lore. 24

But all the glorious action's fame
Illustrates the inventor's name.
Who taught, save Corinth's noble race,
The Dithyrambic hymn to grace,
In festal pride the bull to lead,
Or curb with reins the generous steed?
Or on the temples with expanded wing
Placed the twin semblance of the feather'd king?
Them the sweet-breathing muse inspires,
While Mars in his sublime career,
Their youth with thirst of glory fires,
And gives to hurl the deadly spear. 33

Supreme, wide-ruling Jove, whose sway
Olympia glories to obey,
Through every age with guardian arm
Shielding this happy race from harm,
Conducted by thy prosperous gale,
May Xenophon's light pinnace sail.

16 The Corinthians are so called, as being descended from King Aletes, who came into the Peloponnesus with the Heraclidæ, and obtained the empire of Corinth.

29 There is some obscurity in this passage. It is doubted by the commentators whether the double eagle were sculptured on the pediment, (aëtoma,) or placed inside of the temple. Green is of the latter opinion, but supports it by rather a singular argument, viz., that the word in the original is ενθηκ'; whereas it is evident that the corresponding line in the second epode requires εθηκ' in the first, which is the common and doubtless the true reading.

Pausanias, in his description of the temple of Minerva Εργανη,

Receive th' encomiastic strain,
His tribute, who on Pisa's plain
The pentathletic garland won:
Urged by insuperable force
While he the stadium's lengthen'd course
With rapid foot was first to run.
Of all in that great strife renown'd,
Such wreaths no former mortal crown'd.

His brow, in pride of triumph placed,
Twice has the Isthmian parsley graced—
As oft conspicuous in the Nemean field,
To him the crown his vanquish'd rivals yield—
And by Alphéus' shore his father's name,
Swift-footed Thessalus, is given to fame.
Him the same sun beheld on Pytho's plain,
The stadic and diaulic prize obtain:
And rocky Athens wove her chaplet fair
Thrice in one moon, to deck the victor's hair.

Seven times th' Hellotian palm he gain'd;
But when on Isthmian Neptune's strand
The efforts of his victor hand
Join'd to great Ptæodorus' might,
His sire and partner in the fight,
The glorious prize obtain'd;
More lengthen'd pomps and songs proclaim
Terpsias' and Eritimus' fame.

the Artificer, in the citadel at Lacedæmon, has these words:— *ἡ δε προς δυσμας εχει των ζωων αετους τε δυο, τους ορνιθας, και ισας επ' αυτοις νικας.*

59 The Hellotia was a festival of Minerva celebrated at Corinth; in which was a game called *Λαμπαδοδρομια*, from youths *running with lamps* in their hands. The scholiast informs us that when the Dorians, with the Heraclidæ, invaded Corinth and burned the city, the greater part of the virgins fled; but Hellotia, with her sister Eurytione, perished in the flames of the temple of Minerva.

66 The former was the son of Ptæodorus; the latter the son of Terpsias.

What palms to him from Delphic contests rise!
What honours Nemea's grassy field supplies!
If all his glorious deeds my song would tell,
The shore's unnumber'd stones I might recount as well. 66

Wisdom still follows in the mean,
On every fit occasion seen.
I, when true friendship wakes the string,
Prudence or warlike fame to sing,
Not e'en for Corinth's sires will raise
Strains of exaggerated praise.
Thence Sisyphus, the craftiest son of earth,
His hands endued with more than mortal skill,
And to this race Medea owes her birth,
Whose wedded choice opposed her father's will.
Her ready aid, by love inspired, could save
Argo and all her crew from the remorseless grave.

What time the troops in long array
Appear'd before the Dardan wall,
Anxious to end the doubtful fray,
Begun at the Atridæ's call.
When, aided by their friendly host,
Greece strove her Helen to regain,
And Troy beyond her threaten'd coast
To drive th' invaders to the main.
While Danaus' sons with fear survey'd
Glaucus, from Lycia's field array'd—
The plain, he said with conscious pride,
Where flows Pirene's sacred tide,
That was my sire's dominion fair,
Whose palace tower'd in splendour there. 88

Bold Pegasus, the snaky Gorgon's son,
He strove to curb with many an effort vain,
Where that sweet fountain's bubbling waters run,
Till virgin Pallas brought the golden rein.
In vision to his couch of rest she came,

And cried, " Can still th' Œolian monarch sleep?
The courser with this wished-for bridle tame,
And to the god who rules the stormy deep,
As the white bullock on his altar bleeds,
Display as strong a rein as checks his fiery steeds."

'Twas thus, as plunged in sleep he lay,
The godlike maid, who joys to wield
The terrors of her azure shield,
Seem'd in the shadowy gloom to say.
On eager foot the monarch rose
And seized the wonder glittering near,
Then straight the whole bright vision shows
To Polyidus, native seer,
That when by night retired to rest,
Obedient to the high behest,
Within her consecrated fane,
The virgin progeny of Jove,
Who darts his lightning spear above,
Gave to his hand the golden rein. 111

The prophet bade him swift obey
This passage of the will divine,
A sturdy bull to Neptune slay,
And to equestrian Pallas rear the shrine.
Full oft the gods with power supreme
Have brought the wish'd event to birth,
Beyond the utmost hope or dream
Of the short-sighted sons of earth.
Even thus Bellerophon the bold
With gentle rein thrown o'er his head,
The winged courser's pride controll'd,
And at his potent bidding led. 122

Then quickly mounting, sportive play'd
In brazen panoply array'd.
Borne by his faithful steed, he sought the field,
Where blows the desert air with chilling breath;

Made the brave Amazonian squadrons yield,
And closed their female warrior ranks in death.
Chimæra, breathing fire, his arms o'erthrew,
And the proud race of Solymi he slew.
His death I sing not—while from thraldom freed,
The ancient stalls of Jove receive th' aspiring steed. 132

But 'tis not mine beyond the mark to throw
The whirling arrows from my potent bow.
The high-throned muses' willing slave, I raise
With the just tribute of poetic praise,
The Oligæthidæ's Corinthian train,
Victors at Isthmus and on Nemea's plain.
While in brief tale their glories I rehearse,
True is the oath that sanctifies my verse.
Since thirty wreaths the herald's sweet-toned sound
In either contest won, sings to the world around. 143

Their triumphs on Olympia's plain
Ere now my song has given to fame;
And future crowns the lay shall move,
If true my ardent wishes prove.
But should the natal demon bless,
Since God alone confers success,
To Jove and war's stern lord we leave
The embryo glories to achieve.
For them what verdant garlands grow
On the Parnassian mountain's brow!
What chaplets Thebes and Argos yield,
And green Arcadia's sacred grove!
Where stands as witness of the field,
The altar of Lycæan Jove. 154

142 The scholiast says that these were stars anciently called *ονοι* as well as *φατναι*. Perhaps, therefore, it was the *Præsepe Asellorum*, near the constellation Cancer; which, being a summer sign, answers to the description of it given by Theocritus, (xxii. 21.)—*ονων ανα μεσσον αμαυρη Φατνη, σημαινοισα τα πρὸς πλοον ενδια παντα.*

Pellene, Sicyon, have beheld their might—
Æacidæ's well-guarded grove,
Eleusis, Megara, where oft in fight,
As oft in splendid Marathon they strove.
Eubœa and the wealthy cities spread
Beneath aspiring Ætna's head.
Through Græcia's realm more wreaths to them belong
Than could be number'd in the poet's song.
Still, mighty Jove, preserve their tranquil state,
And may increasing joys the virtuous race await!

THE FOURTEENTH OLYMPIC ODE.

TO ASOPICHUS OF ORCHOMENOS, ON HIS VICTORY IN THE STADIC COURSE, GAINED IN THE SEVENTIETH OLYMPIAD.

ARGUMENT.

This ode begins with a highly poetical invocation to the Graces, guardians of Orchomenos, that they may bless the victor with their propitious influence.—The poet concludes with an address to Echo, enjoining her to carry the news of his conquest to the city of Proserpine, in order to gratify his father Cleodamus with the pleasing intelligence.

Nymphs of Cephisian streams! who reign
Where generous coursers graze the plain,
And rule Orchomenos the fair;
Ye Graces! who with power divine
Protect the ancient Minyæ's line,
Oh listen to my humble prayer.
To you the grateful bard shall raise
His tribute of poetic praise;
Since wisdom, beauty, splendour flow
From your bright sphere to man below.
Not without you the bless'd above
Or join in banquet or in chorus move.
But throned on high, your lovely train
Placed near the Pythian god of day,
Whose golden shafts the beams of light display,
All the high deeds of Heaven ordain,
And praise th' Olympic sire with hymns of endless love.

Aglaia, offspring of his might divine,
Thalia and Euphrosyne, whose ear

The songs of heaven delights to hear,
Ye tuneful sisters, harken now to mine.
As moving on, with agile state,
The festal pomp we celebrate.
To hymn, Asopichus, thy fame,
With Lydian melodies I came;
Since Minyas' prosperous town to thee
Owes her Olympic victory. [27]

Now to Persephonea's hall,
Encircled by its sable wall,
Haste, Echo, bear thy grateful tale
To Cleodamus' ear;
Which in illustrious Pisa's vale
Announced his bright career:
How in life's early bloom his son
The glorious wreath of triumph won;
Encircling with that guerdon fair,
In winged grace his flowing hair. [35]

35 It was usual for the victors at the Olympic games to entwine with garlands the manes of their horses as well as their own hair. To this custom Pindar frequently alludes.

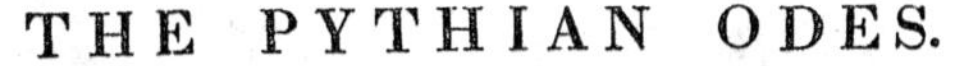

THE PYTHIAN ODES.

OF THE PYTHIAN GAMES.

THE Pythian Games were instituted in honour of Apollo. Conjectures vary with respect to the origin of the word, which some imagine to have been named from the serpent Python slain by that god. So Ovid (Met. i. 445) describing the generation and death of this monster :—

"Neve operis famam possit delere vetustas,
Instituit sacros celebri certamine ludos;
Pythia de domito serpentis nomine dictos."

Others derive the term *απο του πυθεσθαι*, because the serpent lay and *putrefied* there; others again *απο του πυνθανεσθαι*, from *inquiry*, because men in doubt went to consult the Pythian Apollo. But the most probable conjecture is that which derives them from Pytho, the ancient name of the town Delphi, situated in a valley of Mount Parnassus, the scene of their celebration, as the other Grecian games, the Olympian, Nemean, and Isthmian, were denominated from the spot on which they were held. The Pythian contests, which the Greeks regarded with the highest reverence, were instituted many years after the Olympic, and before the Isthmian.

Some authors maintain that they were established by Adrastus, king of Argos, B. C. 1263. At first they were held every ninth, but afterward every fifth year. It is said that in the first Pythiad the gods themselves were combatants; and that Castor won the prize in the stadic course, Pollux in boxing, Hercules in the pancratium, Calais in the foot race, Zetes in fighting with armour, Telamon in wrestling, and Peleus in throwing the quoit; and that the victor's reward was a laurel crown bestowed by Apollo, afterward changed for a garland of palm leaves. Ovid (loc. cit.) says that the wreath was arbitrary.

"His juvenum quicumque manu, pedibusve, rotave
Vicerat, esculeæ capiebat frondis honorem.
Nondum laurus erat; longoque descentia crine
Tempora cingebat de qualibet arbore Phœbus."

The exercises at these games were originally the same as at the Olympic, with the exception of the chariot race, which, however, was at length added. The songs by which the praises of Apollo for his victory over the serpent Pytho were celebrated were, according to Strabo, divided into *ανακρουσις, the prelude*; an allusion to which is probably contained in the opening of the Pythian odes: *εμπειρα, the first experiment; κατακελευσμος, collecting courage and rousing for the fight; ιαμβος και δακτυλος, the insults of the god over his prostrate enemy; συριγγες*, a shrill air expressing the *hisses of the expiring serpent.*

According to some authors, these games were introduced into Rome under the title of *Ludi Apollinares.*

THE FIRST PYTHIAN ODE.

TO HIERO, THE ÆTNÆAN, ON HIS VICTORY IN THE CHARIOT RACE, GAINED IN THE TWENTY-NINTH PYTHIAD.

ARGUMENT.

PINDAR begins this ode with a beautiful and poetical invocation to the lyre, expatiating on its powerful effects on gods and men.—The impious alone are incapable of enjoying its sweetness: among which number is Typhœus, who is described with great sublimity, as struggling under the superincumbent weight of Ætna.—This digression leads to the mention of the town built by Hiero at the foot of the mountain, and named from it.—Of this city he had caused himself to be proclaimed a citizen by the herald, who declared him victorious in the Pythian chariot race. This the poet regards as a presage of future triumphs, and invokes Apollo to take the town, together with the surrounding country, under his especial protection: since, as his pious disposition leads him frequently to declare, all mortal advantages, as wisdom, strength, eloquence, are derived from the gods.—Then follow the praises of Hiero, and good wishes for his future prosperity, together with the mention of his son Dinomenes.—Calling to mind the ancient history of the family and the calamities which they had suffered, the poet invokes Jupiter to be propitious to them in future, and to avert the perils of war by which they were threatened.—Concludes with offering his advice and good wishes.

OH golden lyre! to whose harmonious string
Apollo and the fair-hair'd muses sing,
Glad prelude which the choral train obey,
When moving in the mazy dance
To the sweet strains the band advance,
Their movements guided by thy sovereign sway—
Thine is the potent art to tame
The lightning's everlasting flame.

Jove's slumbering eagle on his sceptre laid,
Rests with swift plume on either side display'd. 12

Thy melting sounds his eyelids close 11
In the dark shadows of repose.
While his curved head and quivering back declare
That even in sleep thy darts have enter'd there.
Mars, as he listens to thy lay,
Gives his impetuous spear to rest—
Thy numbers charm his rage away,
And lull to peace his stormy breast.
Nor less are all the inmates of the sky
Sooth'd by the shafts of harmony;
Whene'er Apollo's skilful hand
Conducts the muses' sacred band. 24

But wretches whom immortal Jove
Deigns not to honour with his love,
Hear in confusion the Pierian strain
On earth or on the mighty main.
As Typhon, he who dared all heaven to brave,
And 'gainst the gods with hundred heads to rise,

9 Casimir appears to have imitated this splendid passage: (Lyric. Ep. ix. 15:)—

"——tibi præpes alti
Civis Olympi
Hinc et hinc pressis reverenter alis
Attulit pacem."

Homer (Il. xxiv. 361,) calls the eagle *Jove's winged messenger*, and *the strong sovereign of the plumed race.—Pope.* Apuleius (Metam. vi. 119,) gives almost a verbal translation of the words of Pindar: "Nam supremi Jovis regalis ales illa, repente, propansis utrimque pennis, affuit rapax aquila."

The English reader will probably call to mind a poetical paraphrase of the celebrated invocation with which this beautiful ode begins, by Akenside, in his hymn to the Naiads:—

"With emulation all the sounding choir,
And bright Apollo, leader of the song,
Their voices through the liquid air exalt," &c.

27 With this description of the hundred-headed Typhon or Typhœus, who is also mentioned in the beginning of the fourth

Nurtured of old in famed Cilicia's cave,
Now whelm'd in black Tartarean darkness lies.
Cumæ's sea-girdled shores below,
And where Sicilia's waters flow,
Crush'd by the island's weight, impress'd
Upon the rebel's shaggy breast,
Ætna his giant form restrains,
Whose towering height the cloud sustains,
Nurse of the sharp perennial snow. 39

Forth from her inmost caverns urge their way
Fountains of pure and unapproached fire,
Rivers of smoke that blot the face of day,
And from their source of lurid flame aspire.
But flashes of bright hue illume
The horrors of nocturnal gloom;
And hurl the rocks with thundering sound,
Whelm'd in the watery gulf profound.
The restless monster from his burning seat
Sends up to heaven the springs of direst heat;
And strikes with mute surprise their eye and ear
Who see the wondrous fire, and sounds prodigious hear. 50

So close his pinion'd form is bound
Beneath dark Ætna's leafy head;
Supported on the rugged ground,
While all his back is torn, reclining on that bed.

Olympic and the eighth Pythian, compare Callimachus, (in Del. 141,) who, like Pindar, appears anxious to clothe so vast an image with appropriate magnificence of language:—

Ὡς δ' ὁποτ' Αιτναιου ορεος πυρι τυφομενοιο
Σειονται μυχα παντα, κατουδαιοιο γιγαντος.

37 See Theocritus, (Id. xi. 47,) where the Cyclop, describing the delights of his Ætnæan residence, says,

There, from deep-shaded Ætna's melting snows
The cooling spring's ambrosial beverage flows.
POLWHELE.

Compare also Euripides—(Phœn. 815.)

Oh! may thy power, protecting Jove,
My humble prayer and deeds approve;
This mountain's guard, whose lofty brow
O'erlooks the fruitful land below,
And to the neighb'ring city gives its name,
Rear'd by the builder of immortal fame,
While the loud herald's shout declared afar
First in the Pythian course Ætnæan Hiero's car

To men who o'er the ocean sail
'Tis sweet to launch before the gale,
And ere they leave the port, discern
The omen of a bless'd return;
So might th' encomiastic lay
Recording these triumphant deeds,
Foretel in many a future day
Of garlands won by conquering steeds;
Which shall th' illustrious city raise
In festal melodies of praise.
Oh Lycian Phœbus! Delian king,
Who lovest Castalia's pure Parnassian spring,
May these warm hopes acceptance find
With Ætna's valiant sons, in thine approving mind!

For by the ruling powers of heaven
All virtues are to mortals given.
Wisdom is theirs—from them are sprung
The active hand, the fluent tongue.
And when, the victor's might to sing,
Eager I wake the lyric string,
I fear not from an erring bow
The brazen-headed shaft to throw,
But scattering far the darts of song,
Hope to confound the rival throng.
Oh! thus may Hiero's happy state
Succeeding ages give to last,

59 Hiero, to whom the first Olympic ode is addressed.

And grant, to crown his prosperous fate,
Oblivion of the sorrows past!

Her solace too Remembrance yields,
Recording in what numerous fields
His hand the noble chaplet gain'd;
While by the favouring powers of heaven
To him were brighter honours given
Than Grecian victor e'er obtain'd:
He still, though with enfeebled might,
Like Philoctetes, waged the fight.
Howe'er oppress'd, the brave contend
To sooth him with the name of friend.

'Tis said that erst the godlike band
Urged with inquiring haste their way
To Lemnos' solitary strand,
Where Pæan's tortured offspring lay;
Without whose bow the fated wall
Of Priam's city ne'er could fall.
Though sickness all his powers opposed,
Yet he the Grecian labours closed.
Thus from the deity may Hiero gain
All future joy and respite from his pain.
Then aid me, muse, the lay to raise,
Sung to Deinomenes' glad ear—
The pious youth a father's praise
From conquering steeds will joy to hear.

Come, let us find a friendly hymn, to sing
The majesty of Ætna's future king:

89 An allusion is here made to Hiero's recovery from a very dangerous illness under which he had been labouring. The transition to the story of Philoctetes, and comparison of that hero with the Sicilian monarch, is highly poetical and just. The scholiast informs us that a covert allusion is here made to Anaxilaus, king of Rhegium; or, as others understand it, to Theron, king of Agrigentum.

To whom that city Hiero rear'd—
Subjected to the bonds of law
Which Doric states from Hyllus draw—
Since heavenly freedom reigns where laws are fear'd.
The heroes who their noble race
From Pamphilus and great Alcides trace,
Who dwelt in distant times below
Taygetus' aspiring brow,
By true allegiance bound would still
Ægimius' high behests fulfil.
From Pindus rushing to the main
'Twas theirs Amyclæ's walls to gain.
In glory as in station near
The heavenly twins from Leda sprung,
Whose milk-white steeds and conquering spear
Throughout th' applauding world are sung.

Still o'er their fortune, Jove, preside,
And may the tongue of Truth proclaim
By Amena's Sicilian tide
Their citizens' and monarch's fame.
Still may the venerable king
Direct his son's obedient mind,
To harmony his subjects bring,
And in firm ties of concord bind.
Saturnian king!—if aught my prayers avail,
Soon will the shouts of hostile Tuscans cease,
Phœnicia's baffled sons from Cumæ sail,
And all our naval contest end in peace.

By Syracusa's lord o'erthrown,
What sad reverses have they known!

118 The colony of Ætna, as well as the Megarensians and Syracusans, were of Doric origin; the latter of whom received their laws from Hyllus, son of Hercules.

142 This naval victory, achieved by the brothers Hiero and Gelo over the Etruscans off the coast of Cumæ, is again mentioned in the ninth Nemean ode, v. 69, et sq, with nearly the

From the swift ships their youth he hurl'd
Deep plunged beneath the watery world;
Setting the land of Hellas free
From the rude bonds of slavery.
To praise th' Athenian name, my muse
From Salamis her lay would choose;
While Sparta glorious in the fight
Waged near Cithæron's towering height;
When her brave progeny o'erthrew
The Median archers' bended yew.
E'en thus, Deinomenes, thy fame
Sounded in hymns of loud acclaim,
Near Himera's well-water'd shore,
Where thy strong arm in glory's field
Made the contending foeman yield,
Thy latest children shall explore. 156

If just, the brief and simple tale
O'er lengthen'd numbers shall prevail:
While loathes the breast and sated ear
Exaggerated strains to hear;
Strains which disgust and envy raise
By superfluity of praise;

same invocation to Saturnian Jupiter to grant continued peace and prosperity to the Sicilians, as well as to the Grecians in general. Pindar ascribes to it the most important consequences, no less than the liberation of Greece, and not merely of Sicily, from the heavy yoke of captivity. The second victory, recorded at v. 154, was that gained by the sons of Deinomenes over the Carthaginians at Himera on the same day with the victory by the Athenians at Salamis, (A. C. 480.) These were themes worthy of the patriotic poet's enthusiasm, and he appears to expatiate on them with peculiar delight. In v. 152 Pindar alludes to the battle of Platæa, gained by Pausanias with the united forces of Lacedæmon and Athens over an army of Persians vastly superior in number, (A. C. 479,) on the same day with that of Mycale. This great victory completed the liberation of Greece; and perhaps in the whole range of descriptive poetry we shall scarcely find a series of victorious actions more concisely yet more appropriately described.

And the dark jealous mind annoy
That hears with pain another's joy.
But unsubdued by envious hate,
(For pity were a lower state,)
Still be thine honest actions sung;
With steady hand direct the helm,
Protector of the peopled realm,
And on truth's whetstone edge thy tongue. 168

For know, a fault of lightest blame 176
Would brand a king with flagrant shame.
Since be thy bearing good or ill,
Unnumber'd eyes survey thee still.
Then tarnish not thy generous mind,
If thy delighted ear rejoice
In honest fame's applauding voice,
Be all thy bounties unconfined.
Like the skill'd pilot, spread thy sail
Before the free and liberal gale. 177

Nor, friend, let flattery's specious wile
Thy better judgment e'er beguile.
When life's brief span is past away,
And closed the transitory scene,
The storied page or poet's lay
Declares how bright that life has been.
Still Crœsus' philanthropic virtue lives;
While Phalaris, who made his victims flame
Within the brazen bull's ignited frame,
To everlasting infamy survives:

170 That is, as the scholiast explains the passage, you had better be praised for your virtues than pitied for your vices or bad actions.

176 A similar sentiment occurs in Fletcher's Thierry and Theodoret, (act i., sc. 1.), where the Prince of Austracia says of royal delinquents,

"The sins we do people behold through optics,
Which show them ten times more than common vices,
And often multiply them."

Nor is the hated tyrant sung
In festal chorus by the youthful tongue.
Success is mortals' chief reward below—
The next when hymns proclaim the glorious prize—
But he whose lot in both triumphant lies
Receives the highest crown that Fortune can bestow.

THE SECOND PYTHIAN ODE.

TO THE SAME HIERO, ON HIS VICTORY IN THE CHARIOT RACE.

ARGUMENT.

Pindar begins this ode with an address to Syracuse, declaring that he brings her a hymn on account of Hiero's victory.—The merits of the victor justly demand this tribute.—By way of illustration, he digresses to the story of Ixion, who repaid the benefits received from Jupiter by base ingratitude, and when placed on the wheel, uttered a memorable saying, in order to deter men from such conduct: this leads to the fabulous birth and history of Centaurus.—The poet then adds various moral sentiments, with a view of confirming the moral truth deduced from this narration, and repels the odious charge of having slandered his patron and benefactor, from which the example of Archilochus would be sufficient to deter him.—Then follow the praises of Hiero, especially on account of his wisdom, and the glory of his martial exploits, in the assistance which he rendered to his brother Gelon, whom Hiero succeeded on the throne of Syracuse, in his contest with the Carthaginians.—In conclusion, he subjoins various precepts and admonitions, especially warning him not to lend an ear to the voice of adulation.

Oh Syracuse! in whom combine
Four towns their might to furnish thine,
Mars' loved abode—of generous steeds,
And men renown'd for martial deeds,
The fostering nurse divine—
To thee from splendid Thebes I come,
And bear the grateful tidings home,

2 These towns are thus enumerated by the scholiast: Acradina, Neapolis, Tyche, Epipolæ: justly, therefore, might the poet address Syracuse by the epithet μεγαλοπολιες.

How Hiero's victor coursers' might
Sped his earth-shaking chariot's flight.
By frequent crowns that shine afar
Resplendent in the Pythian war,
Ennobling high Ortygia's seat,
Where Dian's river shrine Alphéus' waters greet.
Without whose aid his agile grasp in vain
Had check'd his coursers with the varied rein.
For prompt with each assisting hand,
The huntress maid who joys to slay
With certain aim her sylvan prey,
And Mercury whose godhead claims
Dominion o'er the sacred games,
Placed round his polish'd car the shining band.
Taming by bit and curb applied
The docile steeds' impetuous pride;
And calling to the arduous course
The god who wields the trident's force.
Each lyric poet for a different lord
Frames the sweet hymn his valour to record.
The Cyprians thus with acclamations sing
The praise of Cinyras, their glorious king;
Loved by Apollo with his golden hair,
The priest of Venus and her cherish'd care.
Favours of friends conferr'd upon the good,
Lead to a just return of gratitude.

Son of Deinomenes! the Locrian maid
Raises the loud and joyful strain to thee,

13 I. e., the island Ortygia, at the south of Sicily. The scholiast interprets ποταμιας by της Αλφειωσας.

19 The scholiast quotes a fragment of Æschylus in which Mercury is called εναγωνιος, president of the games. In the Agamemnon (v. 521.) the herald invokes Apollo under the titles of σωτηρ καταγωνιος; and in the next verse addresses τους αγωνιους θεους Παντας.

29 Homer, who so often confirms the historical and mythological tales of Pindar, also mentions Cinyras, king of Cyprus, as having given to Agamemnon a breastplate, as a pledge of hospitable friendship: (Il., xi., 19, 20.)

Whose step secure proclaims her nation made
By thy brave arm from war's dire tumults free.
As fame reports, thus by the gods' behest,
Whirl'd on his rapid wheel Ixion cries—
"Mortals, bear this upon your minds impress'd—
Requite their love from whom your blessings rise."

This truth he from experience drew,
Dwelling with heaven's Saturnian train,
His raptured soul unable grew
Such mighty transport to sustain;
When raging with unhallow'd flame
His wild imagination strove
To ravish the celestial dame
Who shares the glorious couch of Jove.
The deed, with peril fraught, he tried,
By fearless insolence impell'd;
But quickly his aspiring pride
Avenging retribution quell'd.
These crimes with double weight pursued
The sinning hero to his doom,
Hands first in kindred blood imbrued,
A father hurried to the tomb. 59

Next his endeavour, rash and vain,
The partner of Jove's bed to gain.
Let this instruct ambitious man
The measure of his might to scan;
Since but disgrace and endless wo
From unallow'd embraces flow.
The fool who grasp'd at heavenly charms
Fill'd with a cloud his cheated arms;
Whose form became the stately mien
That marks the bright Saturnian queen.
The hands of Jove this dire deceit
Framed, for his crimes a guerdon meet.

57 This alludes to the murder of Deioneus by his son-in-law Ixion, which was perpetrated by throwing him alive into a pit filled with burning coals.

There on the deadly circle laid,
Whose fourfold chain himself had made,
His limbs in dreadful torment wound
Th' inevitable wheel around,
The wretch with tardy wisdom fraught,
To all mankind this lesson taught.
Submitting to his strong embrace,
Her proud ungracious son she bore,
Unhonour'd by the heavenly race,
Nor known to mortal birth before.
Centaurus (such the nursling's name)
Mingled in Pelion's shady grove
With the Magnesian mares in love,
And hence a wondrous army came.
Each parent's nature form'd to show—
Bent to the mother's shape below,
While rose the stately sire above.

The god whose speed prevents the eagle's wing,
And moves more swiftly than the dolphins sweep,
Sporting on rapid fin, the watery deep,
Can mortal hopes to prosperous issue bring;
Subdues the pride of one aspiring mind,
And deathless fame to others has assign'd.
But let me not with slanderous tale
Like beast of hostile tooth assail;
For as I saw, though far away,
Archilochus, whose bitter vein
His rancorous spleen could ne'er restrain,
O'erwhelmed in want and misery lay.
Imperial wealth by wisdom graced
In the first lot of bliss is placed;

71 I. e., the wheel with four radii or spokes to which Ixion was bound.

96 The story of this poet, who, by the bitterness of his poetical slander, caused the death of his father-in-law Lycambes, presents a remarkable instance of retributive justice. By *far away* is meant distant in point of time, as Archilochus flourished nearly one hundred and fifty years prior to Pindar.

And this high rank is clearly thine—
Lord of the host and well-built town,
Let thy free mind with blessings crown
Those whom thy fates to thee assign.
Of all thy mighty fathers gone,
Whatever tongue should dare proclaim
Through Greece that any hero's fame
In wealth or honours brighter shone,
With folly's mark would stamp his name. 112

But when thy virtues wake the song,
By flowery ways I pass along.
In youth the valour of thine arm
Shielded thy life from adverse harm.
Hence I declare that thou hast found
A glory which exceeds all bound;
Whether on foot the warriors rage,
Or in equestrian strife engage;
And free from blame my praise shall sound
Thy counsels in maturer age.
Farewell—this hymn across the hoary sea,
As by Phœnician craft, I send to thee.

121 It appears from this passage, which is confirmed by a fragment of Sophocles, as well as one of Aristophanes, that the Phœnicians, like the Canaanites of Scripture, were always distinguished above other nations by their eminence as merchants, which seems to have passed into a sort of proverb. The Castorean song, which Pindar sends across the sea to Hiero, it is probable that nothing more is intended than a hymn commemorative of an equestrian victory, Castor being the god of horsemanship: nor must it be confounded with the Καστορειον μελος, or war song of the Spartans. The purport of the following passage is very obscure, referring, probably, to some story unknown to us. The praise of the righteous judge, Rhadamanthus, which follows, Heyne considers to have been a favourite theme with the ancient poets, and affords another proof of the noble independence of Pindar's mind, and of the value of his friendship, which prompted him to warn even a king with perfect plainness and sincerity against being corrupted by the false praises of venal adulators. The construction of the next four lines is by no means clear, although the sentiment, cautioning Hiero to be-

Thou the triumphant Castoréan song,
With music that th' Æolian lyre shall make,
To which the seven harmonious chords belong,
Skill'd as thou art, with willing candour take.
Let witless boys extol the shape
Of the deform'd unsightly ape:
But we the lofty song of praise
To Rhadamanthus justly raise—
Clear-sighted judge! whose rigorous mind
With wisdom and experience fraught,
Ne'er by the mists of flattery blind,
In her seducing wiles is caught.
How often from her whisper'd lies
Inextricable evils rise!
To him whose lips with foxlike art
The slanderous calumnies impart;
And him who with believing ear
The tale of falsehood joys to hear.
From such deceit what good can spring?
Will this or fame or profit bring?
As in the fisher's watery toil,
Aloft the buoyant cork remains,
While laden with its finny spoil,
The whelming gulf his net retains.
So I from fear and danger free,
Float corklike on the briny sea.

Ne'er is a good and potent word
From lips of treacherous townsman heard.
His wiles that all alike deceive,
A web of endless mischief weave.
Such boldness ne'er can I approve—
Still be it mine a friend to love;
But like a wolf the foe to view,
And in his crooked ways pursue.

ware of being misled by the arts of whispering slanderers, is sufficiently obvious.

151 I have here followed Heyne's emendation, *ατav* instead of the common reading *αγαν*.

Oft from a man of upright tongue
A state's true happiness has sprung:
Whether in solitary pride
A king the reins of empire guide,
Or the grave band of nobles proud,
Or chief of the tumultuous crowd.
Against the potent will of Heaven
'Tis mad ambition to contend,
By whom to these now might is given,
Now others call the god their friend.
But calm content the envious mind
In their delight can never find.
When the preponderating scale
Bids any happier lot prevail,
The rankling wound torments their breast,
Till in the wish'd possession bless'd.
But he, the patient and the wise,
Who to the yoke his neck applies,
Lifts not, like oxen prone to feel
Each casual sting, his angry heel—
Be my complacent temper shown,
Conversing with the good alone.

THE THIRD PYTHIAN ODE.

TO THE SAME HIERO, ON HIS VICTORY IN THE SINGLE-HORSE RACE, GAINED IN THE TWENTY-SIXTH PYTHIAD.

ARGUMENT.

When the intelligence of Hiero's victory in the Pythian games was reported to him, that monarch laboured under a grievous disorder.—Hence the friendly poet takes occasion to express his wish that the centaur Chiron, the preceptor of Æsculapius in the healing art, could return to life, in order to restore health to the afflicted Hiero.—This leads to the fabulous story of Apollo and Coronis, to whose clandestine love he owed his birth.—He then proceeds to the victor's praises, and prays to the gods for his continued prosperity.—Then follows a consolatory exhortation to bear adversity with an equal mind, derived from the uncertain condition of mortality, and the constant interruption to earthly happiness; which truth he illustrates by the examples of Cadmus and Peleus; interweaving the mythological story of the nuptials of Peleus and Thetis. —He concludes by recommending equanimity from his own example.

Oh! could to life my anxious care
Chiron Phillynides recall;
(If my weak tongue may form a prayer
Breathed for the common good of all;)
Celestial Saturn's potent child,
To rule o'er Pelion's valleys still,
Howe'er in form like monster wild,
Yet men approved his friendly will.
He nurtured once the hero kind,
Asclepias, whose assuaging art
For the rack'd limbs relief could find,
And bid each torturing pain depart. 13

Him e'er by Eilithyia's aid
Equestrian Phlegyas' daughter bore,

Transfix'd by Dian's shafts, the maid
Went down to Pluto's dreary shore;
And lifeless in her chamber lay,
A victim to the god of day.
No slight or trivial wounds proceed
From wrath of Jove's immortal seed.
Her sire beguiled—her mind subdued
By folly—with contempt she view'd
The ties that charm'd her heart before;
Loved by the god, whose locks unshorn
His brow with youthful grace adorn,
The fruit of heavenly race she bore.
Her haughty soul could ne'er sustain
To see the marriage table spread,
Or listen to the nuptial strain
By the coeval virgins led;
Whose melody their raptured ear
At evening's hour delights to hear:
But sicken'd with desire to prove
The ardours of an absent love.
Full many share the damsel's pain—
What tribes of mortals, rash and vain,
Blind to the good that courts their view,
Eager some distant joy pursue!
And lured by hope's delusive gleam
Chase but an unsubstantial dream. 41

Fair-robed Coronis' scornful mind
Such fate was justly doom'd to find;
For in the stranger's couch she lay,
Who from Arcadia bent his way.
But Loxias, who on Pytho's shrine
With kingly eye in act divine
Sees many a victim bleed,
He who by wisdom all his own
Makes to himself each action known,
Survey'd the impious deed.

45 Apollo or the Sun, so named from his oblique course through the ecliptic.

No falsehood mocks his piercing sight,
Nor gods nor men elude the skill
Which judges in prophetic light
The open act, the secret will.
Then having known the fraud that led
The nymph to Ischys' foreign bed,
His sister fierce with dire intent
To Laceræa straight he sent.
The maid whose habitation rose
Where marshy Bœbias' fountain flows,
Too soon her alter'd demon drove
The ills that wait on crime to prove.
When by the cruel plague pursued
Her sin the guiltless neighbours rued—
Sad victims of a common tomb—
As from one fatal spark arise
The flames aspiring to the skies,
And all the crackling wood consume.

60 Bœbias, so named from one of the nymphs, is a fountain near Laceræa, in Pelasgiotis. Catullus, (de Nupt. Pel. et Thet. 286, ed. Voss :)—

> "Xyniasi et linquens Doris celebrata choreis
> Bœbiados."

in which passage some editions read *Minosin* and *Nonatios* for *Xyniasi* and *Bœbiados.* Doering reads *Mnemonidum*, and *Nonvacuus* instead of *Bœbiados.* Strabo (Geogr. lib. ix.) appears to confirm Vossius' reading.

61 It is perhaps unnecessary to refer the critical reader to Bentley's Dissertation on Phalaris (p. 216—218) for an excellent elucidation of the expression δαιμων ἑτερος, which *the Examiner* had denied to be poetical. The scholiast explains ἑτερος by ὁ κακοποιος; and quotes a choliambic of Callimachus to confirm his interpretation. To the remarks of our admirable critic, who, if not gifted with any great talent in metrical composition, had nevertheless a very accurate perception of the niceties of poetical expression, I would add the words of Euripides : (Med. 1106 :)—

> ——————ειδε κυρησει
> δαιμων οὗτος :

meaning death.

But when upon the funeral pyre
Her kindred placed the maid,
And curling round the greedy fire,
In vivid lustre play'd—
"My soul," thus spoke the god of day,
"Its own bright race abhors to slay;
O'erwhelm'd by that most wretched death
Which stopp'd the hapless mother's breath."
This said, with one short step he came,
And snatch'd his infant from the flame;
Through whose divided channel trod
The feet of the departing god.
The rescued child he gave to share
Magnesian centaur's fostering care;
And learn of him the soothing art
That wards from man disease's dart.

Of those whom nature made to feel
Corroding ulcers gnaw their frame;
Or stones far hurl'd, or glittering steel,
All to the great physician came.
By summer's heat or winter's cold
Oppress'd, of him they sought relief.
Each deadly pang his skill controll'd,
And found a balm for every grief.
On some the force of charmed strains he tried,
To some the medicated draught applied:
Some limbs he placed the amulets around;
Some from the trunk he cut, and made the patient sound.

But wisdom yields to sordid gain·
Hands which the golden bribes contain
Are bound by them alone.
At their command the grasp of death
Restored the man whose forfeit breath
Had from its mansion flown.

101 Alluding, perhaps, to the fable of the resuscitated *Hippol*.

But quickly heaven's Saturnian lord
Snatch'd with each hand the life restored;
And wing'd his bolt of lurid flame
Once more to crush the mortal frame.
From him let all of human kind
Learn to acquire an humble mind:
Nor 'gainst the rulers of the sky
To vaunt their fleeting destiny. 108

Affect not then, beloved soul,
The life immortal of the bless'd:
Let prudence thy desires control,
In practicable schemes to rest.
If Chiron, of unerring skill,
Dwelt in his Pelion cavern still;
And if the sweet-toned hymns could find
Their wanton passage to his mind,
Then my persuasive tongue had pray'd
(Nor vainly) the physician's aid;
Who should some healing brother give,
Latona's son or Jove's, to gain
Respite from fever's burning pain,
And bid th' afflicted god revive.
In ships that cut th' Ionian sea
I come to my Ætnæan friend.
Mild king! whose cares, from envy free,
O'er Syracusa's sons extend.
Foster'd by him, e'en strangers prove
The blessings of a father's love. 126

If, crossing the Sicilian deep,
Her onward course my bark should keep,
To him my grateful hand would bear
Of twofold joys a garland fair.
Health's golden charm, the loud acclaim
That sings the Pythian victor's fame;

ytus, thence called *Virbius;* some suppose *Tyndarus*, others *Glaucus*, others *Hymenæus*, others *Orion*, or *Capaneus*.

Such triumphs as in days of yore
At Cirrha Pherenicus bore:
And brighter than the airy star
For him my splendour beams afar.

But to the mother would I pray,
Whose altar near my dwelling stands:
There oft the nymphs, who bend their way
To her and Pan, their vows to pay,
Assemble in nocturnal bands.
Thee, Hiero, whose exalted mind
Can to the heights of science rise;
True wisdom, with experience join'd,
And former ages render wise.
When gods or man one good bestow,
That blessing leads to double wo.
While fools can ne'er with decent pride
    Sustain their adverse fate,
Calm patience, outwardly elate,
    Shows but the brighter side.
In the first rank of fortune placed,
Monarch! such happiness is thine;
For kings, with power superior graced,
Must above all conspicuous shine.
Peleus nor godlike Cadmus led
A life exempt from every care;
Who, beyond mortals bless'd, were said
The height of happiness to share.
They heard when Pelion's woody hill
And the seven Theban portals rang
With strains which the melodious skill
Of the gold-netted muses sang.
One fair Harmonia to the nuptial bed,
One prudent Nereus' child, illustrious Thetis led.

To both the hymeneal feasts
Came Saturn's sons, heaven's kingly guests;

139 I. e., the sun. See Ol. i. v. 9.

Whom, seated on their thrones of gold,
They saw the splendid gifts unfold.
Thus every care and labour past,
Rewarded by the fostering love
That guards the favour'd sons of Jove,
Their drooping hearts were raised at last.
But Cadmus, in a later age,
By his three daughters' wretched fate,
Their awful death and frantic rage,
Fell from his bless'd paternal state;
When Father Jove, in radiant flame,
To thy sweet couch, fair-arm'd Thyone, came. 177

While Peleus' offspring, whom on Phthia's shore
Her only son, immortal Thetis bore,
Burn'd on the funeral pyre, in cries of grief
Compell'd the Greeks to mourn their slaughter'd chief. 182

Whoever then of mortal kind
To certain truth directs his mind,
Let him with grateful heart enjoy
What good the blessed gods bestow:
His shortlived pleasures to destroy
Soon will the adverse tempests blow.
How great soe'er, it speeds away,
Though rushing with the tempest's sway.

179 The fate of two of the daughters of Cadmus, *Ino* and *Semele*, has been mentioned before, (Ol. ii. 36.) To these Pindar now adds the third, *Agave*, who, in a fit of madness, slew her son Pentheus. (See Ovid. Met. lib. iii. ad fin.) The history of these three sisters, to whom may be added Autonoe, mother of the ill-fated Actæon, presents a striking instance of the uncertain tenure by which mortal prosperity is held. In v. 184 *Semele* is called *Thyone;* so named, says the scholiast, *απο του περι τον Διονυσον παθους, ὁτι θυει και ενθουσιᾳ κατα τους χορους*; as the name Semele was given, *ὁτι σειει τα μελη των οινουργουντων αυτον* (ὁ Διονυσος scil.)

193, 194 The metaphor is here expressed in nearly the same words as in the last verse of the seventh Olympic ode.

Lowly when in a lot obscure,
But liberal if my fortunes rise;
These blessings I shall render sure,
Obtain'd with all my energies.
If wealth the favouring god should give,
I hope that not unknown to fame
My honour'd and illustrious name
In ages yet to come may live.
We know that glorious powers belong
To the sweet poet's epic song;
What time he wakes the sounding lyre,
And bids departed worth aspire.
Such Nestor's lot. This charm could save
Lycian Sarpedon from the grave:
But few the lengthen'd age obtain
Whose virtue blooms in lyric strain.

THE FOURTH PYTHIAN ODE.

TO ARCESILAUS OF CYRENE, ON HIS VICTORY IN THE CHARIOT RACE, GAINED IN THE THIRTY-FIRST PYTHIAD.

ARGUMENT.

In the opening of this extremely long and highly poetical ode, Pindar, whose subject leads him to the mention of Cyrene, interweaving mythology with historical relation, digresses to the origin of the colony, and the prediction given by Medea to Euphemus, one of the Argonauts, and subjoins the interpretation of it from the Delphic oracle given to Battus concerning the origin of the colony which was to be planted by him in Libya.—This introduces a long and episodical narration of the Argonautic expedition; the slaying of the dragon, and the recovery of the golden fleece,—The simple and beautiful description of Jason's sudden appearance among the citizens of Iolcos.—The remainder of the ode is occupied with admonitions to Arcesilaus respecting the prudent and judicious government of his kingdom.—In this part the piety and wisdom of the poet are conspicuous, although it may be justly doubted whether the conclusion be altogether suitable to the nature of a lyric ode.

This day thy prompt assistance lend,
Muse, to the hero and the friend,
Lord of Cyrene, famed for generous steeds—
To Delphi and Apollo raise
The well-earn'd melody of praise,
As the bright pomp Arcesilaus leads.
In ages past the priestess there,
Who near Jove's golden eagles held her throne,
With voice oracular made known
What truths the present god inspired her to declare.

8 These were placed near the Delphic tripod, and probably gave rise to the story of the two birds sent by Jupiter, one from

That Battus, when he left the sacred isle,
(The colonist of Libya's fruitful land,)
Should rear th' equestrian city's towering pile,
Secure upon its chalky rock to stand. 15

And treasured in his mind should lie
Medea's ancient prophecy.
Which when the seventeenth age was past,
Æetes' vengeful child foretold,
In every point fulfill'd at last,
The sons of Thera should behold.
The Colchian queen inspired to tell
What from her lips immortal fell,
Thus spoke the fates' supreme command
To warlike Jason's naval band:
"From gods and mighty heroes sprung,
Give ear to my prophetic tongue.
Hereafter from this seabeat shore
The child of Epaphus shall move,
By mortals cherish'd as before,
And plant the root where men adore
The majesty of Libyan Jove. 28

Then for the short-finn'd dolphin's speed
Shall they direct the rapid steed;
Instead of oars, their rein shall steer
The cars that mock the storm's career.
That omen issuing from the skies
True will the sure event declare,
When spacious Thera shall arise,
Metropolis of cities fair:
Which at the mouth of the Tritonian lake,
From the great god in human form, whose hand

the east and the other from the west, in order to ascertain the true centre of the earth, and which met at Pytho, or Delphi.

11 The island Thera or Callista.

32–35 I.e., instead of the naval pursuits of islanders, they shall emulate the equestrian skill of their continental neighbours.

To his kind host return'd the fertile land,
Euphemus hurried from the prow to take.
To ratify the sign, Saturnian Jove
Thunder'd auspicious from his throne above.

Now while the brazen anchor's might,
Curb of the rapid Argo's flight,
The sailors o'er the ship suspend,
He comes their labours to attend.
Twelve days from ocean's watery bed
On the earth's desert back we led,
Counsell'd by me, the naval frame.
The cheerful mien assuming then
Of him, the most revered of men,
Alone the mighty godhead came;
As when to each arriving guest
The liberal master of the feast
At first his courteous speech applies.

But sweet desire, our homeward way
To urge, forbade a longer stay.
Eurypylus who traced his birth,
To him who girds and shakes the earth,
Observed our eager haste to move:
Then snatching straight the fertile clod,
Pledge of the hospitable god,
To give it to Euphemus strove.
Obedient to the will divine,
The hero leap'd upon the strand,
Receiving with extended hand
The mystic earth his fates assign:
That whelm'd beneath the briny tide,
When evening's shadows gather'd round,
Was from the vessel heard to glide
Far in the watery gulf profound.

49 The god Triton in the form of Eurypylus.

64 This mythological tale is related at length by Apollonius, in the fourth book of his Argonautics: (1550–1600.)

Full oft had I the menial train
To guard that precious gift enjoin'd;
But dull oblivion seized their mind,
And render'd all my caution vain.
Now in this isle is shed before the time
The immortal seed of spacious Libya's clime;
For when by sacred Tænarus he pass'd,
Whose subterranean mouth to Hades leads,
At home the treasure had Euphemus cast,
Great Neptune's son who rules his potent steeds;
Whom in a former age Europa bore,
Daughter of Tityus, on Cephisus' shore. 82

His children's fourth succeeding race
Had seized, with Grecian arms to aid,
The continent's extended space;
When, exiles from great Sparta made,
Mycenæ and the Argive bay,
The wand'ring train pursue their way.
Now will he find that chosen race
Sprung from the Lemnian dames' embrace,
When honour'd by th' immortal host,
They come to this sea-girded coast,
And there beget the man, whose reign
Shall stretch o'er Libya's clouded plain.
When to the sacred Pythian dome
That glitters with abundant gold,
Battus in after times shall come,
Phœbus will his decree unfold,
That he in ships should bring a numerous band
Far as Saturnian Nilus' fruitful land." 99

83 Virgil appears to have imitated this passage: (Georg. iv. 467:)—

" *Tænarias etiam fauces, alta ostia Ditis,*
Et caligantem nigra formidine lucum
Ingressus, Manesque adiit, Regemque tremendum."

104 The scholiast says that Pindar here mentions Nilus instead of Jupiter, since this river was by the Egyptians worshipped as a god. He also quotes a hemistich from Parmeno, addressing the Nile as the Egyptian Jove: Αιγυπτιε Ζευ Νειλε.

Such were the strains by fate inspired
That dropp'd from sage Medea's tongue,
Silent the godlike men admired,
And round in fix'd attention hung.
Bless'd son of Polymnestus! thee,
Gladden'd by this spontaneous strain,
The Delphic priestess' augury
Bade the sublimest hopes maintain.
Thrice cried her monitory voice,
"Cyrene's destined king, rejoice!"
When thou inquiredst at the Pythian shrine
The doubtful issue of the voice divine. 112

And now, as in the vernal hour
Impurpled glows each opening flower,
So shines his eighth succeeding race,
Arcesilaus' youthful grace.
Apollo in the Pythian field
And just Amphictyons' high decree
To his triumphant coursers yield
The glorious palm of victory.
Him will I to the muses' train
Give with the ram's bright fleece of gold,
For which when sail'd the Minyæ bold,
Honours from heaven 'twas theirs to gain. 123

111 The expression in the original is remarkable, *μελισσα Δελφις*. So Callimachus of the priestesses of Ceres:

Δηοι δ' ουκ απο παντος ὑδωρ φορεουσι Μελισσαι.

See the annotation in Benedict's edition. Perhaps *μελισσα* in this sense may not improbably be derived from the Hebrew מליצי, an intercessor or interpreter, whose office it was to *smooth*, or *render agreeable* the suit of the petitioner:* (Parkhurst ad verb.:) as *μελισσα*, a bee, probably descends from the same root in its primitive meaning of *sweet.* Virgil, indeed, speaking as a Py thagorean, says, (Georg. iv. 253,)

"Hence to the bee some sages have assign'd
A portion of the god, and heavenly mind."
Sotheby's Version.

So Horace of Orpheus, (ad Pis. 391,) *sacer interpresque deorum*

* The word in Genesis, xlii., 23.

To urge their bark's career what cause was found?
In chains of adamant what peril bound?
'Twas doom'd that Pelias should expire
By force or fraudulent design,
Who waked the hero's vengeful ire,
Sprung from the brave Æolian line.
To his quick thought returning still
The oracle of Delphi spoke
In sounds of wo that loud and shrill
From earth's well-wooded centre broke;
And bade his jealous mind beware
The man with foot of sandal bare.
When he from Chiron's high retreat
The stranger citizen should come
To famed Iolcos' western seat,
And gain at length a foreign home.
Then brandishing his double spear,
Approach'd the wondrous mortal near.
Wrapp'd are his limbs of beauteous mould
Within a double vesture's fold—
Magnesian, and the foreign pard,
'Gainst pelting rains the surest guard;
While locks in sacrifice unshorn
His ample back with grace adorn.
Straight coming on with quiet tread,
He show'd a mind devoid of dread. 151

When one among th' assembled crowd
Turn'd to th' unknown, thus spoke aloud:
" 'Tis not Apollo I behold,
Nor Venus' spouse, the god of war,
Who thunders in his iron car.
Long since, as ancient fame has told,
Deceased in fertile Naxos lie
Iphimedeia's progeny,
Otus, and thou, King Ephialtes bold.

163 Homer (Od., iv., 304,) gives the same character of the *Aloidæ gemini.* See also Virg. Æn., vi., 581; and Stat. Theb., x., 850.

" Vidisti Aloidas, cum cresceret impia tellus" &c.

The virgin huntress' rapid dart
From her unconquer'd quiver flew,
And high-aspiring Tityus slew,
That mortals may desire to prove
The transports of permitted love." 164

So they their mutual thoughts impart
Then with his mules and polish'd car
Came Pelias rushing from afar.
Mute wonder held his mind in thrall
Soon as alone the right foot round
He view'd the well-known sandal bound.
But with dissembled fear address'd
The monarch, his unwelcome guest :
" What country boast'st thou thy dear land to call ?
Fair offspring of a spotless womb,
By mortal lineage art thou come ?
Tell quickly thine illustrious race,
Nor by detested lies disgrace." 178

To him the bold and fearless youth
In placid words this answer gave :
" I come from Chiron's shady cave,
Who disciplined my soul to truth.
By Chariclo and Philyra the fair,
Centaurus' daughters, I was nurtured there.
But when the twentieth year had fled,
Homeward my youthful steps I bent.
To them no word of parting said,
Naught that could mark my fix'd intent
To take the sceptre of the land,
Grasp'd by another's lawless hand.
An honour which the king of heaven
To Æolus and to his sons had given. 192

For Fame reports that Pelias bold,
Slave to his wishes uncontroll'd,
My honour'd parents' rightful sway
Has snatch'd with violence away.

They, when I first the light survey'd,
Dreading the haughty leader's pride.
Sent me in purple robes array'd,
(While female shrieks on every side
Raised through the house in solemn show
The mimic note of funeral wo,)
When only dark and silent night
Was conscious of my secret flight;
And to Saturnian Chiron gave,
The nurture of his hand to crave. 205

But all the tale ye know full well—
Where rose my noble sire's abode,
In car with milk-white steeds who rode,
Illustrious townsmen, clearly tell.
Great Æson's offspring, lo! I come
A native to no foreign home.
From Saturn sprung, the heavenly beast
His charge by Jason's name address'd."
He spoke: a father's doting eye
Soon recognised his progeny;
And from his aged lids below
The copious tears began to flow;
Which showed the soul's o'erflowing joy
To see his best and loveliest boy. 219

Attracted by the hero's fame,
To them both Æson's brothers came.
This Pheres from Hyperia's fountain calls,
And Amythaon from Messene's walls.
These soon Admetus and Melampus join'd,
To greet their kinsman with a friendly mind.
Them at the hospitable board
Jason with courteous speech address'd,
And bade the cheer profusely stored
Exhilarate the frequent guest.
Five days and nights their courses roll, 234
While pleasure warms each festive soul. 233

But on the sixth, once more the youth
Repeats his tale in words of truth.
Then follow'd by the kindred band,
In haste he from the mansion went.
Their steps to Pelias' dome they bent,
On rushing with tumultuous stand.
Soon as the sound assail'd his ear
Came bright-hair'd Tyro's offspring near.
From Jason's lips with sweetness fill'd,
The mild and gentle speech distill'd.

" Petræan Neptune's son, the mind
To praise deceit is more inclined,
Than justice, though in grief it end,
And to a bitter issue tend.
Hence let our lawless anger cease,
Be all the future joy and peace.
One mother, as full well ye know,
Bore Cretheus and Salmoneus bold,
And the third race from them who flow,
We the sun's golden might behold.
The fates survey with adverse eyes
When impious kindred feuds arise.

'Tis not for us with sword or dart,
That perforate the brazen shield,
Our fathers' ample wealth to part,
The heritage their glories yield.
I the white flocks that graze the plain,
And yellow herds to thee resign,
With all our parents' wide domain,
Which thou hast seized, enlarging thine.
Nor shall my mind with envy grieve
To see thy house new wealth receive.
But thou the sceptred monarch's throne,
Seat of old Cretheus' royal son,
Whence he the laws with justice fraught
To his equestrian subjects taught—

These without pain that both must rue,
Restore—lest fresher grief ensue!"

When thus the youthful hero spoke,
From Pelias this mild answer broke:
" Such will I be—though tardy age
Now warn me of life's closing stage,
While thou art fresh in youth's gay flow'ret still—
Potent thy vigorous arm shall prove,
Th' infernal godheads' wrath remove,
And murder'd Phryxus' high behest fulfil:
' Haste, from Æetes' chambers bear
My soul, he cried, and golden hair,
On the ram's fleecy back outspread,
That once a certain refuge gave
From stepdame's treachery and the wave.'
'Twas thus the wondrous vision said.
Where the Castalian waters flow,
To search the oracle I go—
When straight the voice prophetic there
Bids me for naval flight prepare.
If thou thy prompt assistance lend,
Which may this arduous contest end,
I swear to make the lot thine own,
To monarchize and rule alone.
Firm witness of the faithful oath
Be Jove, the common sire of both."

They part; this compact ratified,
Jason the herald's trump of fame,
His instant voyage to proclaim,
Urges to sound on every side.
Thither the sons of Leda fair
And of Saturnian Jove repair;

281 Phryxus, whose manes, as Pelias craftily insinuates, are to be appeased by the youthful Jason, was the father of Athamas and Ino, who were driven from their paternal soil and died in Colchis.

Alcmena's too, her eyelids set
Within a silken fringe of jet.
Two heroes of th' earth-shaker's race,
Whose locks in clustering beauty play,
Dreading by fear or dull delay
Their ancient valour to disgrace;
From Pylos one directs his flight,
And one from the Tænarean height.
Be this, Euphemus, to thy glory told,
And thine, oh Periclymenus the bold!
The harper Orpheus join'd the valiant train,
Apollo's vaunted son, and father of the strain.

And Hermes of the golden wand
Sent his twin sons, whose bosoms beat
To join the enterprising band
With fervent youth's impetuous heat.
Prompt at the call, with fearless heart
Echion, Erytus depart
From their loved home, that lay below
Distant Pangæus' lofty brow.
Boreas, whose rule the winds obey,
Arm'd his brave sons, whose back display'd
The ample pinions' purple shade,
Zetes and Calais for the fray.

Great Juno waked the sweet desire
Which bade the demigods aspire
With Argo o'er the deep to roam;
That fix'd in his maternal home
Remote from peril none should stay,
And wear his laggard age away.
But share his fellow heroes' toil,
Death's fairest antidote, the spoil
Soon as to proud Iolcos' town
Came the bright flower of seamen down,
Jason extoll'd with praises due,
And number'd all the valiant crew.

Skill'd in each bird that cleaves the sky,
And sacred lots of augury,
Mopsus enjoin'd the host their sail
To spread before the favouring gale.
But when they hang upon the prow
Their anchors o'er the deep below,
Fix'd at the stern, the chief displays
His sacred vial's golden blaze.
Invoking heaven's great father Jove,
Who wields his lightning spear above;
Waves that o'er ocean's bosom play,
And breezes' every varying way,
Calm nights and days his prayers implore,
And sweet return, their wanderings o'er. 349

Propitious thunder's awful sound
  Heaven's favouring answer quickly spoke,
And lightning's forked darts around
  From all the clouds irradiate broke.
Elated at the prosperous sign,
The heroes glow with joy divine.
The augur issued his command
  To ply their oars with constant force,
Suggesting to the valiant band
  Sweet hopes to cheer them on their course.
Quick gaining with the breezy south
Th' inhospitable ocean's mouth,
There to the god a shrine they rear
Who sways the raging sea's career.
(Of Thracian bulls a tawny herd,
To aid the sacrifice, appear'd,)
And hollow altar's heaven-built pile,
From stony quarry hewn erewhile. 367

Not yet the dangerous pass explored,
They supplicate the vessel's lord
To fly the inevitable shock
That springs from the twin clashing rock.

But now the jarring portals close,
For ever fix'd in dead repose:
Since the proud demigods by fate
Are urged to cross the narrow strait.
And next the wandering heroes trace
To Phasis' flowing streams their way,
Mingling with Colchis' swarthy race,
And great Æetes in the fray.
Venus, whose darts inflict the sharpest wound,
First to mankind the raging songster bore,
Which to the wheel indissolubly bound,
That from Olympus gain'd its magic round,
Taught wise Æsonides her charmed lore; 386

That from Medea's raging mind
All shame of parents left behind
Persuasion's lash might take, and prove
Greece the sole object of her love.
The sum of all the labours dire
Enjoin'd him by her cruel sire
She told; and mingled with the oil
Her antidotes to rugged toil,
Given to anoint his manly frame,
Then in sweet Hymen's bands they vow'd to quench their flame. 397

But when the adamantine plough
Æetes in the midst had set,

386 This is the celebrated ιυγξ, a bird which was supposed to possess the power of inspiring the emotions of love. The scholiast gives us a long explanation of its properties, and in his comment on Nem. iv. 56, where it is again mentioned, gives its allegorical pedigree, by declaring it to have been a daughter of Echo, or, as some assert, of Peitho, the goddess of persuasion, who by filters, or magical incantations, allured Jupiter to the love of Ino, and was transformed by the revengeful Juno into a bird, which by its continued whirling expressed emblematically the raging agitation of love. The classical reader will call to mind the importance attached to its agency by Simætha, in the second Idyllium of Theocritus.

And oxen wont the fires to blow
  From cheeks that rage with constant fret,
While thundering on alternate feet,
The soil with brazen hoofs they beat—
He only their rough spirit broke,
And led obedient to the yoke.
Then straight a cubit's length impress'd
Of furrow on earth's yielding breast,
And thus he spoke: "In this high deed
If the ship's ruler shall succeed,
The fleece immortal let him bear,
Irradiate with its golden hair." 411

He said: his robe of saffron hue
Aside the youthful Jason threw,
And trusting in immortal aid,
His arduous enterprise essay'd.
On him the fire could work no harm,
Awed by his potent hostess' charm.
Then dragging on the rustic load,
Their necks and well-ribb'd haunches bound
With thongs compulsive thrown around,
He urged the sharp and bitter goad;
Then labour'd on with manly strength,
Completing soon his measured length.
O'erwhelm'd at first in speechless wo,
  Æetes view'd the arduous deed;
Then admiration's transports flow,
  And praises unrepress'd succeed. 424

To the brave youth their friendly hands
    Extend the social train,
His brow they crown with verdant bands,
    And greet in courteous strain.
Straight the sun's wondrous offspring show'd
Where was the shining skin bestow'd,
Extended high on Phryxus' sword,
A gift to war's impetuous lord.

But still, these mighty dangers pass'd
He hoped the youth would fail at last.
For in an ambush'd wood 'twas laid,
Kept by a greedy dragon's care,
With whose dire bulk, at large display'd,
No lengthen'd vessel might compare,
Though urged by fifty oars, by strokes of iron made.

Still could I speed my chariot's way,
But time forbids the long delay.
A shorter path I know full well,
In wisdom who the rest excel.
The varied snake of azure hue
He soon, Arcesilaus, slew;
And with it bore Medea home,
Author of murder'd Pelias' doom.
Then mingling in the ocean deep,
The Erythræan sea they sweep;
Thence mid the Lemnian race, who gave
Their youthful husbands to the grave,
A test of corporal strength they made—
(Aside the cumbering garments laid)
And shared their couch of sweet repose. 452

Thus in a foreign region bright
By day or in the peaceful night
Your beams of happiness arose.
For planted there, Euphemus' race
Illustrious shines with endless grace.

453 It would not be an easy task to explain the geographical course which Pindar here describes the Argonauts to have taken on their return from the expedition in quest of the golden fleece. By the *Erythræan Sea*, the Indian Ocean is to be understood, through which it seems they came into Africa, and when arrived on land, carrying the ship on their shoulders until they came to the Tritonian lake, they sailed into the Mediterranean, and touched at Thera; thence through the Ægean they came to the island of Lemnos, and connected themselves with its homicidal women.

To Lacedæmon's fertile seats
  And hardy sons the wanderers come;
Then fair Callista's island greets
  The heroes in a foreign home.
With honour hence derived from heaven
To you Latoides has given
Fair Libya's wealthy plain to crown,
And golden-throned Cyrene's town
With counsel justly framed to sway,
Which her bless'd citizens obey. 466

Now learn the Theban sage's art—
If sharp-edged axe with ruthless stroke
Her branches from the giant oak,
The form disgraced, compel to part,
Though shorn her fruit, enough is there
Her pristine beauties to declare—
If fire be ever sought at last
To shelter from the wintry blast,
Or among pillars straight and tall,
  It now sustain some lordly dome,
Hard labour in a foreign wall,
  Leaving all bare its native home. 479

Thou a most timely healer art,
  Since Pæan's favour crowns thy name—
Then, oh! a tender hand impart
  To heal the state's disorder'd frame:
A city's pride the weakest arm
May shake with danger and alarm.
But hard indeed the task to place
Her glory on its ancient base,
Unless the god with sudden sway
Direct the steersman on his way.

469 Apollo, the son of Latona.

474 Œdipus. In the remaining part of this ode Pindar cautions Arcesilaus against using unnecessarv severity towards his Cyrenean subjects.

For thee in gratitude is wove
The garland of a people's love;
Then still let bless'd Cyrene share
Thy kind and persevering care. 492

Now, monarch, with attentive ear
This maxim of the poet hear;
A virtuous messenger will crown
Each action with supreme renown;
And thus will to the muse accrue
Praise from the herald's message true.
Long time through fair Cyrene's town
Has just Demophilus been known:
And Battus' glorious house confess'd
The graces of his spotless breast.
Ere yet complete youth's narrow span,
Among the boys he shone a man:
In solemn counsel he appears
The Nestor of a hundred years:
Slander's free tongue he bids be mute,
His virtues all her tales confute: 504

Taught the base railer to abhor,
And with the good to wage no war;
Protracting naught by slow delay,
For short with man occasion's stay.
Well can he seize the fitting hour,
No slave to wayward fortune's power.
The heaviest this of human woes,
That he who each fair blessing knows,
Bound by necessity's strong chain,
Must his encumber'd foot restrain.
Like Atlas, tottering with the weight
Of all the bright incumbent heaven,

500 The maxim of Homer, called by eminence *the poet*, to which Pindar alludes, is contained in the fifteenth book of the Iliad, in the exhortation of Neptune to Iris.

520 Alludes to Demophilus, who had been banished by Arcesilaus, and whom Pindar wishes the monarch to recall.

He struggles with oppressive fate,
  From home and his possessions driven.
Immortal Jove the Titan crew
Released at length from thraldom due.
The seaman in a flagging gale
Loosens his idly-fluttering sail. 521

But soon, his deadly troubles o'er,
He prays to see his home once more.
There by Apollo's sacred spring
  To youthful revels yield his soul,
And to his skilful townsmen bring
  The lyre its varied strains to roll.
With them to lead, remote from strife,
The quiet tenour of his life.
And then in Thebes recall'd to dwell,
His grateful tongue shall freely tell
What new fount of ambrosial lays
He struck, Arcesilaus, in thy praise. 533

543 This perhaps alludes to the discovery of the fountain Hippocrene by the horse Pegasus.

THE FIFTH PYTHIAN ODE.

TO THE SAME ARCESILAUS ON HIS VICTORY IN THE CHARIOT RACE, GAINED IN THE THIRTY-FIRST OLYMPIAD.

ARGUMENT.

PINDAR begins by proclaiming the happiness of Arcesilaus, especially in gaining the Pythian victory, for which he exhorts him, in his usual pious manner, to return thanks to the gods, and to his charioteer Carrhotus; at the same time cautioning the victor not to expect sincere and perpetual happiness, since no one is free from trouble.—The reader should bear in mind that this ode was written at a time of civil dissension between the king and people of Cyrene.—Nevertheless the ancient felicity of Battus will attend Arcesilaus, who is protected by the favour of Apollo.—The poet then makes a transition to the predictions of that god, which induced the Heraclidæ to return into Peloponnesus, A. C. 1104, eighty years after the Trojan war; at which time Pindar's ancestors, the Ægidæ, came with the colony to Thera, and thence to Cyrene.—Then follow the praises of Battus, and of his posterity, particularly of Arcesilaus.—The ode concludes with good wishes for their prosperity.

ALL-POWERFUL is the wealth of kings,
The golden store when Fortune brings,
And Virtue her pure radiance blends.
Around, to bless their mortal state,
Attendant crowds obsequious wait
Of clients and expecting friends.
Oh thou! to whom, by favouring heaven,
Arcesilaus, wealth is given,
Which Glory, from life's earliest day,
Illumines with her brilliant ray;
Shining by Castor's aid afar,
Refulgent in his golden car;

Who, the tempestuous winter o'er,
  Returning quiet gives to reign,
When the retreating clouds restore
  Light to thy blessed house again. 13

The gifts that mark Heaven's favouring care,
With brighter grace the prudent bear.
Round thee wealth flows in copious tide;
Whose feet the paths of justice tread;
Whose potent empire, far and wide,
Is over numerous cities spread.
The fairest charms of royal sway,
  Prudence and majesty combined,
In thee their genuine marks display,
  Whose eye declares a kindred mind.
Now happy in thy recent fame,
Won in th' equestrian Pytho's game;
This pomp displaying hymn is thine,
Which leads Apollo's sport divine. 29

Nor thou, great king, forget the lays
That celebrate Cyrene's praise;
Cyrene, round whose fertile soil
The charms of lovely Venus smile.
Ascribe the whole to God above,
And more than all Carrhotus' love!
Who not to Battus' royal court,
Where Justice and her train resort,
Convey'd Excuse, with glozing tongue,
From laggard Epimetheus sprung.

30 **Απολλωνιον Θυρμα.** The Roman *Ludi Apollinares.*

36 The charioteer of Arcesilaus.

39 Epimetheus, the fabled brother of Prometheus, married Pandora, and thus introduced all kinds of evil among mankind. Excuse or Negligence was the daughter of the former, as Prudence sprang from the latter. This passage of Pindar will perhaps bring to the recollection of the reader a similar one in Milton: (Par. Lost, ix. 853:)—

"In her face excuse
Came prologue, and apology too prompt."

But in his victor chariot borne,
Where pure Castalia's waters flow,
He gain'd the envied wreath, thy brow
With honour'd triumph to adorn:
Urging his wheels' uninjured force
Twelve times around the sacred course. 44

For never by unskilful stroke
His car's compacted strength he broke;
But, the Crisæan hill o'ercome,
  This fabric of ingenious hands
Is hung aloft in Phœbus' dome
  That in the woody hollow stands,
Upon the beam of cypress laid,
Where the bright image is display'd;
Which, fix'd by Cretan archers, stood,
A single offspring of the wood;
Conspicuous on its lofty place,
The proud Parnassian fane to grace.
'Tis then thy part, with willing mind,
To meet thy benefactor kind.
Offspring of Alexibius, thee
Extol the bright-hair'd graceful three.
How bless'd to have thy labours past
Long in the poet's record last!
Of forty guides, whose skill would steer
'Gainst thine their chariot's rash career,
Bringing with fearless mind thy car
Alone unbroken in the war.
And now, the strife of glory past,
  Thou art return'd once more

45 The scholiast informs us that forty charioteers contended with Arcesilaus, and all had their cars broken in the course; but Carrhotus preserved uninjured that of his employer: in consequence of which the unbroken chariot was placed in the temple at Delphi, and consecrated to Apollo.

This is one of the earliest recorded instances of the custom of suspending votive offerings in the temples of the gods, as testimonies of gratitude for favours received or calamities avoided.

To thy paternal walls at last,
  On Libya's fertile shore.

But no one is, or e'er shall be
From grief, the lot of mortals, free.
Yet Battus' ancient fortunes wait
His prosperous and his adverse state.
He forms the city's guardian pride,
A shining light to all beside.
Struck with deep awe and panic dread,
From him the roaring lions fled;
When he to speak, divinely taught,
A language o'er the ocean brought.
Apollo struck the beasts with fear,
  Who led the colonizing train,
Lest great Cyrene's lord should hear,
  And find the high prediction vain.

He who to man with healing art
Could blunt disease's heavy dart;
Who gives the lyre's sweet notes to flow,
And muse to still each mental wo;
Bidding within his favourites' breast
The tranquil love of virtue rest,
And ruling the prophetic sound
That issues from his cave profound,
This could in Lacedæmon place,
  In Argos, Pylos the divine,
The chiefs of brave Alcides' race,
  And old Ægimius' noble line.
Let me the fair renown proclaim,
Which from illustrious Sparta came.

My fathers hence to Thera's seat
Th' Ægidæ moved their wandering feet.

79 It is related by Herodotus that Battus, the founder of Cyrene, meeting a lion in Libya, uttered a cry so piercing as to

Heaven and the fates' supreme behest
Impell'd them to the victim feast.
Apollo, taking hence the hoard
Which thy Carnean rites afford,
We raise the strain of fair renown
To hymn Cyrene's well-built town,
Where Trojans of Antenor's race,
All sheathed in brass, have fix'd their place.
For they with Helen came, when they survey'd
Their native soil by war in smoky ruin laid.

Approaching then th' equestrian band,
The courteous natives of the land
Receive with hospitable care,
And sacrifice with presents bear.
These Battus led, when the deep wave
To his swift ships a passage gave.
He to th' inhabitants divine
Rear'd the tall grove and ample shrine,
Making for steeds a smooth and stony way,
That the great god whose potent art
From mortals wards disease's dart,
Might all his festal pomp display;
Where at the forum's utmost bound
Now dead he lies apart in holy ground.

While among men, his life was bless'd;
And when the hero sank to rest,

scare the savage beast, and to restore to him the use of his voice, according to the prediction of Apollo.

104 This is the epithet of Apollo mentioned by Callimachus, and which he prefers to that derived from Claros: (in Apol. 70.) See also v. 88, where he describes the festivities celebrated near the fountain of Cyre, where the men danced in solemn measure with the yellow-haired Libyan damsels.

118 It appears that Aristotle, surnamed Battus, constructed a paved way, (σκυρωταν ὁδον,) by which the sacred pomps were brought to the temple of Apollo. On this passage the scholiast remarks: λεγεται δε σκυρωτη αντι του λιθοστρωτος; the word used

A people's love was still his own;
While other sacred monarchs laid
Apart to death's impervious shade
Before the palace gates are flown.
And now thy mighty valour's fame,
Steep'd in the hymn's mellifluous dew,
Piercing their ear with loud acclaim,
Earth's dark recess shall travel through.
The common bliss of all the race,
Whose wreaths Arcesilaus grace.
His triumphs in the Pythian field
Apollo with his sword of gold
In graceful numbers shall unfold;
A recompense the lyric strain
Recited by the youthful train,
For all his toil and cost will yield.
'Tis said of old the prudent raise
Their voice in such a hero's praise.
Superior to his tender years,
He carries an unshaken mind,
And bold of tongue and heart appears
The eagle of the feather'd kind;
Whose wide-extended wings display
His sheltering valour in the fray.
He from his early youth sublime
Was skill'd to raise the sudden rhyme,
And foremost in th' equestrian war
Guide to the goal his rapid car. [154]

Of native arts through each fair road
His persevering steps have trod;
And still to crown his efforts high
May heaven its ready aid supply;
And grant him, bless'd Saturnian line,
In council as in act to shine!

by St. John (xix. 13) as denoting the same place which the Hebrews called Γαββαθα.

Let not the black tempestuous gale
With hostile force his life assail,
As when th' autumnal fruits are cast
On earth before the wintry blast.
The sovereign majesty of Jove
Guides the bless'd object of his love.
And may Olympia's chaplet grace,
Bestow'd by him, great Battus' race ! 168

THE SIXTH PYTHIAN ODE.*

TO XENOCRATES OF ACRAGAS, ON HIS VICTORY IN THE CHARIOT RACE, GAINED IN THE TWENTY-FOURTH PYTHIAD.

ARGUMENT.

The poet panegyrizes Xenocrates on account of his country and his victory in the Pythian games, promising him the immortality of verse: he then addresses Thrasybulus, the son of the victor, whom he celebrates on account of his piety and filial affection, comparing him in these respects to Antilochus the son of Nestor.—Concludes by praising Xenocrates for his moderation and proper use of wealth his evenness of temper and suavity of manners.

Give ear—for either through the plain
Of Venus with the laughing eyes,
Or through the Graces' fair domain,
The bard's poetic journey lies.

* This short poem, which the scholiast asserts to be monostrophic, and which, both in its construction and metrical arrangement, has much embarrassed the commentators, opens with a declaration on the part of the poet to proceed to the temple of the Delphian god, placed in the centre of the earth, in order to celebrate the praises of Xenocrates, father of his friend Thrasybulus, which had before been sung by Simonides, and are again recited in the second Isthmian ode. The periphrasis for Delphi in the third verse, *ομφαλος επιβρομου χθονος*, may be illustrated by Euripides: (Orest. 323:)—

τριποδος απο, φασιν, ἀν δ Φοιβος
ελακε, δεξαμενος, ανα το δαπεδον,
ἱνα μεσομφαλοι λεγονται μυχοι.

Again v. 584, 585:—

Απολλων ὃς μεσομφαλους ἑδρας
ναιων βροτοισι στομα νεμει σαφεστατον.

The allusions to the central situation of Pytho or Delphi are o

To thundering earth's prophetic dome,
In the just centre placed, we come;
Where, guarded by the holy shade,
Apollo's golden grove contains
The treasure of the Pythian strains
Which there, Xenocrates, is laid
The bless'd Emmenidæ to crown,
And watery Acragas' renown. 9

This nor the wintry storm's array,
The roaring cloud's terrific host,
Nor winds and whirling sands convey,
Beneath the depths of ocean lost.
And thou, with countenance serenely bright,
To thy great sire shalt tell the pleasing tale,
Oh Thrasybulus! when in Crissa's vale,
Thy race ennobling, sped his chariot's flight. 18

Firmly thou hold'st the precept fair
Which erst they say with guardian care
Upon his mountain station wild
The son of Philyra impress'd
On Peleus' vigorous orphan child,
To reverence Jove, the chief of all the bless'd.
Lord of the thundering bolt and lightning's flame,
And through the term allow'd by heaven,
Such honour be to parents given
As may not rob them of their rightful claim. 27

very frequent occurrence among the ancient poets. See Pyth viii. 82, where the expression

γας
ομφαλον παρ' αοιδιμον

is doubtless of parallel import to

ομφαλος επιβρομου χθονος

in this ode.

13 Thus paraphrased by Casimir, (Lyric. iii. 31, 6:)—

"Quam neque turbidus
Auster, neque emotus refuso
Subruat Oceanus profundo."

This noble mind in days of yore
Antilochus the valiant bore,
Who Æthiop Memnon's deadly strife
Sustaining, saved his father's life;
For struck by Paris' dart, the steed
Slack'd the Nestorean chariot's speed;
While he the powerful spear urged on,
And the Messenian sage, his breast
By agitating fear oppress'd,
With no vain effort call'd his son. 36

Thus the firm hero's yielded breath
Redeem'd his much-loved sire from death.
Of all who in a former age
E'er trod the world's eventful stage,
Him first this wondrous act will prove
In virtue and parental love.
But his renown has pass'd away.
Among the heroes of the day
Shines Thrasybulus, whose fair deeds proclaim
His steps have reach'd the height of sire and uncle's
fame. 46

His youth, exempt from fraud and pride,
Collects deep wisdom's ample store,
Wont in the muses' haunts to hide,
And cull their scientific lore;
While thy sweet arts his willing mind,
Equestrian lord, earth-shaking Neptune, bind;
And his sweet soul, in social converse free,
Transcends the honey'd labour of the bee. 54

31 See Homer, Il., viii., 100; Od., iv., 255; Pope's version In the former of these passages the incident mentioned by Pindar is related, and in the latter the death of Antilochus, son of Nestor, is alluded to by his brother Pisistratus.

THE SEVENTH PYTHIAN ODE.

TO MEGACLES THE ATHENIAN, ON HIS VICTORY WITH THE QUADRIGÆ, GAINED IN THE TWENTY-EIGHTH PYTHIAD.

ARGUMENT.

THIS short ode opens with an address to Athens, whence the victor derives a great portion of his fame, tracing his lineage to Alcmæon; his triumphs in the different games of Greece are enumerated.—The poet expresses his concern that the happiness of Megacles should be diminished by the envy of his rivals, and the mutability of human fortune, which, however, affects all men alike.

THE fairest prelude to my strain
Athena's noble walls contain;
Whence struck, thy steeds the lyre shall grace,
That hymns Alcmæon's potent race.
What house, what country shall I name
Through Greece of more illustrious fame,
When all the various cities round
Erectheus' townsmen's praise resound?

They who in Pytho the divine,
Apollo, rear'd thy wondrous shrine.
Five triumphs in the Isthmian field
Urge me the lyric song to yield—
Oh Megacles! one glorious crown,
  In Jove's Olympic strife obtain'd,
And two from Cirrha's sacred town,
  By thee and thy forefathers gain'd.

I joy that merited success
Should all thy recent efforts bless.

But I lament that envy's cloud
Must thy victorious actions shroud.
Yet such they say is man—whose fate
By weal or wo is checker'd still;
No constant happiness his state
Attends without approaching ill.

THE EIGHTH PYTHIAN ODE.

TO ARISTOMENES OF ÆGINA, ON HIS VICTORY WITH THE CÆSTUS, GAINED IN THE THIRTY-FIFTH PYTHIAD.

ARGUMENT.

Pindar begins this ode with a beautiful invocation to Tranquillity; then expatiates on the might of Apollo, by whose favour Aristomenes, the son of Xenarces, gained his Pythian conquest.—Then follow the praises of Ægina, the mother of heroes, especially from the descendants of Æacus.—He then resumes the commendation of Aristomenes, applying to him the saying of Amphiaraus, that innate valour is hereditary, and interweaves that seer's prediction respecting the Epigoni, descendants of Adrastus and the Argive chiefs, who should besiege Thebes.—To these he subjoins the expression of his affection for Alcmæon, and the esteem with which he regards him.—Returning to the victory, he supplicates Apollo to crown him with success in future, reminding him that he is indebted to the favour of the gods for his past glory, the several instances of which he proceeds to enumerate.—Expatiates on the felicity of those who conquer in the games, which is sufficient to counterbalance the miseries of short-lived mortality.—And concludes with an address to Ægina.

Bland Quiet! who preserv'st the state
In tranquil peace serene and great,
Daughter of Justice, whose high sway
Council and war alike obey,

1–5 This metaphor, denoting the well-ordered tranquillity which distinguishes Ægina, is highly poetical, and is in many other passages applied by Pindar to the same state, the origin of which he traces to Æacus. (See particularly Ol., viii., 28; Nem., iv., 19; Isth., v., 24, &c.)

4 In v. 4, how scriptural is the expression—

Εχοισα κλαϊδας Ὑπερτατας,

to denote the height of power! (Matt., xvi., 19) Και δωσω σοι τας

The Pythian hymn that now I weave
For Aristomenes receive;
Since well thou know'st thine active aid to lend,
Or mildly to the fit occasion bend. 9

When ruthless anger fills the breast,
Severe and hostile to the foe,
Thy power soon lays the storm to rest,
And plunges in the wave below.
Thee, ere he felt the deadly stroke,
Reckless Porphyrion dared provoke;
But learn'd at length the dearest gain
From willing owners to obtain. 18

And she by her superior strength
The boaster's pride o'ercame at length.
Her nor Cilician Typho fled,
That dire and monstrous hundred-head.
Nor he who ruled the giant brood:
For by the lightning's deadly blow,
And arrows of Apollo's bow,
Were the rebellious tribe subdued.
'Twas he that with propitious mind
Received Xenarces' son,
From Cirrha's walls, his brows entwined
With the Parnassian bays in Doric triumph won. 29

And not, as by the Graces scorn'd,
Have Æacus' bright race adorn'd

κλεις της βασιλειας των ουρανων. Again, in Apocal., ix., 1, *Και εδοθη αυτῳ ἡ κλεις του φρεατος της αβυσσου.* See also cap. i., 18.

21 The chief of these are briefly enumerated by Horace: (Od., III., iv., 53:)—

"Sed quid Typhœus, et validus Mimas,
Aut quid minaci Porphyrion statu,
Quid Rhœcus, evulsisque truncis
Enceladus jaculator audax?"

The scholiast informs us that verse 15 alludes to an attempt made by Porphyrion to take away the oxen of Hercules against the will of that hero.

In vain with virtuous deeds the isle
Where cities ruled in justice smile;
Since from old time her glorious name
Excites her sons to deeds of fame:
Great heroes nourish'd to the fight
Of swiftness and victorious might;
And tribes of meaner mortals round
Throughout the earth her praises sound.
But all my vacant hours will fail;
  Ere to the lyre and dulcet strain
I can commit the lengthen'd tale
  Satiety the mind will pain. 46

Thy triumphs now, heroic boy,
The labours of my muse employ,
Who shall convey with winged speed
The record of thy latest deed;
For in th' Olympic wrestler's game
Tracking thy noble uncle's fame,
Thine efforts Theognotus not disgrace:
And in the strong-limb'd Isthmian fray
The wreaths thy vigour bore away
The glories of Clitomachus efface.
Thy deeds, the tribe of Midylus that raise,
Deserve Oïcleus son's prophetic praise;
Who erst in Thebes beheld with prescient sight
The martial youth still constant in the fight,
When having now twice left their Argive home,
To the seven-portall'd town th' Epigoni were come.

When thus he spoke: "Of those whose heart
  Nature with generous ardour fires,
I see th' impetuous youth depart,
  Warm'd with the spirit of their sires.

54 Amphiaraus, the Theban prophet, whose son Alcmæon, called by Pindar *Alcman*, bears on his shield the *insigne* of a dragon, prefiguring, according to the scholiast, the death of his father, who was to descend alive into the grave, as that animal goes into the holes and caverns of the earth.

Alcman on his refulgent shield
Whirling the dragon's varied form
Clearly I view, while in the field
Foremost at Cadmus' gates he bides the battle storm.

And he who in the former fray
Fatigued and vanquish'd urged his way,
Adrastus of heroic might
Now views a better omen's flight;
Howe'er in his domestic state
Vex'd by the storms of adverse fate.
To him alone of all the Grecian band
With his uninjured host by equal heaven,
His dead son's bones, collected through the land,
To bring to Abas' spacious streets 'tis given."
'Twas thus Amphiaraus said:
And I around Alcmæon's head
The verdant chaplet joy to place,
Sprinkled with hymns' mellifluous grace.
He, guarded by whose neighb'ring fane,
All my possessions safe remain,
To earth's prophetic centre as I went,
By his paternal art convey'd
The answer in night's gloomy shade,
Which to my charmed ear Apollo sent. 87

Far-darting god, whose glorious dome
Within the Pythian hollow stands,
Receiving from all distant lands
Whatever suppliants thither roam,

76 Argos is thus denominated by Pindar, as having been built by Abas, son of Lynceus, and father of Adrastus, whose son Ægialeus was the only one of the Epigoni, i. e., the descendants of the seven Argive chiefs who did not return safe to their native land after the Theban war.

81 The house of Pindar stood near the temple or shrine of Alcmæon; and as the poet went to consult the oracle of the Pythian Apollo, the answer was conveyed to him in a dream by that hero, who appears to have been worshipped with great reverence—συγγονοισι τεχναις, i. e., by the art of vaticination, practised by his father.

'Twas there thou deignedst to bestow
The greatest joy of man below,
And gav'st him at thy feast, oh king,
Snatch'd with an eager hand, to bring
The high pentathlic guerdon home.
With willing mind accept my prayer,
And view the numbers which declare
In honey'd pomp, but words of truth,
The deeds of this victorious youth.
Your fate, Xenarcidæ, to bless
I ask the gods' perpetual love. 103

For should a hero's might success
With no laborious effort prove,
His prosperous life the witless tribe
To his own prudent aims ascribe.
The vigour of a mortal hand
Such happiness can ne'er command.
For by the gods' superior power
  To hope and joy the vanquish'd rise,
While he whose boundless wishes tower,
  Beneath their arm defended lies.
Thy valiant deeds unknown to fail,
  Delighted Megara proclaims,
And Marathon's sequester'd vale;
  Thee too in Juno's kindred games
Thrice crown'd th' applauding circle sees,
Victorious Aristomenes! 116

Triumphant in the wrestler's hardy toil
Thy frame upon four prostrate bodies lay—
No wish'd return from the dire Pythian fray
The gods decreed to their loved native soil.

115 Alluding, probably, to the Heræan contests, established in Ægina, by imitation of those at Argos, the favoured city of the queen of gods. The Æginetæ were a colony from the Argives; hence the epithet *kindred*. Didymus, as the scholiast informs us, says that the Hecatombæan contests are here alluded to.

121 I think there can be little doubt that the right reading

No mother's smile of joyful praise
Could their desponding spirits raise;
But as their steps in coward flight
Shunn'd the proud adversaries' sight,
Harass'd by shame and grief they trod the darkest ways.
But he who has obtain'd the meed
That crowns each fair and noble deed,
With hope and joy transported glows.
Him swift-wing'd valour gives to rise,
And a superior good supplies
To all the bliss that wealth bestows. 131

Full often with increasing light
Glitters each mortal pleasure bright,
And shortly dash'd upon the ground
By some unhappy stroke 'tis found.
Man, the frail being of a day,
Uncertain shadow of a dream,
Illumined by the heavenly beam,
Flutters his easy life away.
Ægina! guardian of the land
Peopled by freedom's generous band,
Preserve this city with a mother's love.
Thee may King Æacus behold,
Peleus and Telamon the bold,
With bless'd Achilles and immortal Jove. 145

here is κριθη, (pro εκριθη,) *was decreed*, although some commentators prefer εν Πυθιαδι κριθη: founding the interpretation on a notion, which I believe to be quite gratuitous, of the victors in the Pythian games being sent home, crowned with a barley chaplet. Besides that the first syllable in the Homeric word κριθη, *hordeum*, is long; (Il., xi., 69; Od., ix., 110; xix., 112, &c.;) whereas the corresponding verse in the antistrophe requires a short one:—

ανο-
ρεαις, εχων κρεσσονα πλουτον.

THE NINTH PYTHIAN ODE.

TO TELESICRATES, THE CYRENÆAN, ON HIS VICTORY IN THE ARMED COURSE, GAINED IN THE TWENTY-EIGHTH PYTHIAD.*

ARGUMENT.

The poet begins with celebrating the praises of his hero, which leads him to a digression concerning the early history of Cyrene, the forcible abduction of the nymph from whom that city was named, and the birth of Aristæus, the fruit of her connection with the god Apollo.—Returns to his subject, with which he unites the story of Iolaus, a friend of Hercules, who, having had his life renewed for one single day, made use of his recovered existence to overcome and slay Eurystheus.—Excuses the episodical style of his narrative by the wish that all poets entertain to celebrate the praises of Hercules.—Returns to the victor, and enumerates his triumphs.—Recalls the memory of an old contest, in which Antæus, the Libyan, proposed as a reward to the victor the hand of his daughter, which was gained by Alexidamas, a fellow-towns man, or ancestor, of Telesicrates.

The hero of the brazen shield,
Victorious in the Pythian field,
Great Telesicrates my lays
Would with the deep-zoned Graces praise:
Bless'd man! Cyrene's joy and crown,
Equestrian seat of high renown.
Her in his golden car of yore
Ravish'd from Pelion's sylvan dell,
Where storms with ceaseless fury swell,
Latona's bright-hair'd offspring bore;

* The armed course was one in which the contending heroes ran with brazen shields, as the first line indicates. This ode is remarkable for the flowing beauty of its diction and general simplicity of construction.

Giving the huntress virgin's hand
  Empire o'er Libya's realm to keep,
Third portion of the peopled land,
  That teems alike with fruits and sheep.

The silver-footed Cyprian dame
Received her Delian guest,
And with a touch ethereal press'd
The heaven-built chariot's frame;
And o'er his genial bed she threw
Sweet modesty of virgin hue;
Joining the god in nuptial tie
With powerful Hypseus' progeny:
He who then made his regal sway
Th' impetuous Lapithæ obey:
The second hero whose bright line
From ocean drew its source divine.
Him erst in Pindus' valleys fair
Peneus' bed well-pleased to share,
Daughter of earth, Creüsa bore,
While he a father's tender love
His white-arm'd child, Cyrene, gave to prove.

Not fond with dull delay to pore
The web's repeated progress o'er,
Nor hallow with domestic rites
The banquet's festival delights.

13 Alluding to the ancient division of the habitable globe into Asia, Europe, and Libya, or Africa.

25 Peneus was the son of Oceanus, and Hypseus, the father of Cyrene, was the son of Peneus, and of the nymph of Creusa, daughter of Tellus. The description given by the poet in this passage of the martial disposition of Creusa will remind the classical reader of the character of Camilla as sketched by Virgil: (Æn., vii., 805, sq:)—

"Bellatrix; non illa colo calathisve Minervæ
Fœmineas assueta manus; sed prælia virgo
Dura pati, cursuque pedum prævertere ventos."

But with her dart and brazen spear
The beasts of savage brood to chase,
And render free from every fear
Her father's herds of quiet race;
Permitting the dull weight of sleep
But lightly o'er her lids to creep;
When on her sweet and tranquil bed
The early beams of morn were shed.

Her, as unarm'd she waged the fight
'Gainst an impetuous lion's might,
Apollo found, whose matchless art
From his broad quiver wings the dart.
Then Chiron from his mansion straight
He bade the potent call await.
"Hasten, Phillyrides, to leave
The dark and venerable cave,
In mute astonishment survey
What mind a woman dares display;
Fearless of heart, what perils dread
She brings to her courageous head,
A damsel whose unconquer'd soul
No labours tire, no fears control!
What mortal gave her vital air?
Sprung from what source, a scion fair
Holds she th' umbrageous mountain's breast,
With more than human valour bless'd?

Is it a hallow'd action, say,
By fraud to seek the virgin bower,
And pluck with ruthless arm away
The sweetness of her hallow'd flower?"
To him the sturdy centaur, while
From his relaxing brow a smile
In placid sweetness softly broke,
Without delay his counsel spoke:

"The key that opes persuasion wise
Conceal'd in mystic darkness lies;

Since gods and men alike approve,
Oh Phœbus! that ingenuous shame
Should hide the deeds of sacred flame,
And all be secrecy in love. 74

But thee, whom falsehood ne'er can reach,
Some motive of a doubtful kind
Has with feign'd ignorance inclined
To utter this ambiguous speech.
For whence, oh king! thy fond desire
The damsel's lineage to inquire?
Whose eye of all events surveys
The fated end, the various ways;
Who to what leaves the teeming earth
In spring's prolific hour gives birth,
What sands are moved when waves tempestuous swell,
Canst number with omniscient mind,
And every future period find
Which time's revolving course shall e'er impel. 89

But if with thine I must compare
My wisdom, this I will declare.
Her husband thou who seek'st this vale
Shalt o'er the paths of ocean sail;
And to the verdant plain of Jove
Convey the object of thy love.
Thou shalt appoint Cyrene there
The ruler of a city fair,
Collecting all the island train
To the steep hill that crowns the plain.

86 Thus Apollo with oracular voice declares of himself: (Herod., Clio, xlvii.:)—

Οιδα δ' εγω ψαμμον τ' αριθμον, και μετρα θαλασσης.

94 A figurative expression, denoting the amenity of the soil and climate of Libya; or so called on account of the worship paid there to Jupiter Ammon.

Now sacred Libya's empire wide
Possesses thine illustrious bride,
Who her fair residence shall hold
That glitters with imperial gold.
Justly to her that fertile field
Will its unceasing produce yield,
A land with fruits abundant crown'd,
Where beasts unnumber'd graze around. 103

She shall produce an offspring there,
  Whom to the high-throned Hours and Earth
Illustrious Mercury shall bear
  From the dear authors of his birth.
They on their knees the babe shall place,
Bidding his young and tender lip
Sweet nectar and ambrosia sip,
And with immortal honour grace;
Making the rustic shepherd boy,
Whom mortals Aristæus name,
Skill'd to pursue the savage game,
His friends' delight and dearest joy;
Adored with almost equal love
To sacred Phœbus or to Jove." 116

Thus having said, he moved his breast
In wedlock to be fully bless'd.
But when the gods to action speed,
Short is the road and swift the deed.
That very day's revolving sun
Beheld the fated purpose done:
Saw them on Libya's golden strand
Join'd in the hymeneal band;
Where she protects that beauteous town
Which in each contest gains renown.
Once more upon the Pythian plain,
Carneades, thine offspring brave
By the bright wreath which fortune gave,
For her new lustre joys to gain.

Glory for her his conquests weave
Who shall with willing mind receive
The hero from the Delphic toil,
In his loved female-beauteous soil. 132

Great virtues ask a lengthen'd song—
But to adorn a high emprise
Briefly, is grateful to the wise;
Since its due limits to each act belong.
Seven-portall'd Thebes great Iolaus knew
The fitting opportunity pursue.
Him, when the proud Eurystheus' head
His vengeful sword had severed,
By charioteer Amphitryo's tomb
Earth hid within its tranquil breast,
Whither in ages past had come
His grandsire, th' earth-sown warrior's guest;
Who dwelt where milk-white coursers' feet
Sounded in the Cadmæan street. 147

Compress'd by his and Jove's embrace,
With the same pang Alcmena bore
Of sons a twin heroic race.
Mute and unskill'd in sacred lore
Were he who would refuse to raise
His voice in great Alcides' praise;
Forgetting the Dircæan spring,
That nurtured him and Iphicles, to sing.
To them will I the hymn address
Who crown my efforts with success.
Ne'er let the vocal Graces' ray
Cease to illuminate my lay.
Already has the victor's fame
Oft raised this glorious city's name,
Once in Ægina's day of fight,
And thrice on the Megarean height;
Forbidding o'er the victor's tale
Silence to draw her dusky veil. 163

Then let the friendly townsmen tell,
  Nor e'en the candid foe conceal
What his strong arm hath wrought so well,
  Laborious for the common weal.
The words of ocean's hoary sage
Submissive reverence should engage
"Crown e'en an enemy's fair deed
With approbation's honest meed."
Thee too at Pallas' stated feasts
  Full often have my eyes survey'd
Triumphant o'er th' assembled guests,
  While many a silent gazing maid
Her husband or her offspring thee
Has wish'd, oh Telesicrates, to be! 176

To him in bright Olympia's day,
And in deep-bosom'd Rhea's fray,
And heroes on his native field
The palm in every contest yield.
From me, then, who the debt would pay,
  Slaking my thirst of song, they claim
Once more to build the lyric lay,
  And hymn thy great forefathers' fame:
As to Irasa's walls the suitors came,
To seek the Libyan nymph, Antæus' fair-hair'd dame. 187

Kinsmen with many a stranger vied,
Illustrious throng! to call her bride—
Eager to crop of form sublime
The flow'ret in its golden prime:
But her ambitious sire, whose ear
From Argive Danaus joy'd to hear
That he had bound in wedlock's tie
His numerous virgin progeny

195 Named by the scholiast Barce, or Alceis. Irasa was a city in the Tritonian lake. The Antæus here mentioned is not to be confounded with the gigantic antagonist of Hercules.

Ere yet the sun's resplendent light
Had travell'd its meridian height,
For his own daughter hoped to gain
A brighter hymeneal chain. 200

For in the stadium's farthest end
To the whole choir he fix'd a place,
And bade the amorous train contend
By skill in the pedestrian race,
Where each aspiring hero strove
To win the object of his love.
'Twas thus the Libyan sire allied
The husband to his destined bride.
Adorn'd in all her bright array
Close to the goal he bade her stay. 208

Sweet issue of their manly toil—
"Her garments," thus he cried aloud,
"Who touches first, of all the crowd,
Shall bear away the lovely spoil."
Alexidamus then, who press'd
Through the swift course before the rest,
Seizing the noble virgin's hand,
Led her through Libya's warlike band.
To him in many a strife before
The leafy crown they gave, on victory's wing to soar! 220

227 The metaphor here is the same as at the conclusion of the fourteenth Olympic ode, and at v. 129 of the eighth, and the last of the ninth Pythian, on which passage the scholiast considers the expression as simply a periphrasis for victory. It appears to be a favourite image with Pindar to denote the exultation produced by victory on the ardent mind. West, however, in his note on the fourteenth Olympic ode, maintains the opinion, founded on a passage in Plutarch, that the word *wings* is to be taken in its literal sense, to denote some emblematical ornaments added to the Olympic wreaths, &c. Let the reader decide.

THE TENTH PYTHIAN ODE.

TO HIPPOCLEAS, THE THESSALIAN, ON HIS VICTORY IN THE RACE OF TWO STADIA, GAINED IN THE TWENTY-SECOND PYTHIAD.

ARGUMENT.

THE poet, tracing the victor's lineage to Aristomachus, the descendant of Hercules, attributes his conquest to the favour of Apollo, and the example of his father Phricias.—Expresses his wishes for the perpetuity of the good fortune which both father and son have acquired, and which is so great that no mortal can surpass it; as the traveller who has arrived at the Hyperborean regions can proceed no farther.—This leads him to a digression on the mythology of the Hyperboreans.—Pindar then checks himself, and concludes with renewed commendation of the victor, and his kinsmen and brothers, Thorax, &c., whose glorious deeds ennoble their native Thessaly.

BLESS'D Lacedæmon! Thessaly the bless'd!
Whose sceptred kings their potent race
To the same valiant Hercules can trace,
Why should my ardent spirit raise
Strains of unseasonable praise?
But me prophetic Pytho's wall,
Aleva's sons and Pelinæum call;
Wishing Hippocleas to grace
With strains of high renown by tuneful bards express'd.

6 Aleva was an ancient king of Thessaly, from whom the inhabitants were named. Pelinæum was the native city of the victor. It is doubted by commentators whether the word 'Αριστομαχου be used by Pindar as an epithet to Hercules or to

For in the contests as he tried his strength,
Amphictyon's host and the Parnassian cave
Pronounced him foremost of the youthful brave,
Contending in the double stadium's length.
  Apollo! if thine aid befriend,
  Sweet is man's onset and his end;
  This deed the youth achieved through thee,
  And thine auspicious deity.
  Twice from the field, by kindred fire,
  Urged in the footsteps of his sire,
  Th' Olympic chaplet he convey'd,
  In martial panoply array'd. 23

  And where, upon her sheltering plain,
    Beneath the rock fair Cirrha lies,
  Swift-footed Phricias joy'd to gain
    The Pythian contest's glorious prize.
  In times to come may prosperous fate
  Exalt, as now, their blissful state!
  Nor, having gain'd an ample share
  Of all that Greece esteems as fair,
  May envious blasts from Heaven assail
  The victims of a backward gale. 31

  Still may the god with liberal heart
  Unshaken happiness impart!
  Hymn'd is that man in poets' lay
    Who with strong hands or rapid feet
  Has borne the noblest palms away;
    In whom firm strength and valour meet.
  Still living, by his youthful son
  Who saw the Pythian garlands won.
  Not yet to them the lot is given
  To scale the brazen soil of heaven:

denote one of the Heraclidæ, from whom Aleva derived his origin. The scholiast asserts the former.

41 This epithet of Olympus is repeated in the seventh Isthmian: (v. 72.) It will probably remind the reader of that ter

But the remotest point that lies
Open to human enterprise
Their course has gain'd, well skill'd to sweep
The wide expanse of glory's deep;
But not along the wondrous way
To Hyperborean crowds can ships or feet convey

Of old, as at their sacred feast,
  Whole hecatombs appeased the god,
The steps of an illustrious guest,
  Perseus, their habitation trod;
Whose festivals and songs of praise
Apollo with delight surveys;
And smiles to see the bestial train
In wanton pride erect and vain. 56

Yet never will th' impartial muse
To dwell with minds like these refuse:
Around them move the virgin choirs,
The breathing flutes and sounding lyres;
And twining with their festive hair
The wreath of golden laurel fair,
With temperate mirth and social glee
They join in solemn revelry.
Nor dire disease, nor wasting age,
Against their sacred lives engage:
But free from trouble and from strife,
Through the mild tenour of their life

rible prophetic denunciation of the Jewish lawgiver: (Deut., xxviii., 3:) "Thy heaven that is over thy head shall be brass."

46 This digression to the Hyperborean regions, which Pindar here seems to consider as the western boundary of the world, and to the story of Perseus, who came suddenly on the pious inhabitants as they were sacrificing hecatombs of wild asses to Apollo, is greatly censured by the scholiast as an unreasonable deviation from the original scope and design of the ode. But these irregularities are so characteristic of our poet, that whatever place or persons the progress of his story leads him, however slightly, to mention, we look as a matter of course for any mythological record connected with them.

Secure they dwell, nor fear to know
Avenging Nemesis their foe.
Erst, breathing with a heart of flame,
The valiant son of Danae came;
Who by divine Athena's hand,
Led to the bless'd heroic band,
Slew Gorgon, and her dire head bore
With dragon locks all cover'd o'er;
And thus, with stony ruin fraught,
Death to the islanders he brought. 75

But when the gods their power display,
How strange soe'er the mighty deed,
Firm rev'rence and belief to pay,
Nor doubt nor wonder shall impede.
Restrain the oar; and from the prow
Fix, to secure against the shock
Of many a sea-imbosom'd rock,
Your anchor in the deep below.
For now th' encomiastic lay,
Like bee that flits on changeful wing,
To fresher glories hastes away. 84

But ardent hope inspires my breast,
That while the Ephyræans sing
My sweet lays by Peneus' spring,
Hippocleas above the rest,
Mindful of each triumphant crown,
Among the old, the virgin train,
And fellow-combatants, the strain
Shall dignify with bright renown.
In various minds far different objects move
The cares and fond solicitudes of love. 94

But he whose fortune can obtain
The object of his strong desire,
Calm and contented should remain,
Nor to uncertain good aspire;

Since veil'd in doubtful gloom appear
The issues of the coming year.
I trust in Thorax' friendly care,
Who wishing my kind deeds to share,
Has yoked for me the muses' car,
By its four coursers whirl'd afar;
Urging, with like affection'd soul,
The willing poet to the goal. 104

As gold to Lydian stone applied,
Thus shines the upright mind when tried.
Then to his virtuous brother's praise
Let us the joyful tribute raise;
Since their bright deeds Thessalia's state
On wings of fame have borne elate;
Enrich'd by whose paternal sway,
Her children glory to obey. 112

THE ELEVENTH PYTHIAN ODE.

TO THRASYDÆUS, THE THEBAN, ON HIS VICTORY IN THE STADIC COURSE, GAINED WHEN A BOY, IN THE TWENTY-EIGHTH PYTHIAD.

ARGUMENT.

The poet begins this ode with an invocation to the deities of his country—Semele, Ino, and Alcmena—entreating their presence when the pomp of triumph is to be brought to the temple of Ismenian Apollo, and naming the field of conquest the rich plain of Pylades, he digresses to the story of his friend Orestes, and the murder of Agamemnon by Clytemnestra.—Returns to his subject, commending the victor and his father on account of his numerous triumphs.—Declares his preference of the moderate but secure fortune which they enjoy to the unstable pomp by which tyrants are surrounded.—Concludes by citing the examples of Iolaus, son of Iphiclus, Castor, and Pollux.

Daughters of Cadmus! Semele the fair,
    Companion of th' Olympic train,
And Ino, now Leucothea, given to share
    The couch of Nereids in the main;
Go with the mother of Alcides brave
To Melia's dark and sacred cave,
    Where lies the golden tripod's store,
    To which unerring Loxias bore

1 The opening of this ode affords another proof of the fondness with which Pindar alludes to the story of the daughters of Cadmus and Harmonia; Semele, now an assessor or companion of the gods, and Ino, deified as Leucothea, or Matuta, goddess of the morning, whose rites were only approached by freeborn matrons. (See Ol., ii.; Pyth., iii. and xi.)

6 Melia was an ocean nymph, who became the mother of Ismenus and Tenerus by Apollo.

Superior love, and bade the hallow'd fane,
Seat of prophetic truth, Ismenus' name retain.

Harmonia's children! ye whose heroine band,
Assembled by the god's command,
At close of day he bids in social state
Pytho and Themis celebrate,
With earth's truth-speaking centre—to proclaim
Seven-portall'd Thebes and Cirrha's game,
Where Thrasydæus by the third won crown
Hath his paternal hearth's renown
Exalted where great Pylades' command
(Spartan Orestes' friend) ruled o'er the fertile land. 24.

Him, when his slaughter'd father lay,
By Clytemnestra's hand subdued,
The nurse Arsinoe stole away
From the dire scene of fraud and blood;
What time with Agamemnon's soul
She, whom no pity could control,
Urging the sharp and glittering blade,
Dardanian Priam's daughter hurl'd
Cassandra to th' infernal world,
Where flows sad Acheron through realms of shade.

Did her to the unhallow'd stroke
Iphigenia's doom provoke,
Who died, far from her native land,
A victim on Euripus' strand?
Or lust of an adulterous bed,
That to the nightly dalliance led?

17 One by his father, one by his uncle, one by himself. Orestes is called Spartan, (v. 20,) since, although a native of Mycenæ, he was made king of Sparta. The following digression, relating his story, with the adultery of Clytemnestra, &c., is also reprehended by the scholiast as irrelevant to the subject of the ode.

The same narration is made by the shade of Agamemnon to Ulysses in the infernal regions: (Od., xi., 404–434.) Compare the tale as related by Sophocles: (Electra, 94, et seq.)

A crime of most abhorrent die
  In her whose wedded bliss is young!
The violated marriage tie
  Is told by every foreign tongue—
Since naught to hide the guilty tale
From slanderous townsmen can avail. 44

Envy is wealth's perpetual foe,
'Gainst which the humble mutter low.
Ev'n when the great Alcides came
To Sparta, seat of ancient fame,
Bringing destruction on the prophet maid;
He fell, who saw the wasting fire
For Helen's baneful charms aspire,
And low in dust Troy's splendid fabrics laid.
Orestes with his youthful head
To hospitable Strophius fled,
His aged friend, who dwelt below
Parnassus' elevated brow.
At length with valiant arm he gave
His mother and Ægisthus to the grave. 57

Now, friends, in devious track I stray
From the direct and beaten way;
Slave to some arbitrary gale,
That guides the pliant vessel's sail.
Muse, if by compact or for gain
  A mercenary voice thou raise,
Exaggerate in varied strain
  The subject of thy venal praise.
Let Trasydæus now inspire
Thy lay, or his triumphant sire,
The Pythian victor, they whose fame
Shines with a bright and glorious flame. 69

Late conquerors in th' Olympic car,
And the renown'd equestrian war,
With naked limbs in Pytho's race,
They rushing through the stadium's space,

The Grecian host in speed o'ercame.
Such blessings as the gods impart
Still may I love with tranquil heart,
Seeking in life an easy state—
I find the middle ranks endure
In lasting happiness secure,
And blame th' exalted tyrant's fate. 81

The virtues of a common kind
Engage my unambitious mind,
Since loss o'er envy still impends.
He who has gain'd the summit fair,
Living remote from anxious care,
Nor to injurious wrong descends,
Reaches black death's most wish'd-for bound,
Shedding, to bless a lovely race,
The richest of possessions round
His noble deeds' illustrious grace; 90

Such as in hymns transmits to fame
Triumphant Iphiclides' name.
Thee, kingly Pollux, and great Castor's might—
Sons of the gods! who one day dwell
Within Therapne's gloomy cell,
Another on Olympus' towering height.

93 This part of the history of Castor and Pollux, who underwent for each other the alternate vicissitudes of life and death, is also related by Homer: (Od., xi., 371, seq.:)—

> "By turns they visit this ethereal sky,
> And live alternate, and alternate die."—*Pope.*

So Virgil: (Æn., vi., 121:)—

> "Si fratrem Pollux alterna morte redemit,
> Itque reditque viam toties."

Therapne was a town of Laconia, where Castor and Pollux were born. Heyne conjectures, and I think with great probability, that this fable of the Dioscuri owed its origin to some confused notion of the daily rising and setting of Luciferus and Hesperus. Pindar again relates the story: (Nem., x., 100, et seq. 173, seq.)

THE TWELFTH PYTHIAN ODE.

TO MIDAS OF ACRAGAS, ON HIS VICTORIES IN THE MUSICAL CONTEST, GAINED IN THE TWENTY-FOURTH AND TWENTY-FIFTH PYTHIAD.

ARGUMENT.

THE poet in this beautiful ode first invokes the city of Agrigentum, personifying her under the character of a goddess.—Proceeds to describe the invention of the flute, which he attributes to Minerva, who by its shrill tones imitated the cry of the Gorgon slaughtered by Perseus.—He then expatiates on its various other uses, in exciting the combatants to the field, &c.—Concludes with a highly poetical reflection on the mutability of human fortune.

THEE, shining on the well-built mountain's head,
Fairest of mortal cities, I entreat,
  Proserpina's imperial seat,
By Acragas' sheep-feeding banks outspread,
  With gods' and men's propitious love,
  Accept this crown from Pytho's plain,
  Won by illustrious Midas' strain,
  And him who conquers Greece approve;
  In that high art Athena found of old,
Which mimick'd in their howl the Gorgon sisters
    bold. 14

10 The name *Athena*, ἡ διαπλεξαισα, *the weaver*, in its literal sense, may probably be deduced from אטן, *filum texuit*. The origin of the Gorgonian strain is here finely related. The triple monster surrounded by its dragon locks is described by Æschylus : (P. V. 796, seq. :)—

πελας δ' αδελφαι τωνδε τρεις καταπτεροι,
δρακοντομαλλοι Γοργονες, βροτοστυγεις

The names of the three Gorgon sisters were Stheno, Euryale, Medusa : and each head is afterward described (v. 35, &c.) as

As from the triple virgin's head,
By dragon locks encompass'd round,
She heard the voice, ere life had fled,
Elaborate a mournful sound;
When Perseus' valiant arm had slain
The third part of the sister train;
And whelm'd beneath her people's grave,
Seriphus bosom'd in the wave;
Obscuring, by the foul disgrace,
Phorcys' imperishable race;
When he to Polydectes brought
The festal gift with ruin fraught:
Who long his mother Danae held
Captive in wedlock's chain compell'd,
Bearing the head that show'd Medusa's beauteous face. [29]

He who is call'd in legends old
The offspring of self-fallen gold.
But when from each laborious deed
Her much-loved hero she had freed,
The virgin goddess made to sigh
The flute's sonorous melody;
That soon as left the mournful note
Euryale's rapacious throat,
Her instrument's shrill sounds might flow
In tones of imitative wo.
But when she deign'd the heavenly art
For mortal pleasure to impart,
She bade the high and glorious strain
The name of many heads retain,
Memorial of that stubborn fight
Which roused the adverse people's might. [42]

Such as with dulcet voice proceeds
From slender brass and vocal reeds;

uttering its separate lamentation, which was imitated in a separate strain.

Which near the Graces' temple spring,
Where festal choirs exult and sing,
To witness in Cephisus' grove
The bands in measured cadence move.
What bliss soe'er to man is known,
Laborious efforts gain alone.
Such as the god will crown to-day,
Or brighten with to-morrow's ray.
Though fix'd th' irrevocable doom,
Yet soon or late the time shall come
That either cheats th' expecting mind,
Or leaves its wishes far behind.

47 The river Cephisus empties itself into the lake Copais, here designated by Καφισις, a nymph sprung from that river.

53 This moral conclusion arises naturally from the subject, as we are informed by the scholiast that Midas gained the victory against his expectations, since his pipe became broken in the contest.

THE NEMEAN ODES.

OF THE NEMEAN GAMES.

THESE games were probably so called from Nemea, a town of Argolis, with a wood in which Hercules when a youth is fabled to have killed a lion which infested that region; and in commemoration of this exploit the games were instituted, about the same time with the Olympic. They were among the most celebrated in Greece, and are said to have been originally held by the Argives, in memory of Opheltes, or Archemorus, son of Lycurgus, and king of Nemea, whose death was occasioned by the bite of a serpent, and to have been renewed by Hercules.

According to Pausanias, (in Phocaicis,) Adrastus was the author, and his descendants, the Epigoni, were the restorers of these games, which were held every third year, on the twelfth day of the month called by the Macedonians *Πανεμος*, by the Athenians *Βοηδρομιων*, answering to our August. The Argives, Corinthians, and Cleonæans were alternate presidents of these games, in which were exhibited chariot, horse, and foot races, boxing, wrestling, and all the usual exercises, whether gymnastic or equestrian. The reward at first bestowed on the conqueror was a crown of olive, afterward changed for one of parsley, which being a funereal plant, served to commemorate the death of Archemorus, in whose honour an oration was usually pronounced, and the distributors of prizes at these games were clad in mourning garments. A magnificent account of their celebration is contained in the opening of the sixth book of the Thebais of Statius.

THE FIRST NEMEAN ODE.

TO CHROMIUS, THE ÆTNÆAN, ON HIS VICTORY IN THE CHARIOT RACE.*

ARGUMENT.

The poet begins this ode with an address to Ortygia, an island in the bay of Syracuse, which anciently formed one of the four quarters of that city: with this he connects the praises of the victor, and the celebration of his virtues, particularly his hospitality.—He then digresses to the story of Hercules, from his birth to his apotheosis and marriage with Hebe, with which he concludes the ode.

From noble Syracuse, Ortygia, sprung,
Where breathes again Alpheus' long-lost head,
Sister of Delos, Dian's natal bed,
From thee the sweet-toned hymn is sung,
To praise the steeds whose feet like tempests move,
By favour of Ætnæan Jove. 6
Me Chromius' car excites on Nemea's plain
With his proud deeds to join th' encomiastic strain.

* Chromius, whose victory is here celebrated, was the son of Agesidamus, and married a sister of Gelon. Virgil appears to have imitated this passage, where he describes the situation of Ortygia and the reappearance of Alpheus after his subterranean wanderings at the mouth of the fountain Arethusa, hence called by Pindar αμπνευμα σεμνον Αλφεου, which Cowley translates inaccurately, *the first breathing place.*

"Sicanio prætenta sinu jacet insula contra
Plemmyrium undosum; nomen dixere priores
Ortygiam. Alpheum fama est huc Elidis amnem
Occultas egisse vias subter mare; qui nunc
Ore, Arethusa, tuo Siculis confunditur undis."
Æn., iii., 692.

Ortygia is called the *sister of Delos*, as having originally been known by the same appellation.

From the great gods to man arise
The springs of valorous enterprise.
Success affords the brightest meed
Of every great and glorious deed:
Such contests as on lyric string
The mindful muse delights to sing.
Now to the isle some tribute raise,
Which Jove, Olympus' sovereign lord,
Pledged with a nod his sacred word
(When to Persephone's command
Was given Sicilia's fertile land)
To gild with wealthy cities' towering praise.

To her, besides, Saturnius gave
A people arm'd, equestrian, brave;
And oft encircled with th' Olympic crown.
The olive wreath that victory weaves
Resplendent with its golden leaves,
Full many a time I've aim'd, nor e'er at random thrown.
Now at the hospitable gate
Chanting the hero's deeds I wait,
Where for his poet spread, the feast
Adorns the hall that never wants a guest.

As water drowns th' opposing flame,
So shall thy virtues' constant ray
Chase the calumnious mists away
That vainly would obscure thy fame.
Mankind by various arts ascend
The paths to eminence that tend—
In action, manly strength is shown;
In counsel, the reflecting mind;
To whose sagacious foresight known,
Lies the dark future unconfined.

31 This passage is rather obscure, although it appears to me that the general sense of it can be only that which is given in the translation. Λελογχε, placed absolutely, must denote the natural property which water possesses of extinguishing fire.

Son of Agesidamus! thee
To crown both might and skill agree.
A hidden and superfluous store
  Of wealth I wish not to possess;
But while they sing my praises o'er,
  With ready hand my friends to bless; 47

Since men to arduous deeds who soar
Hope the same glory and success.
When valour's lofty arts are sung,
Alcides prompts my willing tongue,
Rehearsing ancient fame.
The hero whom in radiance bright
Maternal throes sent forth to light,
With his twin brother came.
Him Juno on her golden throne survey'd,
In swaddling clothes of saffron hue array'd. 58

Then quickly raging at the view,
  The gods' bright queen her dragons sent;
And they, the open portals through,
  Deep in the spacious chamber went;
Eager the infants to compress
Within their rapid jaws' caress.
But he, with head in proud array
Stretch'd forth, began the deadly fray;
Daring the double snake to clasp
In his inevitable grasp;
And soon compress'd, the spirit flies
Their members of gigantic size.
Struck with intolerable dread,
The women trembled round Alcmena's bed:
While she with naked foot arose,
Prompt to repel the rage of her tremendous foes. 76

The chiefs of the Cadmæan band
In brazen arms tumultuous went,
And bold Amphitryon in his hand
Quick vibrating the unsheath'd brand,

Thither his sorrowing footsteps bent.
Since with an equal weight on all
Calamities domestic fall,
How soon soe'er from foreign grief
The heart uninjured finds relief. 84

By admiration's power subdued,
Though mingled with concern, he stood;
When his son's fearless pride he saw,
Exceeding moderation's law.
But as declared the immortal train,
The messenger's report was vain.
Then, straight he call'd Tiresias near,
Jove's truest, most illustrious seer;
Who to the chief of all the host
Show'd by what adverse fortunes cross'd,
How many ravening monsters slain
By land or on the trackless main;
And him that with unhallow'd pride
Should turn from virtue's path aside,
Alcides by a hateful doom,
He said, should hurry to the tomb. 99

And when the gods on Phlegra's plain
Wage combat with the giant train,
These monsters of terrestrial birth
Would soil their splendid locks with earth;
While he, his mighty labours past,
Quiet and peace should gain at last;
Enjoying in the mansions bless'd
A long eternity of rest;
Receiving to his godlike side
Hebe, his ever-blooming bride;
And seated near Saturnian Jove,
The nuptials o'er, his dome approve. 112

94 Antæus or Busiris, who for their arrogance and violent disposition were both punished with death by Hercules.

THE SECOND NEMEAN ODE.

TO TIMODEMUS, THE ATHENIAN, ON HIS VICTORY IN THE PANCRATIUM.

ARGUMENT.

THE poet declares this to be the first victory which Timodemus has obtained, considering it as a presage of future success in the Pythian and Isthmian games. This is the more probable, as his ancestors have rendered the family illustrious by their numerous victories gained in many preceding contests, several of which he enumerates.—Concludes with an exhortation to the citizens to celebrate with hymns the glorious return of Timodemus to his country.

As bards of the Homeric train
From Jove preluding, weave the strain,
So has this hero the foundation laid
Of conquests in the sacred games,
And now his earliest chaplet claims
Where Nemea's grove expands her hallow'd shade.

1 The scholiast, in commenting on the opening lines of this ode, gives a variety of conjectures on the origin of the phrase ῥαπτειν ωδας, and quotes a fragment of Callimachus, (cxxxviii. Bentl.,) whence some consider ῥαψωδους and ῥαπδωδους as synonymous. The author of the Etymologicum Magnum says that ωδη was anciently used as a generic term for a poem; and in all probability nothing more is meant by a *rhapsodist* than a composer of verses. The scholiast quotes Hippostratus as his authority for asserting that Cinæthus the Syracusan was the first who rhapsodised or wove together the scattered portions of Homer's divine poems. The same expression occurs in Isth. ii., 66, on which passage the classical reader will do well to consult Heyne's elaborate comment (in vv. lect.) Sudorius's paraphrase is *opere expolito.*

Still oft as onward age proceeds,
And in the track paternal leads,
Adorning spacious Athens with renown,
Triumphant in the Isthmian fray,
Timonous' son shall bear away
Her brightest wreath, and oft the Pythian crown. 16

As where the mountain Pleiads burn,
Not far they see Orion turn.
How potent, Salamis, thy might
To nourish heroes for the fight!
Hector perceived, in Troy's sad hour,
Thy son, intrepid Ajax' power;
And the sustain'd pancratium's praise
Shall thee, oh Timodemus, raise! 24

Acharnæ's glorious tribe of old
Have flourish'd with their heroes bold;
And foremost in each solemn game
The Timodemidæ proclaim.
They near Parnassus' height obtain'd,
Four times the victor's meed have borne,
And from Corinthian judges gain'd
In glades where valiant Pelops reign'd,
Eight several wreaths their brows adorn.

13 The scholiast has a very long note on this passage, relating the mythological story of the Pleiades, whom Pindar designates under the epithet ορειαν, as being the daughters of Atlas, who was metamorphosed into the famous African *mountain.* It appears that Orion, being violently enamoured of Pleione, who is sometimes understood as denoting the whole cluster of the Pleiades, and having pursued her for a considerable time, Jupiter recorded their history by converting them into neighbouring constellations; the former lying to the northwest, and the latter to the southeast of Taurus. The scholiast further informs us, that Crates read θερειαν instead of ορειαν, as the rising of the Pleiades was to Greece the indication of approaching harvest: in like manner the Nemean crown is the precursor of Isthmian and Pythian victories, to be achieved hereafter by Aristoclides.

Seven chaplets in the Nemean field—
  But to recount each various meed
Which Jove's Olympic contests yield,
  The power of numbers would exceed.
Him, citizens, in revels sing,
As Timodemus home you bring
With glorious pomp, and let your voice
In strain, as honey sweet, rejoice!

THE THIRD NEMEAN ODE.

TO ARISTOCLIDES OF ÆGINA, VICTOR IN THE PANCRATIUM.

ARGUMENT.

This ode opens with a beautiful address to the muse, whom the poet invites to pass at Ægina, which was a Doric colony, the sacred month in which the Nemean festival is held.—This leads to the praises of the island Ægina, which the victor, son of Aristophanes, has exalted by his triumphs, as much as if he had sailed to the Pillars of Hercules, and thus gained the extreme point attainable by human exertion.—The poet then checks himself, and enters on a theme more closely connected with his subject, the panegyric of the native heroes of Ægina, Peleus, Telamon, Achilles.—He then returns to the victor, declaring him to have fulfilled the various duties of boyhood, manhood, and more advanced age.—Concludes with bidding adieu to his friend, whom he pronounces worthy of the meed which the poet sends him, on account of his triumphs at Nemea, Epidaurus, and Megara.

Oh sacred muse!—on thee I call,
Mother of our poetic band,
Come to Ægina's Doric strand,
So throng'd at Nemea's festival;
For near Asopus' hallow'd wave
The youths who frame their choral lay,
And sweet-toned minstrelsy display,
Thy voice with eager fondness crave.
Each deed a different object claims—
While the proud victor in the games
To the sweet strain his wishes bends,
That still his virtues and his wreath attends. 13

Then grant this vocal boon to me
In unrestrain'd satiety.

Th' accepted hymn, oh child of Jove,
Who dwells enthroned in clouds above,
Begin, for I to chant his praise
Their voice and social lyre will raise.
The fruit of my delightful toil
Shall crown the glory of the soil.
Where dwelt the Myrmidons of yore,
Whose ancient and illustrious race
Aristoclides with disgrace
Of tarnish'd fame ne'er cover'd o'er;
Subdued in the pancratium's fight,
Where heroes strive with valiant might.

He who on Nemea's fertile plain
  The palm of conquest wins, has found
An antidote to labouring pain,
  A healing balm for every wound.
With his sweet form's unequall'd grace
  The valour of his arm agrees,
And onward bears in glory's race
  The son of Aristophanes.
No farther o'er the trackless main
An easy passage hope to gain
Than where Alcides' pillars stand.

Placed by the hero god, to stay
The wandering seaman on his way,
And witness the proud naval band
What time on the Herculean main
The mighty monsters he had slain.
Impell'd by his adventurous mind
The springs of marshy lakes to find,
Proceeding far as he could roam,
He traced the realm and voyage home.
But to what distant headland, say,
Waft'st thou, oh mind, my sail away?
To Æacus I charge thee bear
And to his race the chaplet fair;

For Justice adds her flower to raise
A tribute to the good man's praise. 50

Unjust the love that only views
With pleasure names of foreign lore—
Wouldst thou a worthy hero choose
To raise and ornament thy muse,
Domestic chronicles explore.
His royal virtues thus prolong
King Peleus' fame in ancient song;
Who his hewn spear exulting shook,
And all alone Iolcos took;
Then with aspiring labour strove
To win the seaborn Thetis' love ;
While Telamon's far-potent might
With Iolas o'erthrew Laomedon in fight. 63

Him to the Amazonian band,
Whose bow of brass twang'd in their hand,
He follow'd—nor subduing fear
Quench'd his impetuous mind's career;
For true nobility of soul
Prevails beyond all weak control.
The man that darkling gropes his way,
But for his borrow'd wisdom blind,
With foot uncertain where to stray,
And hopes that various objects sway,
Grasps all alike with feeble mind. 74

Meanwhile in Philyra's abode
  Achilles of the golden hair
In sports of active childhood show'd
  The ripen'd hero's manly care;
Shaking his iron-headed dart
In hands that play'd the warrior's part.
He combated with lions wild,
And swift as storms destruction wrought.
The boars he slew when scarce were fled
Six winters o'er his youthful head,

And to Centaurus, Saturn's child,
Their palpitating bodies brought.
Him ever wonder'd to behold
Diana and Minerva bold,
Without or dogs or nets' deceit,
O'ercome the stags with rapid feet. 89

I find it thus in legends old:
Wise Chiron in his stony cave
Long since to Jason nurture gave;
And taught Asclepias there to gain
The manual art that softens pain;
Then bound in matrimonial tie
Nereus' fair-handed progeny;
Storing her noble offspring's mind
With every excellence combined. 100

That soon as to the Trojan coast
Him winds and urging waters bore,
He might sustain the battle roar
Of Lycia's and of Phrygia's host.
Mingled with Æthiopia's band,
On high the martial spear who wield,
Combining mind with active hand;
That ne'er returning from the field
Should Helenus' brave kinsman roam,
Memnon their liege, and trace his journey home.

Jove, from this source the glories shine
Of Æacus' illustrious line,
Since from thy sacred blood they spring;
While thy great influence rules the game,
Which native youths with loud acclaim,
And hymns of joy tumultuous sing.
Shouts which the victor's triumphs tell
Become Aristoclides well;

110 Tithonus, father of Memnon, and Priam, father of Helenus were brothers.

Whose noble deeds this island raise
To heights of glory and of praise;
Gracing with Phœbus' Pythian strain
Thearion's venerable fane.
The issue of the contest tells
In what high efforts each excels.
When with the stripling band a boy,
  A man with men of riper age,
He made triumphant aims employ
  Each period of life's mortal stage;
And lengthen'd time with wisdom fraught
Prudence, the fourth best virtue, taught;

That can success on each design bestow.
Then hail, my enterprising friend;
To thee this beverage sweet I send,
Where the white milk and mingled honey flow.
Thus with the dew of song aspire
Soft breathings of th' Æolian lyre,
Though tardy be the lay.

Swiftest of birds, the eagle wends
Her flight, and with sharp talon rends
On high th' ensanguined prey;
While daws, below, a chattering brood,
Inglorious crop their earthly food.
For thee, if high-throned Clio raise
In thy victorious spirit's praise
The hymn, from Nemea shines the light,
From Megara and Epidaurus bright.

THE FOURTH NEMEAN ODE.

TO TIMASARCHUS OF ÆGINA, VICTOR IN THE PALÆSTRA.

ARGUMENT.

In this ode the sweetness and soothing effects of encomiastic poetry are beautifully described.—It is dedicated by the poet to the praise of the victor, his native island, and to the memory of his father, Timocritus.—Then follows a digression to the heroes of Ægina—Telamon, Alcyoneus, and especially Hercules.—Here he recalls his wandering muse, from fear of being reprehended by envious tongues, and indulges himself in anticipations of future excellence which shall be matured by time.—Nevertheless he returns to his digression, and describes the extent of dominion possessed by other heroes of Ægina—Teucer, Ajax, Achilles, Neoptolemus, and Peleus.—Recalls a second time his digressing strain, which he expresses metaphorically by bringing back his vessel from the darkness of Gades to the continent of Europe; since to relate the whole story of the Æacidæ were a fruitless endeavour.—He therefore enters on the praises of the tribe of Theandridæ, to which the victor belonged; of his maternal uncle Callicles; his grandfather Euphanes; and his alipta, or preceptor, Melesias, with whom he concludes the ode.

Hilarity, thou sovereign balm
And remedy of labours o'er,
Whose pain by arts untried before
The muses' vocal daughters calm—
What time they wake the lyric string,
  Not such delight the tepid wave
Can to the soften'd members bring,
  As praise, the meed of efforts have,
Which poets to the harp symphonious sing—
Beyond events of transient worth
  Long their recorded acts shall live —
Drawn from the mind's deep treasures forth,
  Such as the favouring Graces give.

Oh! may it be my happy fate
To Nemea and Saturnian Jove
Where wrestling Timasarchus strove,
The prelude hymn to consecrate.
May Æacus' well-guarded seat
With candid mind this tribute greet,
Where Justice rears her sheltering arm
Of power to save each guest from harm.
Were still Timocritus thy sire
  Warm'd by the genial solar ray,
Intent upon the varied lyre
  He oft had framed the victor's lay,
That should his numerous wreaths proclaim
Won in the Cleonæan game,
In Athens, rich with fair renown,
And the seven-portall'd Theban town. 31

When near Amphitryo's splendid tomb
For him with no unwilling hand
Their chaplets the Cadmæan band
Gave for Ægina's sake to bloom;
As to his kindred city's walls
With hasty steps the hero went,
Seeking the bless'd Herculean halls,
On amicable purpose bent. 39

With him to aid, in days of yore
Troy the bold Telamon o'erthrew,
Invaded Merops' Coan shore,
And the stupendous warrior slew
Alcyoneus—but first he broke
With a huge stone's vindictive stroke
Twelve chariots by four coursers whirl'd,
And heroes to destruction hurl'd
Who tamed the steed and urged the car
Of twice that number to the war.
Unskill'd in fight must he appear
To whom the moral is not clear;

Since he that can in aught prevail
Must in his turn expect to fail. 52

But the strict law that rules my song
And hours which urge their course along,
This thought prohibit, and restrain
Within just bounds the wandering strain.
Though fond desire my heart impel
Such tales at the new moon to tell;
Thee though the deep sea wave convey
Adventurous on thy middle way;
  Yet, mind, resist the snare;
Then far superior shall we rise
To all our slandering enemies,
  And walk in splendour fair;
While they of envious eye and soul
On earth their empty purpose roll. 66

To me what energetic power
Fate gave me in my natal hour,
Full well I know advancing time
Shall ripen to its destined prime.
Then haste, sweet lyre, the lay to weave
With Lydian melody combined,
Such as Œnone shall receive,
And Cyprus with enraptured mind;
Where, banish'd from his own domains,
The Telamonian Teucer reigns.
But Ajax his paternal soil
Yet holds—the Salaminian isle. 78

Achilles rules the shining land
Whose splendour gems the Euxine deep.
Phthia owns Thetis' high command:
While each sublime and beaked steep

78 I. e., the island *Leuce*, or *white*, so named from the abundance of herons with which it appears to glitter from afar. The poets describe it as an Elysium where the souls of deceased

That rises eminently o'er
Epirus' wide-extended shore,
And from Dodona lifts the brow
To where the Ionian waters flow,
Giving in numerous herds to graze,
Young Neoptolemus obeys.
Iolcos, fair Thessalian town,
Which Pelion's woody summits crown,
Attack'd by hostile hand, a slave
Peleus to his Hæmonians gave. 91

He whom Acastus' crafty dame,
Hippolyta, by guile o'ercame;
While Pelias' son's Dædalian blade
For him the fatal ambush laid.
But Chiron far the peril drove,
Fulfilling the decrees of Jove. 100

He the dread fire's all-potent might,
The terrors of the sharpen'd claws
And teeth that arm the direful jaws
Of lions raging for the fight,

heroes enjoy perpetual repose. In the celebrated scholion o. Callistratus, (εν μυρτω κλαδι, &c.,) Harmodius is addressed as dwelling in the islands of happy spirits with Diomed and the swift-footed Achilles.

94 The obscurity of this passage has greatly embarrassed the commentators. By the *sword of Dædalus* the scholiast simply understands a fraudulent design, sharpened for the destruction of its victim. The poet must be understood to institute a comparison between the craft of Acastus and that of Dædalus, who slew Minos by pouring on him a stream of boiling water with the co-operation of the daughters of Cocalus, king of Sicily. In like manner Peleus was subdued by stratagem, and his country Magnesia made subject to the Thessalians, through the treacherous instrumentality of Cretheis, daughter of Hippolytus, and wife to Acastus. The following lines allude to the various shapes of fire, lion, &c., into which Thetis is said to have transformed herself, with the vain hope of avoiding the matrimonial affinity of Peleus. Pindar relates the story again in Nem., v., 53, et seq., more at large and with greater clearness.

Subdued, and to his humbler bed
A lofty-throned Nereid led.
His eye beheld th' assembled train
Who rule in heaven and in the main,
Seated on high, and bless his race
With the rich gifts of power and grace. 111

To Gades none can urge his sail,
Which clouds and western darkness veil.
Approaching that most distant strand,
Return the bark to Europe's land;
For never can my tongue avail
To sing, Æacidæ, your lengthen'd tale.
But faithful to my compact, I
Hither a ready herald came,
To celebrate those triumphs high
In sports that knit the hardy frame;
Which Isthmus and Olympia's field
To the Theandridæ with Nemea's yield. 117

There having made a first essay,
Homeward again they bend their way,
But not without the frequent crown
That bears the fruit of high renown.
Thy tribe on thee we hear in solemn state
With songs of triumph, Timasarchus, wait. 129

If whiter than the Parian stone
A monument thou bid me raise
To Callicles thine uncle's praise—
As fires that sparkling gold refine
Give all its purest beams to shine—

108 Sudorius thus paraphrases the original expression, which is very peculiar:—

"Sufficit nautas penitus remotas
Visere Gades,
Cæca nox ultra est, tenebræque densæ—
Quas licet nullis penetrare remis."

So shall the hymn's triumphant tone
The hero's glorious deeds that sings
Exalt him to the rank of kings.
Though now by Acheron he dwell,
Yet shall my tongue his conquests tell;
When Corinth round the victor's brow
In thund'ring Neptune's game her parsley bade to glow. 142

He by thy willing grandsire's tongue,
Old Euphanes, has erst been sung,
Coevals, youth, in other days;
For best, as in heroic deeds,
By Fortune aided, each succeeds,
Each his bright eloquence displays;
As he Melesias who commends
At once the doubtful strife suspends:
Weaving the melodies of song,
Unconquer'd in the wrestler's toil,
Mild to the good and friendly throng,
But rough his enemies to foil. 156

THE FIFTH NEMEAN ODE.*

TO PYTHEAS OF ÆGINA, VICTOR WITH THE CÆSTUS.

ARGUMENT.

THE poet charges his song with the celebration of the victory which Pytheas, son of Lampo, has achieved in the Nemean games.—Hence he digresses to the heroes of Ægina, descendants of Æacus, especially Peleus, Euthymenes, Pytheas, the Athenian Menander his alipta, and Themistius.—Concludes with an address to his muse, exhorting her boldly to sing the triumphs of Pytheas at Nemea and in the festivals which were held at Epidaurus in honour of Æsculapius.

MINE is no statuary's fame,
Whose art constructs the mimic frame,
Forever standing on the selfsame base.
But leave, sweet song, Ægina's port,
On long-deck'd ships and cutters short,
To tell that Lampo's mighty son
Pytheas the Nemean crown hath won,
Whose honours the pancratium's victor grace.
Incipient manhood's tender flower
Not yet his downy cheek array'd
When his triumphant deeds display'd
Th' Æacidæ's victorious power—

* The opening of this ode contains an indirect reproach of the kindred of Pytheas, who wished to procure from Pindar an ode to commemorate his victory for a less sum than three drachmæ, (about ten pounds,) asserting that it would be preferable to purchase a statue for that sum: but afterward, sensible of their error, they request the bard to furnish them with an ode. He therefore begins very appropriately by instituting a comparison between the immobility of a statue and the universal celebrity which verses would obtain for the victor, by penetrating the most distant regions of the habitable world.

Heroes whose warlike glories spring
From Saturn and the heavenly king,
And Thetis' golden Nereid train;
Illustrating with high renown
The parent city's walls that crown
Ægina's hospitable plain. 16

Her they implored, as near the shrine
Of their Hellenian sire they stood,
That bless'd with sons in battle good
And naval strife her fame might shine;
Then raised their suppliant hands on high
Endeis' noble progeny,
Together with King Phocus' might,
Whom erst bright Psamathea bore,
A goddess, on her sandy shore.
I dread to speak with lofty tongue,
And show what direful ills have sprung
From slighted sense of right.
By what avenging god expell'd,
Their glorious isle the valiant band
Deserted—but my song withheld
From the sad theme, will make a stand.
'Tis not for every truth to show
Its undisguised and open brow—
Oft the best prudence of the wise
In silent meditation lies. 33

But would my song a tribute raise
Their wealth or manual strength to praise,
And iron firmness in the war,
I'd leap beyond the rest afar,
Proving with lightly bended knee
My supple frame's agility;
While rushes my adventurous strain
On eagle wing beyond the main.

24 I. e., Telamon and Peleus, sons of Æacus, and Endeis, he daughter of Chiron.

The ready muses' lovely choir
To them on Pelion's mountain sang,
And in the midst Apollo's lyre,
Struck by his golden plectrum, rang,
As the great leader sounded high
Its varied seven-toned harmony. 45

They hymn'd, beginning first from Jove,
Peleus and Thetis' sacred name,
And how the fair Cretheis strove,
Hippolyta, to soil his fame.
Magnesia's lord, her spouse, she led
By many a lure and artful wile,
Feigning a tale of treacherous guile,
That he Acastus' nuptial bed
Attempted basely to defile. 56

'Twas false—for him with raging mind
And suppliant prayer she oft address'd:
Yet her warm speech no love could find
Responsive in his tortured breast.
But he refused the nymph's desire,
Dreading His wrath the stranger's sire.
Heaven's mighty king, immortal Jove,
Who guides the clouds that roll above,
Observed the deed, and gave a sign
That from the golden-sceptred line
Of Nereids sporting in the main
The hero should a consort gain;
Persuading Neptune to approve
The social bond of kindred love; 67

The god who oft from Ægæ's height
To Dorian Isthmus speeds his flight.

67 I. e., Jupiter the protector of strangers.
74 Neptune and Peleus married Amphitrite and Thetis, two of the Nereids; they were therefore brothers-in-law.

Him there receive the festal choir
With sound of the melodious reed,
And in firm strength of limb aspire,
The native test of every deed;
While thou, Euthymenes, at rest
On the fair goddess Victory's breast,
Raisest the varied hymn to crown
Thine own Ægina with renown.
Now Pytheas' rapid footsteps trace
His uncle's fame in glory's race; 80

Illustrating his kindred line.
Such fame the strife of Nemea's field
And the month's circling periods yield,
Which Phœbus views with love divine.
At home and on green Nisus' height,
His equals, rushing to the fight,
He conquer'd—I exult to view
The city these fair deeds pursue. 86

To brave Menander's presence, know,
Thy toils their sweet requital owe.
Who fits the athletes for the ring
Should like himself from Athens spring.
No longer let chill fear control
The generous purpose of thy soul,
Themistius if thou come to sing.
But raise thy voice—and to the end
Of the tall mast thy sails extend—

90 I. e., the month Delphinius, in which a contest was celebrated by the Æginetans, sacred to Apollo, called the Hydrophoria.

99 This and the following line are thus paraphrased by Sudorius :—

"Cecropidam decet
Fortem exercitiis præesse virilibus."

It appears from this passage that the Athenians were as preeminent for their skill in athletic exercises as in arts and arms.

Loudly his double palm proclaim,
 Which in the Epidaurian field
The hardy wrestler's glorious game,
 And the pancratium's contests yield.
Assisted by the nymphs of auburn hair,
To Æacus' high fane 'twas his the wreaths to bear

THE SIXTH NEMEAN ODE.

TO ALCIMIDAS OF ÆGINA, VICTOR IN THE PALÆSTRA, IN THE CLASS OF BOYS.

ARGUMENT.

THIS ode begins with a moral reflection on the emanation of divinity by which the mind of man is enlightened, being of the same origin with the divine race.—This is illustrated by the example of Alcimidas, who, though a mere youth, treads in the footsteps of his grandfather Praxidamas.—His victories in the different games are enumerated, by which he has restored the glory of his house, that had been tarnished by the inactivity of his father Theo.—The victories of the tribe of Bassidæ are celebrated.—Pindar then proceeds to expatiate on the glories of the Æginetan heroes.—Returns to the victor, whose five-and-twentieth triumph is celebrated in this ode.—His kinsman Timidas, and his alipta, or charioteer, Melesias, whose rapid skill in guiding the car is compared to that of a dolphin cleaving the waves.

OF mortal or immortal race,
From the same mother earth we trace
Our lives—but not the same degree
Of power and vital energy
To man of transient space is given,
As in the brazen soil of heav'n.
Yet some resemblance can we find
Of nature or the mighty mind
That links us to the powers divine,
Howe'er 'tis not in us to know
When shall stern fate's recorded blow,
By day or night, our course define. 13

Now by Alcimidas is found
  The kindred excellence display'd,
As fields with rich luxuriance crown'd,
  To mortal life subservient made.

Renew their annual vigour, bless'd
With due vicissitudes of rest.
Warm from the pleasing Nemean game,
'Twas thus the hardy stripling came,
This contest, which began from Jove,
Pursuing with unwearied pace,
He for the wrestler's chaplet strove,
Eager as huntsman in the chase;
Tracking his grandsire's bright career,
Praxidamas, his steps appear.
He, where Alpheus' waters flow,
Olympia's wreath around his brow
To grace th' Æacidæ entwined,
Five times on him the Isthmian crown
And Nemea's thrice conferr'd renown;
No longer in oblivion pined
Soclides, plant of elder shoot
From Agesimachus, the parent root. 37

Since they, the triple chaplet gain'd,
To valour's summit have attain'd—
With labour and triumphant might
Contending in the glorious fight.
More numerous palms by favouring Heav'n
Have to no other house been given,
Won in the pugilistic fray,
Than such as on the Isthmian strand,
Recess of all the Grecian land,
This noble tribe has borne away. 45

With lofty eloquence of speech
The destined mark I hope to reach.
Thither, oh muse, from out thy bow
The shaft of epic sweetness throw.
To them the bards of other days
Have given the meed of honest praise;
Since frequent acts transmit to fame
The Bassidæ's illustrious name.

A race renown'd in ancient lore,
Who their own high encomium bore,
And by their vigorous deeds could yield
To such as till Pieria's field
Full many a hymn—his hands around
The cæstus' leathern safeguard bound,
From the same tribe in Pytho's fray
Brave Callias erst the prize obtain'd,
And Phœbus' high approval gain'd,
From golden-sceptred Lato sprung;
Whose triumphs at the close of day
The Graces' choir in bright array
Have by Castalia's waters sung. 66

And where the Isthmian bridge divides
Th' unwearied and opposing tides,
To him the Amphictyons' high decree
Assign'd their palm of victory,
Who by triennial bullocks slain
Appeased the monarch of the main.
Him too the lion's parsley crown'd
Triumphant on that sacred ground
Which lies beneath the shade outspread
Of Phlius' ancient mountain's head. 74

Open to bards on every side
Is the fair theme, the entrance wide,
Who to this glorious island raise
The tribute of poetic praise.
To them the Æacidæ have shown
Their mighty virtues' ample fame;
While far o'er earth and sea has flown
The sound of their illustrious name.
Even to the distant Æthiops' seat,
Ere Memnon homeward urged his wand'ring feet.

62 The epithet here given to Latona is the same by which Thetis is distinguished—(Nem., v., 65;) and Amphitrite, wife of Neptune—(Ol., ii., 168.)

On them fell strife and heavy war,
What time Achilles from his car,
Leaping with hasty step on earth,
By wrathful spear's ensanguined head
The monarch number'd with the dead,
Who to bright morning owed his birth.
Poets of other ages here
Have urged their chariots' swift career:
And I in this pursuit am join'd—
The waves that near the rudder flow,
While the ship cleaves the depths below,
First occupy the steersman's mind.

But I on willing shoulders bear
A double load of anxious care,
And come a herald to proclaim
The glories of the sacred game,
Whose five-and-twenty garlands grace
Alcimidas' illustrious race.
Thee, boy, and Timidas, who strove
By the Saturnian monarch's grove,
The guerdon of Olympia's fray
Thy lot forbade to bear away.
E'en like the dolphin race that sweep
On rapid fin the watery deep,
Melesias would I name, whose force
And hands direct the chariot's course.

THE SEVENTH NEMEAN ODE.

TO SOGENES OF ÆGINA, VICTOR WHEN A BOY IN THE PENTATHLIC GAMES.

ARGUMENT.

THIS ode opens with an address to Eilithyia, the goddess who presided at parturition, declaring that Sogenes, the son of Thearion, was at his birth gifted with so robust a frame as should enable him while yet a boy to conquer in the pentathlum.—The muses, by celebrating in song the glorious actions of heroes, confer on them a celebrity more than commensurate with their importance; nor would Ulysses have acquired such fame but for the praises of Homer.—To them is owing the renown of Neoptolemus, son of Achilles, one of the heroes of Ægina, to whose history the poet digresses.—Then checking himself, from the fear of exciting satiety in his hearers, he returns to Ægina, Thearion, and the victor Sogenes; invoking the continued favour of Jupiter, to whom the Nemean games were sacred, of Æacus, and especially of Hercules, whom he entreats to become an intercessor with Jupiter, Juno, and Minerva, that they may grant their protection to the conqueror and to his latest posterity.—Concludes with declaring his intention not to insult the memory of Neoptolemus by renewing the story of his death; but deprecates repeated apologies to his adversaries.

OH thou, to whom a seat is given
The deep-revolving Parcæ near,
Child of the potent queen of heav'n,
Prolific Eilithyia, hear!
Without thine aid we ne'er should claim
In the clear day or sable night
To gaze upon the genial light,
And view thy sister Hebe's hardy frame.

4 The precise object of Pindar in this opening address to the goddess of parturition has been variously explained by different

Not subject all to equal law,
The vital energy we draw.
But thou, as different fates prevail,
Urgest our ever-varying scale.
With thee his valiant arm to bless,
Young Sogenes, Theario's son,
Shines in renown and high success
Mid those who the pentathlic wreath have won.

He in th' Æacidæ's fair city dwells,
Who shake the spear, and rouse with kindred flame
The sons to emulate their fathers' fame,
Where the song oft the pomp of triumph swells.
On him, whom fortune's smiles befriend.
The muses' honey'd streams descend;
While o'er the deeds that want their tale
Darkness extends her dusky veil.
We in what polish'd mirror know
Illustrious deeds reflected glow,
If with resplendent fillet bound
Mnemosyne permit to share
That sweet reward of toil and care,
The epic lay's illustrious sound.
Three days ere yet the tempest rise
The skilful mariner descries.

ancient commentators. It has been suggested by some, with a great appearance of probability, that Thearion, the father of Sogenes, was in the habit of sacrificing to Eilithyia, to whom a temple was erected near his residence. Callimachus (hymn. ad Del. 257) speaks of a lay peculiar to this divinity :—

ειπαν Ελειθυιης ἱερον μελος.

The reciting of which is noticed by Madame Dacier as a very unusual circumstance, but is not commented on by Spanheim. In the Iliad, (xi., 348,) the Eilithyia are mentioned in the plural, as daughters of Juno Lucino, in which passage Pope takes no inconsiderable liberty both with the quality and orthography of this venerable sisterhood, by calling them *the fierce Ilythiæ.*

31 Pliny in his Natural History (lib. iii.) relates that the inhabitants of the island of Lipara can foretel from the course of the smoke which ascends from it what will be the direction of

Both rich and poor one common doom
Calls undistinguish'd to the tomb.
If right I deem, one ampler fame
Exalts the great Ulysses' name,
From Homer's sweet poetic song,
Than to his deeds could e'er belong. 31

Since genius' bright and airy vein
Hallows the fictions of his strain;
And wisdom in sweet fable dress'd
With potent charm allures the breast.
Meanwhile the crowd in error stray,
Darkness still brooding o'er their way;
For had their mind the truth perceived,
Brave Ajax, mad with anger's smart,
When of the arms by them bereaved,
Ne'er with smooth sword had pierced his heart.
Him, rivalling Achilles' might,
Chief of the Grecian host, in fight,
For bright-hair'd Menelaus' bride,
Propitious-breathing zephyrs bore
To Ilus' walls on Phrygia's shore,
In ships that swiftly plough'd the tide. 44

Gulf'd by the same infernal wave,
The bright and lowly seek the grave.
Yet heroes live beyond the tomb—
Whene'er the muse augments their fame.
To earth's deep-bosom'd centre came,
Soon as he wrought Troy's final doom,
Young Pyrrhus, with the Greeks to aid,
And in the Pythian plain was laid.
Destined to see his purpose fail,
From Scyros when he urged his sail;
Till wandering o'er the watery way,
To Ephyre the warriors stray. 55

the wind three days afterward. It is probable that Pindar here alludes to some such tradition.

Short time he in Molossia reign'd
Whose sceptre still his race retain'd;
And bearing from the conquer'd soil
The first fruits of the Trojan spoil,
Approach'd the god—but fell in deadly strife,
Himself a victim to the hostile knife. 62

The Delphians mourn'd with heavy wo;
But fate in vengeance urged the blow,
By whose decree a king should come
Of Æacus' high line, to rest
Within the grove's time-hallow'd breast,
Near Phœbus' wall-encircled dome;
Where his presiding eye might still survey
Chiefs with heroic pomp the sacrifice display.

Three potent reasons will avail
To justify the murderous tale.
No fraudful witness he who claims
Dominion o'er the sacred games.
The race that springs from thee and Jove
Will by their virtues' shining beam,
Ægina, my bold speech approve,
And hallow the domestic theme. 76

But sweet the moment of repose
That brings each labour to its close;
Since e'en excess of honey cloys,
And flow'r of Aphrodisian joys.
By nature various lots are thrown,
But perfect happiness to none.

71 According to the scholiast, it is related of Neoptolemus that while sacrificing at Delphi, and endeavouring to prevent the people from snatching away the offerings, according to their custom, he was slain by them in a tumult of indignation. Virgil (Æn., iii., 330) relates that Neoptolemus was slain by Orestes, in revenge for the loss of his kingdom and affianced bride Hermione.

Nor can I tell whose prosperous state
On constant height is raised by fate:
That, bless'd Thearion, gives to thee
Due portion of felicity. 87

Since prudence ne'er deserts thy mind,
With glorious hardihood combined.
May I, a stranger, still be pure
From reprehension's tale obscure!
As rills convey'd into the field
Their fructifying moisture yield,
So I with just and liberal praise
The friendly hero's name will raise.
Such is the guerdon of the brave. 93

Nor let a Greek attack my name,
Approaching near, with voice of blame,
Who dwells beyond th' Ionian wave. 95

Trusting their hospitable love,
  Among the townsmen's social throng
With look serene and bright I move,
  And foot estranged from force or wrong.
Advancing time new bliss convey!
And let the man who knows me say
If to the strain my tongue impart
The slanders of a rancorous heart. 102

Oh Sogenes! who from the tribe art sprung
  Of brave Euxenidæ, (I swear
  That like the brass-tipp'd javelin, ne'er
I sent beyond the mark my rapid tongue,)
  Who carriedst from the wrestler's toil
    A sinewy neck and corporal might
  Which labour's dew could never soil,
    Nor sun oppress with noonday light.
  And though full arduous were the deed,
  More sweet succeeding triumph's meed.

Permit me for the victor's sake
A strain of louder note to wake.
No churlish bard sings thy renown.
'Twere easy for the victor's brow
To twine a leafy wreath—but thou
Expect the muse's golden crown;
Who plucks the flower of ivory hue,
And coral steep'd in ocean dew. 117

But, tranquil mind, a bolder lay
Must hymn great Jove and Nemea's fray;
Since on this soil the heavenly king
'Tis fit with voice divine to sing;
For, Hercules, thy brother guest,
Whose mild sway rules my country bless'd,
From him and the maternal seed
By fame is stated to proceed. 127

If man to man assistance lend,
  What joy so grateful shall we find
As that of neighbour and of friend
  Who loves us with a constant mind?
And if the gods are prone to feel
The same desire for others' weal,
Near thee, who couldst the giants quell,
Securely Sogenes might dwell,
Tending his sire with pious care
In his forefathers' city fair. 136

For as the doubly yoked steed
Urges the rapid chariot's speed,
On either hand thy neighb'ring dome,
Alcides, guards his humbler home.

136 For as the brightness and warmth of the sun bring the vegetable coral to its matured state of hardness, so does the muse bestow on the victor his best reward in her perfect strain of encomiastic melody.

141 Æacus was the son of Jove and the nymph Ægina, and brother to Hercules.

'Tis thine, bless'd hero, to persuade
Jove, Juno, and the blue-eyed maid.
Thou oft in troubles canst impart
Strength to the fainting mortal heart.
Oh! may their lives thy care engage
In shining youth and hoary age,
That present honour and more bright success
Henceforth his children's children may possess!

Never my tongue with bitter sound
Brave Neoptolemus shall wound.
But to repeat this thrice-told truth
Can want of language only prove;
As babbling sires instruct their youth,
"Corinthus was the son of Jove."

168 Pindar's reverence for Neoptolemus was strengthened by the constant sight of the altar raised at Delphi to that hero, near to which was placed the seat whence the poet chanted his hymns in honour of Apollo.

THE EIGHTH NEMEAN ODE.

TO DEINIS, SON OF MEGAS, VICTOR IN THE STADIC COURSE.

ARGUMENT.

This ode opens with an address to the flower of youth, the harbinger of successful as well as calamitous love.—This leads to the happy amour of Jupiter with the nymph Ægina, the fruit of which was the valiant Æacus, from whom he supplicates as great a degree of prosperity for the Æginetans as was enjoyed by Cinyras, king of Cyprus.—Returns from his digression, lest he should excite envy and blame.—This was the cause of the death of Ajax, who by an unjust decree was deprived of the arms of Achilles, and of many other mischiefs.—The poet addresses a prayer to Jupiter that he may never indulge this malevolent disposition.—On the other hand, he delights in celebrating by his verses the valour of Deinis, his father Megas, and the tribe of the Chariadæ; since the framing of poetical encomia has always afforded a pleasing alleviation of the heaviest calamities.

Bless'd prime of youth! the herald sweet
Of Aphrodite's golden joys,
Who on the eyelids hast thy seat
Of tender nymphs and amorous boys;
While one in gentle arms is borne,
And from th' embrace another torn.
How pleased who in each deed of love
Occasion's fair advantage prove,
Seizing with a successful aim
The objects of their happy flame. 9

Such were the guards of Venus' gifts, who shed
Their genial influence round Ægina's bed;

From whom and mighty Jove was given to spring
In arm and counsel strong, Œnone's king.
Him many oft begg'd to survey,
Since of the nations dwelling round,
The flower of that heroic train
Who led their armies on the plain
By rock-protected Athens crown'd,
And they of Pelops' valiant band
Scatter'd throughout the Spartan land,
Would fain his lordly will obey. 21

While I in suppliant action seize
Great Æacus' time-honour'd knees,
Imploring the loved city's weal,
And citizens' with anxious zeal.
To Deinis now the wreath I bring,
With Lydian melodies entwined,
And Nemea's double stadium sing,
His father Megas' praise combined.
From bounties which the god bestows
More lasting bliss to mortals flows;
Who royal Cinyras erewhile
Loaded with wealth in Cyprus' isle. 31

Now on suspended foot I rest,
Pausing ere I my tale unfold—
Since they who carry to the test
Whate'er by ancient bards is told,
Seeking to feign a story new,
All that is perilous pursue.
Such fictions give the envious food,
Who spare the feeble, but assault the good. 38

Pierced by the sword, through these undone,
Died Telamon's heroic son.
Unskill'd in speech, though brave in soul,
Oblivion's waves his deeds control;
While varied falsehood in the fray
The mighty guerdon bears away.

For by the fraudulent decree,
When sought the Greeks Ulysses' love,
Reft of the golden panoply,
With fate in vain brave Ajax strove. 47

Yet dealt their arms far different blows
On the warm bodies of their foes,
Under the man-defending spear—
Some for Achilles newly slain,
Some they for other toils sustain,
That mark those slaughterous days' career.
But among men of old had sprung,
Companions of the glowing tongue,
Deceit and hatred's foul disgrace ;
Which often with insidious blow
Lays fortune's towering minion low,
And gives th' obscure his glorious place. 58

Never, oh Father Jove! be mine
Manners so stamp'd by false design ;
But let my steps, life's journey through,
Simplicity's straight paths pursue;
That my surviving sons may claim
Inheritance of spotless fame.
While some for golden treasures pray,
Others for land's unbounded sway,
May I acquire the townsmen's love,
  Ere in the earth my limbs are laid—
Boldly their virtuous deeds approve,
  But be their sins with blame repaid! 68

Virtue her growing strength renews,
  Nurtured by poets' fostering care,
As the tree fed by tender dews
  Shoots proudly through the liquid air.
The aid of friends man ever needs,
But chiefly in laborious deeds.
A faithful mirror true delight
Requires to place before the sight. 75

'Tis not in my imperfect art
  Thy soul, oh Megas! to restore;
And empty hopes can but impart
  The issue vain they ever bore.
But a musæan stone to raise
To thee, and in thy tribe's high praise,
The brave Chariadæ, 'tis mine—
With joy I hail thy double speed,
And to reward the glorious deed
Send forth the tributary line.
Full oft before the child of grief
Has found in song a sure relief.
Th' encomiastic hymn was rife
Before Adrastus' and the Thebans' strife. 87

THE NINTH NEMEAN ODE.

TO CHROMIUS THE ÆTNÆAN, ON HIS VICTORY IN THE CHARIOT RACE.

ARGUMENT.

Pindar invokes the muses to bring the Pythian pomp from Sicyon to the new-built city of Ætna in honour of Chromius, who has obtained a victory in these games when celebrated at the former city.—Digresses to the history of Adrastus the Argive chief, by whom they were instituted, and the fate of Amphiaraus, together with reflections arising therefrom.—Returns to his subject, and offers up prayers to Jupiter for the welfare of the Ætnæans.—Concludes the ode with the praises of Chromius, and supplications to Jupiter that he will crown the victor with future triumphs.

From Sicyon, ruled by Pytho's king,
The pomp, oh muses! we will bring
To new-built Ætna, Chromius' mansion bless'd,
Whose doors are open to the frequent guest.
But weave a dulcet epic strain—
For when he mounts the victor car,
The mother and her offspring twain
Hail the triumphant voice from far;
Whose joint-inspecting eyes survey
From Pytho's height the glorious fray. 12

By man's consenting voice 'tis said
No act to prosperous issue brought
Should on the earth in scorn be laid.
The song with boastful praises fraught

7 I. e., Latona with Apollo and Diana.

Offers the due, the noblest meed
To recompense the victor'sdeed.
The sounding harp then let us raise—
And in th' equestrian contests' praise
Give the sonorous flute to blow—
Those contests which in Phœbus' name
Adrastus consecrates to fame,
Where pure Asopus' waters flow.
These my recording muse shall trace,
And with illustrious wreaths the hero grace.

Who ruling then with sceptred sway
In contests of corporeal might,
And in his polish'd chariots' flight,
Raised his loved city's name on high
With new and festal revelry.
From bold Amphiaraus far
Fell discord and intestine war,
And Argive home he urged his way.
No more by this dire fiend oppress'd,
Their empire Talaus' sons possess'd:
But a good man composes hate,
And enmities of ancient date.

As when the firmest pledge of truth,
Adrastus to Œclides' bed
His sister Eriphyle led,
Her who subdued the hapless youth—
Over the bright-hair'd Grecian train
'Twas theirs dominion to obtain.
When they to Thebes' seven portals bring
(Cheer'd by no bird's auspicious wing)
Their numerous host—Saturnian Jove,
Who hurls his lightning shafts above,
Exhorted their mad haste to stay,
Nor urge from home their lengthen'd way.

34 The children of Talaus were Adrastus, Parthenopæus, Pronax, Mecistheus, and their sister Eriphyle, who was married o the prophet Amphiaraus.

With brazen arms and steeds elate
The crowd rush'd on to open fate;
And vanquish'd on Ismenus' banks,
Cut off from hope of sweet return,
The bodies of their slaughter'd ranks,
Fattening the lurid volumes, burn;
For, placed on seven funereal pyres,
The youthful heroes feed the fires.
Jove the earth's solid bosom broke
By his all-potent thunder stroke,
And low Amphiaraus laid
In chariot with the steeds array'd,
Ere, Periclymenus, thy spear
Controll'd his warlike mind's career,
And on his wounded back a trace
Fix'd of indelible disgrace. 63

For when the gods with fears excite,
Their very sons are moved to flight.
Oh! that my prayers, Saturnian Jove,
The dire essay and warlike boast
That rouses the Phœnician host
Could far from Ætna's walls remove,
Of thee a long and prosperous fate
I for her children supplicate; 75

Whose favour can the people crown
With civic honour and renown.
A race of men inhabit there,
  Well pleased the generous steed to train,
Who an exalted spirit bear,
  That soars above the thirst of gain.
Incredible my words must prove
For shame and glory's noble fire,
Quench'd in unequal strife, expire
With lucre's mercenary love.
Oh! hadst thou stood by Chromius' side
In the pedestrian battle's tide,

And when his coursers whirl'd the car,
And vessels waged the naval war,
Then had thine eye discern'd aright
The peril of that deadly fight;
And how that goddess' power endued
His warlike mind with fortitude,
The terrors of the dire affray
And Mars' assaults to drive away. 88

But few by strength or prudent mind
From their own threaten'd ranks can find
Of present death to turn the cloud
Backward upon the hostile crowd.
Hector's bright fame is said to glow
Near where Scamander's waters flow. 95

By steep Helorus' banks of stone,
Where men Area's traject name,
In his first youth with glory's flame
Agesidamus' offspring shone.
His labours wrought in other days,
Whether upon the dusty plain,
Or islands of the neighb'ring main,
With due encomium will I praise.
Such as in fervid youth are wrought,
  If justice sanctify the deed,
Through life with sweet enjoyment fraught,
  To age's latest hour proceed.

99 The Helorus was a very rapid river in the southeast of Sicily, mentioned by Virgil, (Æn., iii., 698,) on the banks of which the scholiast informs us that Gelon, with the assistance of Chromius, obtained a victory over the Carthaginians. *Area's traject* is not so clearly defined by geographers. The scholiast is of opinion that it was a name given to that part of the Fretum Siculum contiguous to Rhegium, in commemoration of the war like events which took place on that coast, and tells us that it is a doubtful point whether the true reading be Αρειας, or Ρεας. One edition gives *αρειας*, from *αραις*, as denoting the *traject of threats*—(viz., of the Carthaginians.)

From heaven's immortal rulers know
Such wondrous happiness must flow.

If ever wealth's abundant store
  Illustrious glory should convey,
No higher eminence explore,
  No farther mortal feet can stray.
As the convivial board is crown'd
By jocund youth's enlivening sound,
Thus the soft luxuries of song
To recent conquest's praise belong.
Where'er the festal cup is shown
The voice assumes a bolder tone.
Let this by any mingled be,
Sweet harbinger of revelry!

Let him in silver goblets pour
The potent offspring of the vine;
With which the steeds in days of yore
Enrich'd triumphant Chromius' store;
While Phœbus gloried to entwine
For him the justly woven crown
From Sicyon's venerable town.
To thee, oh Father Jove! I pray
Grant me this conquest to display,
Assisted by the Graces' choir—
Oh! may I honour in my strain
The various wreaths his efforts gain,
And to the muses let my shafts aspire.

THE TENTH NEMEAN ODE.

TO THIÆUS, SON OF ULIAS, VICTOR IN THE PALÆSTRA.

ARGUMENT.

ADDRESSING this ode to Thiæus, who had conquered at Argos in the Hecatombæa, or Herea, games sacred to Juno, the poet begins by recounting the ancient histories, and celebrating the heroes and other noted characters connected with that ancient city of Danaus, Perseus, Medusa, Epaphus, Hypermnestra, Diomedes, Amphiaraus, Amphitryo, and Hercules.—Recalls himself to his subject, and enumerates the various triumphs of the victor, as well as those which have at different times graced his family.—From the mention of Pamphaes, one of his maternal ancestors; who hospitably entertained Castor and Pollux, he is led to relate the history of the Dioscuri, with which he concludes the ode.

ARGOS, old Danaus' towering seat,
And fifty high-throned daughters' home,
Where rises Juno's stately dome,
Graces, with hymns of triumph greet;
Whose deeds her shining glories raise
With endless arguments of praise.
Long is the tale how Perseus sped
With dire Medusa's gorgon head;
And how o'er Egypt's land appear'd
The towns by Epaphus uprear'd;
Or Hypermnestra pure remain'd,
Whose sheath alone the sword retain'd. 11

The goddess of the azure eye
  Immortal Diomedes made;
And pierced by Jove's artillery,
  The Theban earth's funereal shade

Received Œclides, hapless seer,
Who urged the stormy war's career,
Nor less in nymphs with lovely hair
Refulgent shines the city's fame.
This Jupiter's descents proclaim
To Danae and Alcmena fair:
He who to harmony inclined
Adrastus' sire and Lynceus' mind; 22

And rear'd Amphitryo to the fight;
But he who rules supreme in might
Grafted upon the parent tree
His own immortal progeny:
For when in brazen armour dight
He the repulsed Teleboans slew,
His hall th' immortal ruling god,
Robed in the hero's likeness, trod,
Bearing the intrepid seed to view
Herculean—him whose youthful bride,
  Fairest among the goddess train,
Walks by the genial mother's side,
  Throughout Olympus' high domain. 34

Brief my song's limits to declare
What Argos holds of good and fair;
And hard the labour to control
In man satiety of soul.
But the well-chorded lyre awake,
And as a theme the wrestling take.
Oft as adjudged the brazen prize
Draws crowds to Juno's sacrifice.
Whence Ulias' son twice victor bore
Oblivion of his labours o'er. 45

17 The death of Amphiaraus, which story might perhaps be founded on some vague tradition of the similar fate of Korah, Dathan, and Abiram, was related in the last ode, (l. 57, et seq.)

23 The cause of strife between Lynceus, who had succeeded his father-in-law Adrastus, and Talaus, the father of Adrastus, was related in Nem., ix., 35, et seq.

At Pytho, from the Grecian train
  Of old he bore the meed away.
With like success on Nemea's plain
  He strove, and in the Isthmian fray,
And to the muses gave to sow
The wreaths that should adorn his brow.
Three the sea's narrow portals yield,
And three the venerable field
That owns Adrastus' sway.
Oh Jove ! his tongue will not declare
The object of his mental prayer.
Yet never with a slothful heart
Thy grace he begs thee to impart,
Since his own boldness will the glory share. 56

Known to the god the truths I sing:
And he who soars on venturous wing,
In the high contest to prevail,
Can verify o'er all my tale.
Pisa the highest honour claims,
Alcides rules her sacred games.
Him the sweet intervals of song
Have twice proclaim'd in Athens' festal throng.
In earth concocted by the flame,
To Juno's manly people came,
The sacred olive's produce, brought
In vessels with devices wrought. 68

Glories thy steps, Thiæus, trace
From thy maternal uncles' race,
Whose honours make the Graces fair
And high Tyndaridæ their care.
Were I in kindred's social chain
  To Thrasyclus and Antias bound,

57. I. e., He is not so presumptuous as openly to express a wish to conquer in the Olympic games.

71 Pindar here alludes to the custom of carrying before the victor at the Panathenaic games a sculptured earthenware vase, filled with oil from the sacred olive tree.

In Argos never would I deign
  To hide my free looks on the ground.
How many triumphs shed renown
On Prœtus' steed-producing town!
As well in Corinth's narrow strand,
As four times o'er the Cleonæan band. 79

From Sicyon came in bright array
They who the silver bowls convey;
And from Pellene's walls in vest
Of the sheep's downy softness dress'd:
But never could my hasty verse
The brazen ornaments rehearse,
Since to complete this arduous task
Would more extended leisure ask;
  Which near the altars of Lycæan Jove
Achaia's lofty cities place,
  While Tegea and Clitorium strove,
The first in speed of foot and strength of hand tc grace. 90

To Pamphaes when Castor came,
  His hospitable board to share,
And first in pugilistic fame
  His brother Pollux tarried there,
No wondering doubts the mind should move
That athletes they by nature prove,
Guardians of Sparta's wide domain,
  With Hercules' and Hermes' aid,
Since they the contest's laws maintain,
  Whose bright success themselves have made;
And ever faithful to their trust,
The race divine protect the just.
Now with alternate change they move,
One day to spend with Father Jove,
And one below earth's secret breast,
Within Therapne's cave to rest.

110 See the conclusion of the eleventh Pythian ode.

Fulfilling thus an equal fate ;
Since Pollux, scorning to remain,
For ever with the heavenly train,
Sharing his much-loved Castor's state,
Redeem'd his life in battle slain. 111

Him for his lost herds furious made,
Idas transfix'd with deadly stroke,
Aim'd by his spear of brazen head,
Whom, seated on a trunk of oak,
He from Taïgetus survey'd, whose ken
In lynx-eyed sharpness conquer'd mortal men.
Then straight, devising deeds of might,
Approach'd with rapid step and light
The sons of Aphareus, whom heaven's high sire
Chastised with hands that sent afflictions dire ;
For Leda's offspring swift in flight pursued,
While near their father's tomb the brothers stood;

And, snatching thence a polish'd stone
With Pluto's effigy impress'd,
They aim'd the massy fragment, thrown
With force that stirr'd not Pollux' breast,

131 This stone, which the sons of Aphareus hurl with such impotent force against the breast of Pollux, was perhaps part of the decoration of a stony sepulchre, not *a statue*, for this was prior to the age of statuary. Sudorius, in his metrical paraphrase, calls it a funereal or deadly stone :—

> " Immane saxum funereum manu
> Audace vibravere duri
> In stomachum medium Laconis."

Theocritus, who relates the same story in his twenty-second idyllium, calls the stone *σταλαν*.

The passage describing the vain and impious attack of Idas is thus translated by Polwhele :—

> " Vindictive of his brother's doom,
> He tore a column from Aphareus' tomb,
> Aiming its massy vengeance at the foe,
> With wild uplifted arm, in act to throw ;
> Heaven's sovereign lord elanced a flaming brand
> That dash'd the shatter'd marble from his hand !"

Nor to a backward step could move
The hero who with deadly blow
Against the sides his javelin drove,
Impetuous of the wary foe;
While Jove who dwells on Ida's head
Brandish'd his bolt of smoky red,
And fired the hapless pair.
Mortals in arduous strife engage,
Who with superior force to wage
Unequal contest dare. 136

To aid his fainting brother's might
Tyndarides resumed his flight;
And found him not subdued by death,
But gasping out his fitful breath.
Then pouring forth a fervid tide
Of tears, with mingled sighs he cried,
"Saturnian father! what relief
Shall terminate my bitter grief?
The stroke, oh king, that slays my friend
At thy behest on me descend!
He whom the social train have left,
Of honour is at once bereft;
And few of mortals will sustain
A faithful share in others' pain." 147

He said—when Jove his form display'd,
And this consoling answer made:
"Thou art my son; while of terrestrial race
He to a hero must his lineage trace:
Then take the proffer'd boon, for I
Give thee detested age and death to fly:
To dwell with Pallas on Olympus' height,
And Mars, who shakes his sable spear in fight. 158

This choice is thine: but if the strife
Still arm thee for thy brother's life,

161 Pollux and Helen were the reputed children of Jupiter; Castor and Clytemnestra the offspring of Tyndarus.

And strong affection move thy heart
To grant of all an equal part,
Beneath the earth thy half breath draw,
And by the same impartial law,
Half in the golden domes of heaven."
'Twas thus the immortal father spoke;
Nor could weak doubts his mind provoke
To slight the generous offer given.
The god anew the eye and voice unbound
Of Castor, with his brazen helmet crown'd.

THE ELEVENTH NEMEAN ODE.

TO ARISTAGORAS THE PRYTANIS OF TENEDOS, SON OF ARCESILAUS.

ARGUMENT.

In this ode the poet supplicates Vesta to receive propitiously Aristagoras and his colleagues, who were entering on their annual dignity at Tenedos.—Commends him on account of his father Arcesilaus, his own beautiful form and numerous triumphs, blaming his parents, whose cautious fears would not allow him to engage in the more illustrious Pythian and Olympic contests.—Details the origin of the victor's ancient family from Pisander and Melanippus; but his race having been for a time obscured and inglorious, he concludes the ode with reflections on human vicissitudes, exhorting his hero to aim at attainable objects.

Hail, Vesta, Rhea's offspring! thou whose care
The hearths of Prytanæan mansions share,
Sister of Juno, throned on high
With Jove in kindred majesty—
Let Aristagoras and social train
A friendly welcome entertain,
Where thine illustrious sceptred sign is found,
Who guard fair Tenedos and thee adore,
Slay the fat victims, the libations pour,
While lyre and song, thee, first of gods, resound;
And at the constant board they prove
The rites of hospitable Jove.

2 The Prytanæum was the place at Athens where the council of five hundred held their deliberations, and where the sacred fire of Vesta was kept—(*πυροταμειον*.) In this part of the city they who had deserved well of their country were maintained at the public charge.

May they with heart unwounded still
Their annual dignity fulfil. 12

But I the joyful song will raise
In his great sire Arcesilaus:
That beaüteous form I hail with glee,
And kindred intrepidity.
Let him with rich possessions bless'd,
Whose form excels above the rest,
Seen in the varied contests bright
With glory and surpassing might,
Survey his frame of mortal limbs composed,
Doom'd at the last to be in common earth enclosed.

'Tis just his fellow-townsmen should proclaim
In words and varied songs' mellifluous tone,
Great Aristagoras' victorious fame,
For sixteen palms from neighb'ring rivals won.
His noble country these with high renown
In the pancratium gain'd and wrestler's contest crown. 27

But their son's might the parents' sluggish fear
From Pythian and Olympic fields restrain'd—
Fix'd in my sentiment, I firmly swear,
That when the hero's footsteps have attain'd
The waters of Castalia's fount,
And Saturn's wood-encircled mount,
Again he seeks his native land,
More honour'd than the rival band,
Observes the laws, a frequent guest
Of Hercules' quinquennial feast;
And gayly revelling has bound
The purple boughs his hair around. 37

But oft through empty-minded boast
Mortals th' expected good have lost;
While he by diffidence oppress'd,
Failing of bliss he once possess'd,

Sudden withdraws his backward grasp,
Nor dares in mind the blessing clasp.
'Twere easy his high birth to trace
From old Pisander's Spartan race;
For hither as he bent his course,
He from Amyclæ's walls convey'd,
With bold Orestes' friendly aid,
His brazen-arm'd Æolian force;
And by his mother near Ismenus' flood
From Melanippus drew his mingled blood. 47

Oft since their pristine strength renew'd
Shines forth in after times vicissitude.
Not loaded with perpetual grain,
The fields their yellow hue retain:
Nor trees an ample harvest bear
Of flowers and fruit through all the year;
But with just change—thus equal fate
Man's faded strength can renovate.
No sign proceeding from above
Makes clear the fix'd intent of Jove. 57

But swell'd by many a vain desire,
Too high our mortal thoughts aspire;
For bound in hope's adhesive chain,
The vital energies remain.
The foresight of the human mind
By narrow limits is confined.
Seek not unbounded wealth—nor prove
The raging pangs of hopeless love! 63

THE ISTHMIAN ODES.

OF THE ISTHMIAN GAMES.

These games received their name from the isthmus of Corinth, the scene of their celebration. The traditional account of their origin is, that they were instituted by Sisyphus, king of Corinth, and brother of Athamas, B. C. 1326, to commemorate the metamorphosis of Melicerta, son of Athamas and Ino, into a sea deity, named afterward Palæmon by the Greeks, and Portumnus by the Latins, whom his mother had in her phrensy thrown with herself into the sea; after which the name of Ino was changed to Leucothea. (See the opening of the eleventh Pythian ode.) Melicerta was saved from death by the Nereids, one of whom appeared to Sisyphus, and enjoined him to institute games in order to commemorate this event. They were sacred to Neptune, as the Olympic were to Jupiter, the Pythian to Apollo, and the Nemean to Hercules. Some time after their first celebration they were interrupted by the incursion into Greece of a band of robbers, headed by the fierce and cruel Sciris and Scyron; but at length Theseus,* son of Ægeus, cleared the country of these marauders, who terrified strangers from being present at these games, and reinstituted them about B. C. 1220. He changed the time of their celebration from night to day, and they were held after an interval of three years. (See Nem., vi., 69.) Every kind of combat was exhibited at these games, and the reward of the victor at first consisted of a wreath of pine leaves, which was afterward changed to parsley, as being a funereal plant, and therefore more appropriate to games instituted in honour of the drowned Melicerta. The Corinthians originally presided at them; but on the capture of Corinth by Mummius, A. C. 146, this honourable office was transferred to the Sicyonians. Afterward, however, it was restored to the Corinthians, and enjoyed by them as long as the celebration of these games continued. It is to them that St. Paul so finely alludes: (1 Cor., ix., 24-27.)

* This and other exploits of a similar nature performed by Theseus are mentioned by Ovid: (Met., vii., 433, &c.)

"Great Theseus! thee the Marathonian plain
Admires, and wears with pride the noble stain
Of the dire monster's blood, by valiant Theseus slain"

Tate's version.

THE FIRST ISTHMIAN ODE.

TO HERODOTUS OF THEBES, VICTOR IN THE CHARIOT RACE.

ARGUMENT.

THE poet, having laid aside the task which he had on hand, declares his wish to compose an ode to the conqueror Herodotus, after the example of Castor and Iolaus, in praise of whom he digresses.—Justice of celebrating the victor's triumphs, which are recorded in the remaining part of the ode.

OH mother, Thebes with golden shield,
My theme shall to thy glory yield.
Let rocky Delos not disdain,
For whom I late have pour'd the strain.
Aught happier can the virtuous prove
Than venerated parents' love?
Bless'd by Apollo's fostering care,
Resign, oh isle, thine envied place.
With the gods' aid, a double grace
To happy issue will I bear.
Hymning the unshorn Phœbus' might,
  Round Ceos where the waters flow,
And Isthmus, that with giant height
  Uprears her ocean-girded brow. 11

Since on the brave Cadmæan band
  Six chaplets his victorious arm
Bestow'd, to grace his native land
  With conquering valour's brightest charm.
Alcmena there in days of yore
Her own intrepid offspring bore;
Him whom Geryon's monsters bold
With terror shudder'd to behold.

But I who the bright meed prepare,
Herodotus, to grace thy car,
Who with no foreign hands' control
Thy four steeds urgest to the gaol,
The Castorean hymn would raise,
Or song in Iolaus' praise;
For they who the triumphant chariot drove,
In Thebes and Sparta born, all heroes rank'd above.

First in the numerous contests, they
Adorn'd their halls with tripods rare,
With golden caldrons, goblets fair,
And bore the victor's wreaths away.
In naked stadia shines their valour clear,
As in the armed course, whence sounds the martial spear. 32

And when they whirl'd the dart on high,
Or gave the stony disk to fly—
For yet no crown pentathlic gain'd,
Each deed its due success obtain'd.
Their locks with frequent chaplets bound,
Erst in these contests won,
Where Dirce's streams refresh the ground,
And near Eurotas' wave was found
Iphicles' noble son;
Who to the earth-sown Theban race
Could his illustrious lineage trace,
And Tyndarus', whose loved retreat
Was in Therapne's high Achæan seat. 43

All hail! while I compose the song,
Whose strains to Neptune's power belong,
That rules the sacred Isthmian band,
Protector of the Onchestian strand.

53 Onchestus was a maritime region of Bœotia, consecrated to Neptune. It is here put for the Copiac lake, or any part of the neighbouring country. Heyne remarks that it is customary with Pindar to celebrate at the same time the victor, the game

Connected with this hero's name,
Will I his sire Asopodorus' fame,
And thy paternal soil, Orchomenos, proclaim. 51

Propp'd on a wreck that 'scaped the boundless wave,
A refuge from his dire mischance she gave;
And now once more congenial fate
Has raised him to his ancient state;
While prudence arms his mind to bear
The heavy load of adverse care.
But if to purchase valour's meed,
Expense and toil must crown the deed,
Ne'er should the victor's praise be sung
By an unjust and envious tongue. 61

The poet's recompense is light
His various labours to requite;
Who by the honest meed of praise
A common monument will raise.
To mortal toils of various kind
Are sweet but different gifts assign'd.
The fowler, he that tends his sheep,
Who tills the soil, or ploughs the deep,
All by laborious efforts strive
Hunger's dire pest away to drive.
But he whose valour in the fight,
Or contests of superior might,
Hath borne the splendid prize away,
Shall hear his panegyric sung
By citizens' and strangers' tongue,
And gain of highest worth convey. 75

Be mine the task with loud acclaim
Saturn's earth-shaking son to name,

in which he conquered, and the god who particularly presided over it. It appears that the father of Herodotus had been expelled from Thebes in a civil commotion, and banished to Orchomenos.

Whose near protecting godhead leads
The chariot with its rapid steeds.
And thine, Amphitryo, to address
Eubœa, Minya's green recess,
Ceres' famed Eleusinian grove,
Along whose winding course the chariots move.

With these, Protesilaus, I combine,
Rear'd by the Greeks in Phylace thy shrine:
But to recount what numerous meeds
Herodotus' triumphant steeds
From Hermes, patron of the games,
Have won, more ample limit claims
Than bounds my narrow hymn—the mind
In silence greater bliss can find.

Let him on lofty pinions soar
Of the Pierian vocal band,
With choice boughs pluck'd from Pytho's store,
And where flows on Olympia's shore
Alpheus, let him fill his hand.
So shall his triumphs with renown
Thebes of the seven high portals crown.
But he who nourishes a soul
That hopes of secret wealth control,
Thinks not, while others are his scorn,
How his inglorious life to Pluto speeds forlorn.

92 Phylace was a town in Thessaly, where Protesilaus reigned, and where funeral games were celebrated at his tomb.

THE SECOND ISTHMIAN ODE.

TO XENOCRATES OF AGRIGENTUM, SON OF ARCESILAUS, VICTOR IN THE HORSE RACE.

ARGUMENT.

PINDAR addresses this ode to Thrasybulus, son of the conqueror Xenocrates.—This he professes to do after the example of the old poets, who did not write, as was now done, urged by the sordid incitement of gain.—The triumphs of Xenocrates, his ancestor Ænesidamus, and his charioteer Nicomachus are sung, and Nicasippus is charged with the safe conveyance of this ode, sent in the form of an epistle.

OFT have the men of other days
From the gold-netted muses' car,
Oh Thrasybulus ! hurl'd afar
The lyre's soft-sounding notes, to praise
Youth's ardent prime, that harbinger most sweet
Of Venus throned upon her lofty seat.
For then, not amorous of gain,
The muse sent forth no venal strain—
The honey'd lays not then, as now,
From sweet Terpsichore that flow,
Upon the shining front display'd
The silver emblem of their trade. 14

Now she suggests with heedful care
The Argive's words in mind to bear ;

14 These words are attributed by the scholiast to Aristodemus the Lacedæmonian, whose constant doctrine it was tnat wealth was always to be sought, and that poverty could never be honourable. This saying afterward passed into a proverb, like Horace's

" O cives, cives, quærenda pecunia primum,
Virtus post nummos "

Who with loud speech to truth allied,
Importunate for money cried,
Bereft of all his wealth and friends,
I sing to one who comprehends.
To him when on the Isthmian field
Neptune the triumph deign'd to yield,
And bound his coursers' flowing mane
With Doric parsley's verdant chain,
In his victorious chariot bright
He honour'd Agrigentum's light. 25

Him too, engaged in Crisa's fray,
Beheld the potent god of day,
And gave him glory there;
While old Erectheus' noble race
Adorn'd his brow with verdant grace
In Athens' city fair.
Nor would he blame the proud career
Of his steed-urging charioteer,
Nicomachus, whose hands control
The reins that guide him to the goal. 33

Him too supreme in conquering pow'r,
The heralds of th' Olympic hour,
Priests who to Jove libations bring,
(Elean and Saturnian king,)
Sharing the hospitable feast,
With gratulating voice address'd;
As he fell prostrate at the knee
Of golden-imaged Victory.
Around their land, which they the grove
Designate of Olympian Jove; 41

There, with immortal honours crown'd,
Ænesidamus' offspring shone;

41 We may imagine an image of Victory in a sitting posture to be placed at the extremity of the goal, into whose bosom, as it were, the victor would rush after having completed his course. (See Nem., v., 81, &c.)

For in thy halls the revel's sound,
Oh Thrasybulus! oft is found,
And all the pomp's enlivening tone;
Since no steep hill, no rugged way
Rears its opposing front on high,
Where bards to noble mansions stray,
The honour'd guerdons to convey
Of Heliconian poesy.
Far must my venturous javelin move
Ere I could reach the height of fame,
Where soars Xenocrates above
The rest in nature as in name. 54

View'd by the citizens with awe,
He train'd his coursers by the Grecian law;
Frequenting at each solemn feast
The liberal tables of the bless'd.
Nor ever has the flagging gale
Straiten'd his hospitable sail,
That pass'd in summer hour to Phasis o'er,
In winter veer'd to Nilus' southern shore. 62

Not now, when thoughts with envy blind,
Hang darkling o'er the mortal mind,
His father's valour let him hide,
Nor pass these hymns in silent pride;
Since, unrecited to remain,
I framed not the triumphant strain.
Such, Nicasippus, be thine errand home,
When thou to my familiar host art come. 69

65 These lines are explained by the scholiast as a figurative description of the unbounded hospitality of Xenocrates, which afforded a shelter to guests of the most remote regions.

THE THIRD ISTHMIAN ODE.

TO MELISSUS OF THEBES, VICTOR IN THE QUADRIGÆ.

ARGUMENT.

THE poet in this short ode declares that illustrious deeds ought to be celebrated by poetical praises, such as are due to the present Isthmian, and the former Nemean victory achieved by Melissus, by which he emulates the deeds of his ancestors.

WHOE'ER of men with bliss is crown'd,
Or in the glorious strife renown'd,
Or can in potent wealth rejoice,
And mental insolence restrain,
This man is worthy to obtain
The citizens' applauding voice.
From thee, oh Jove! to man below
Success and valiant efforts flow.
They who revere thy sacred name
A greater happiness may claim.
But not to wayward minds secure
Through life that fortune will endure.

Fair actions due rewards await;
The good 'tis just to celebrate;
Just too the victor's name to raise
With solemn pomp and liberal praise:
While twofold victories impart
Sweet transport to Melissus' heart.
First in the wooded Isthmian dell,
The wreaths of triumph he obtain'd,
In the deep-breasted lion's cell,
Proclaiming Thebes, th' equestrian crown he gain'd.

His glorious deeds will not disgrace
The kindred valour of his race.

Full well ye know what ancient fame
Cleonymus' triumphant chariots claim
Through Labdacus' illustrious line
Their source his sires maternal trace,
And with ancestral riches shine,
Devoting their heroic life
To the four steeds' laborious strife :
While fleeting scenes by turns engage
This ever-varying mortal stage,
Uninjured by the shocks of time,
The gods' bless'd children dwell sublime. 31

THE FOURTH ISTHMIAN ODE.

TO THE SAME MELISSUS.

ARGUMENT.

This ode begins with the praises of Melissus' ancestors, and relates the melancholy consequences of a defeat sustained by his family; whose good fortune, however, again shone forth in this triumph gained by Melissus.—The panegyric of his ancestors and of himself is resumed, and continued with digression to the story of Ajax and Ulysses, Hercules and Antæus, &c.—Apotheosis of Hercules, and divine honours paid him by the yearly sacrifices of the Thebans.—The ode concludes with the praise of Melissus and his charioteer Orseas.

Bless'd by the gods, to me belong
A thousand avenues of song;
Thy triumphs in the Isthmian field,
Melissus, fair occasion yield
The hymn of victory to frame
That all thy virtues shall proclaim;
With which the god delights to grace
Through life Cleonymus' high race;
While by the ever-varying blast
Mankind are still at random cast. 10

For they at Thebes with honour crown'd,
From times of ancient date were said
To be the hosts of all around,
And free from strife's discordant sound,
By every deed to make their own
What tests of glory wide had flown
Among the living or the dead.
Brave in the valour of their race,
They touch'd at the remotest land,
Where the Herculean pillars stand:
Nor let ambition ask an ampler space. 22

They loved to train the generous steeds,
While brazen Mars approved their deeds.
But in the course of one short day
The rough and sanguine cloud of war
Four heroes had impell'd away
From their deserted hearth afar:
And now, the wintry darkness o'er,
Soon as the vernal months succeed,
Serene they flourish as before;
Thus crimson roses cover o'er,
At Heaven's behest, the alter'd mead.

While he, the earth-disturbing god,
Who makes Onchestus his abode,
And the sea bridge that bids the tide
From Corinth's walls at distance glide—
Granting this hymn their noble race
With wondrous potency to grace,
Sings their high deeds, whose loud acclaim
Wakes from her couch primeval fame.
Aroused, her fair form glows with splendour bright,
As mid the other stars shines Phosphor's nobler light.

She who in Athens' verdant field
Proclaim'd the triumphs of his car,
And bade the bards of Sicyon wield
Their vocal lyres, to tell afar
What wreaths the Adrastean contests yield.

34 See note on ode i., 53. By the *sea bridge* in the next verse is to be understood the isthmus of Corinth, which Claudian describes in similar terms: (de Bel. Get. 188:)—

"Vallata mari Scironia rupes,
Et duo continuo connectens æquora muro
Isthmus."

So Ovid: (Med. Jasoni, 104:)—

"Quique maris gemini distinet isthmos aquas?"

(See Nem., vi., 65.)

They when the whole assembly strove,
Like them their crooked chariot drove;
Contending with the Grecian train
Whose costly steeds the palm should gain.

While they in contest never shown,
Are pass'd with silence and unknown.
Obscure their fate, too, who contend
Ere they attain the wish'd-for end,
And this their glorious toils bestow.
Oft the superior in the fray
Has seen his guerdon snatched away
By fraud of some inferior foe.
Ye know that Ajax' deadly might
By his own sword at dead of night
Cut off untimely, reprehension bore
To Hellas' sons, who sought the Trojan shore.

But Homer's songs with honour grace
Him among men of warlike race;
Those strains divine his valour raise,
Heralds of after ages' praise:
For this immortal sound proceeds
When bards proclaim triumphant deeds;
While through the fruitful earth and main
This beam its deathless splendour shall maintain.

Propitious be the muses' care!
As we the torch of song illume,
And to Telesia's offspring bear,
Melissus brave, the chaplet fair,
Worthy upon the victor's brow to bloom.

56 I have adopted Heyne's conjectural emendation of *τουτο* and *κλεος* instead of the common reading *τωνδε* and *τελος*, from which I think none but a weak sense can be elicited.

65 The remarkable expression of the original, *κατα ῥαβδον εφρασεν*, probably means nothing more than that Homer delivered his rhapsodies in a consecutive series of lines. See the opening of the second Nemean ode. Sudorius' paraphrase is *opere expolitor*.

His mind, by labour unsubdued,
Rivals the roaring lion's might,
Or like the fox in crafty mood,
That stays the whirling eagle's flight.
'Tis just the foe's imperious will
By force to conquer or to foil by skill. 81

For not to him Orion's fame
Had been assign'd by partial fate.
Though mean to view, with ponderous weight
Fell from his arm the massive spear.
Erst to Antæus' mansion came
From Thebes to fertile Libya's land,
Of stature short, but dauntless soul,
He that should struggle to control
The bloody monster's fierce career,
Who could delight with savage hand
The fane of Neptune to adorn
With scalps from hapless strangers torn,
Alcmena's son—who took his flight
Up to Olympus' sacred height,
Exploring earth, and through the hoary wave
To mariners a tranquil passage gave. 98

Now by the ægis-bearing god
In bliss he holds his fair abode
With Hebe his celestial bride,
Honour'd and graced by love divine,
King of the domes with gold that shine,
And to heaven's queen in filial bonds allied.
To him above th' Electran gates
The new-constructed altars rise;
On him the genial banquet waits,
With all the pomp of sacrifice.
His shrine we citizens surround
With the eight lifeless bodies crown'd,
Who by the sword there slaughter'd lie,
Alcides hapless progeny,
Whom Megara, great Creon's daughter, bore. 109

To them, when sets the solar beam,
The rising fire's continual gleam
Is given night's darkness to explore;
While lambent smoke's thick volumes rear
Its fumes of incense through the air. 113

The deed of strength, the second day
Still terminates the annual fray:
Where round this victor's honour'd brow
Chaplets of pallid myrtle glow;
Rewarding past and present fame,
Which boyhood's threefold triumphs claim.
In his skill'd driver he confides,
Who, steersman-like, the chariot guides.
Him, then, with Orseas will I praise,
Distilling grace from my mellifluous lays. 124

THE FIFTH ISTHMIAN ODE.

TO PHYLAOIDES OF ÆGINA, VICTOR IN THE PANCRATIUM.

ARGUMENT.

THIS ode opens with an invocation to Thia; who, according to the ancient theogony, was the mother of the Sun, Moon, and Aurora.—Under this name the poet designates glory and renown; for the sake of which men achieve the most illustrious deeds.—He then makes a transition to the victor, with a digression commemorating the heroes of Ægina.—Then to the battle of Salamis.—Returns to Phylacides, and concludes by the praise of Pytheas, his alipta: (the person whose office it was to train and anoint the combatants for the games.)

ILLUSTRIOUS mother of the solar beam,
Mankind, bright Thia, for thy sake esteem
The first of metals, all-subduing gold;
And ships, oh queen! that struggle in the deep,
With car-yoked coursers o'er the plain that sweep,
To honour thee, the wondrous contests hold.
Through thee in every warlike game
Heroes the frequent meed of fame
Achieve, whose hair the wreath around,
By strength or swiftness won, is bound.
When two events propitious meet,
They make the span of life most sweet,

1 Pindar, in this magnificent exordium, addresses Thia, the goddess of splendour, and, according to Hesiod, cited by the scholiast, the mother, by Hyperion, of Sol, Luna, and Aurora. By this invocation he intimates the glory of the Æginetans, to whose exertions in the battle of Salamis the victory over the Persian fleet was mainly attributable. (See l. 56, et. seq.)

If any combatant success
And fair report united bless. 17

Then seek not Jove's immortal state,
Since thine is all this prosperous fate.
Mortals in mortal thoughts should rest.
The Isthmian plain and Nemea's fray
To thee, Phylacides, convey
Their double wreaths, and Pytho's day,
Whose heroes the pancratium's meed contest.
But hymns shall never touch my heart
If Æacus receive no part.
To this fair city have I come,
Which law and justice make their home,
To Lampo's offspring, by the muses' aid.
Envy not him whose foot proceeds
In the pure path of heavenly deeds,
If by a mingled song his labours are repaid. 31

Brave warriors of heroic race
Ere now have won the meed of fame,
Whom harps and sounding flutes proclaim
Victors through lengthen'd ages' space;
Affording to the vocal train,
From Jove, high matter for their strain.
Th' equestrian chaplet Iolaus gain'd
At Thebes, in Argos Perseus' skill obtain'd;
And where the waters of Eurotas flow
Castor and Pollux' spear dealt the triumphant blow. 43

But in Ænone's island bright
Th' Æacidæ's high natures shone,
They by whose conquering arms in fight
Twice were the Trojan walls o'erthrown.

31 The metaphor in this line is repeated with greater amplification in the opening of the next ode, addressed to the same hero.

First tracking Hercules' career,
Then ranged beneath th' Atridæ's spear.
Now urge thy chariot o'er the plain,
And say by whom was Cycnus slain;
By whom great Hector? tell whose blade
In death the fearless Memnon laid,
Chief of the Æthiopian ranks,
Who by his spear's impetuous force
Arrested Telephus' bold course,
And smote him near Caïcus' banks?
To them Ægina's beauteous isle
Report assigns the native soil. 56

That tower was built in ancient time,
To which their virtues soar sublime:
Sounding their praise, my fluent tongue
Can hurl full many a dart of song.
And now shall Ajax' city prove
A witness in the dire affray;
Fair Salamis, whose seamen strove
In the destructive shower of Jove
The deadly hail of countless hosts to stay. 64

But let forgetful Silence veil
In her cold dews the boasting tale;
For Jove, the lord of all, at will
Directs alike the good and ill.
These honours, gain'd by each triumphant deed,
Delight to win the poet's honey'd meed.
Let him who labours to this end
Like Cleonicus' race contend:
Never in dark oblivion's shade
The heroes' lengthen'd toils shall fade;
Nor care distract the mind that views
What cost the wish'd-for palm pursues. 74

Now Pytheas' praise demands the strain,
Who foremost in th' athletic train

With dexterous arm and mind as free
Directs the blows to victory.
Then for his temples weave the crown,
  To him the woolly chaplet bear,
The winged strain of high renown,
  As to Phylacides, prepare. 74

THE SIXTH ISTHMIAN ODE.

TO THE SAME PHYLACIDES, AND TO HIS MATERNAL UNCLE EUTHYMENES.

ARGUMENT.

PINDAR begins this ode with the praises of the victor, with which he combines the expression of his good wishes.—Digresses to the fabulous story of Telamon and his son Ajax; for whom Hercules had offered up his prayers and consulted the auguries.—Concludes with celebrating the triumphs of his relations and townsmen of the same tribe.

As at the hospitable board
With flourishing profusion stored,
We mix the second cup of lays
To Lampo's valiant offspring's praise;
In Nemea's field the first best crown
Received, oh Jove! we make thine own.
And now upon the Isthmian plain
To Neptune with his Nereid train
Phylacides' bright palms entwine,
Youngest of that heroic line.
And may the third libation flow
To him who guards Olympus' heights,
While on Ægina we bestow
Mellifluous poesy's delights.

For he that by expense and toil
Erects his virtues' heavenly pile
Beholds the much-loved glory shine,
Fair progeny of root divine:
And honour'd by th' immortal train,
E'en now his anchor casts, th' extreme of bliss to gain.

Versed in these arts, the hour of fate
Will Cleonicus' offspring wait,
Patient till hoary age shall come,
The guide to Pluto's dreary home;
While Clotho on her lofty seat,
And her dread sisters, I entreat
The friendly hero's life to bless,
And crown his wishes with success. 26

Æacidæ, who shine afar,
Refulgent in your golden car,
The plain injunction I declare
When to this isle my steps repair,
To sprinkle her illustrious name
With dews of honourable fame:
Since in long line a thousand ways
Extends his fair deeds' ample praise;
Beyond where Nilus' waters flow,
Or realms of Hyperborean snow.
Nor can a city e'er be found
So rude and barbarous of tongue
Where Peleus' glory is not sung,
Whom in bless'd filial ties th' immortals bound; 37

Where Telamonian Ajax' name
And his great sire excites no fame.
Whom led, in brazen armour dight,
With his Tirynthians to the fight,
Of Troy the bold and prompt ally,
(That heroes' scourge, whose valiant host
Laomedon by treach'ry lost,)
In ships Alcmena's progeny.
With him the citadel o'erthrew,
And the vast Coan nations slew,
And him who fed his fleecy train
Like some huge mount on Phlegra's plain,
Alcyoneus—nor spared the foe
The string of his deep-twanging bow,

But when the social board was spread,
Æacides to join their fleet he led. 52

Him standing on the lion's hide,
The nectar'd draught he bade to pour,
Amphitryo's warlike son adore,
And at the sacred rites preside.
To him then Telamon the brave,
With gold enchased, a goblet gave;
His hands extending to the skies,
Invincible Alcides cries—
"From thee, oh father Jove! if e'er
With willing mind thou heardst my pray'r,
E'en now this hero's offspring bold,
Our guest, by fate's decree foretold,
Of Eribœa sprung, my supplications crave. 67

That frame's insuperable might,
(As the huge monster's skin is bound
In ample folds my limbs around,
Whom erst I slew in Nemea's soil,
Achieving there my earliest toil)
With an intrepid mind unite."
Thus, while he spoke, Jove bade from high
The king of birds, his eagle, fly.
Sweet pleasure o'er his soul was shed,
When thus with prophet voice he said—
"Thine shall hereafter be the son
Whom thou entreat'st, oh Telamon!
And name him Ajax, since in might
The bird that hither wing'd his flight
To him will just resemblance yield,
Tremendous in the martial field."
This said, he paused, and rested straight;
But all their virtues to relate,
From me a lengthen'd tale would claim.
Dispenser of the sacred feast,
Muse, to Phylacides a guest,
To Pytheas and Euthymenes I came.

Th' encomiastic strain shall be
Pronounced with Argive brevity. 87

Three crowns in the pancratium's fray,
Victorious on the Isthmian shore,
And some from Nemea's plain away
Th' illustrious sons and uncles bore.
What theme for lyric glory bright
Their valiant deeds have brought to light!
And with the Graces' fairest dew
Your tribe, Psaleuchidæ, imbue:
Themistius' house their love shall crown,
Dwelling in this Heaven-favour'd town;
While Lampo strives by deeds to prove,
  And efforts of laborious care,
How much the words of Hesiod move
  His warm approval to declare;
Exhorting his remotest race
Their common city's fame by valiant acts to grace.

Bless'd in the cherish'd strangers' love,
Retain'd within the mild control
Of mediocrity of soul:
His tongue ne'er wont beyond the mind to move.
His name among the athletes known,
  Who oft were taught his might to feel,
Sounds like the hardy Naxian stone,
  Which best subdues the temper'd steel.
To slake their thirst, them will I lave
In Dirce's pure and hallow'd wave,
Which the fair nymphs to light have brought,
Mnemosyne's assiduous train,
Whose costly robes with gold are wrought,
Where Cadmus' gates the well-built walls main-
tain. 111

THE SEVENTH ISTHMIAN ODE.

TO STREPSIADES THE THEBAN, VICTOR IN THE PANCRATIUM.

ARGUMENT.

Pindar begins this highly poetical ode with an address to Thebes ; concisely enumerating her ancient glories, and the most remarkable events in her history.—Praises the maternal uncle of Strepsiades, who had fallen in battle.—Then returns to the victor, and mingles good wishes with his commendations.—Concludes with beseeching Apollo to add a victory in the Isthmian games to the other triumphs of Strepsiades

---

Oh happy Thebes ! of all thy former joys,
Which now the most thy mind employs ?
Is it the hour when first to light of day
The fair-hair'd Bacchus sprang,
By Ceres throned, whose priests their homage pay
With cymbals' brazen clang ?
Or think'st thou of the midnight hour
When veil'd within a golden shower
The chief of the celestial band
Deign'd at Amphitryo's doors to stand ?

1 Dodwell, in his classical Travels in Greece, (vol. i., p. 271,) has a passage in which the glories and heroic characters of Thebes are enumerated, apparently in illustration of the highly poetical exordium of this ode.

"The early or heroic history of Thebes is particularly splendid ; and neither Athens, Lacedæmon, Argos, nor Mycene, were so much celebrated as the capital of Bœotia for great events, for heroes, and for demigods. The names of Kadmos, Semele, Bacchus, Antiope, Zethes, Amphion, Amphitryon, Alcmena, Hercules, Laius, and his unfortunate race, furnish strong evidence of the early power and original lustre of this country. No part of Greece produced characters of more exalted

To aid, while sojourning on earth,
His spouse at the Herculean birth,
Or of Tiresias' counsels wise,
Or Iolaus, skilful charioteer,
Or earth-sown heroes, wielding as they rise
The indefatigable spear:
Or when thou sent'st Adrastus far
From the rude shout and din of war,
Reft of his numerous friends, to roam
Back to equestrian Argos home:
Or when from distant Doris' land
Thou gavest on foot erect to stand
The colony of Spartan line—
Thy sons besieged Amyclæ's wall,
Ægidæ, faithful to the call
Of the prophetic Pythian shrine. [22]

But mighty deeds of old renown
Sleep unremember'd and unknown,
Save when enrich'd the record lie
In the sweet dews of poetry.
Then lead the pomp, the hymn's soft lays
Awake, Strepsiades to praise,

fame than Hesiod, Pindar, Pelopidas, Epaminondas, Plutarch, and Sextus Chæronensis. The dulness, therefore, which the rest of the Grecians ascribed to the Bœotians, on account of the density of their atmosphere, was not always agreeable to truth or consonant with experience. The conscious sublimity of Pindar repelled the imputation."

15 This origin of the Thebans, who were fabled to spring from the sown teeth of the dragon, is frequently alluded to by the ancient poets. So Ovid: (Amor., iii., 12. 35:)—

"Protea quid referam, Thebanaque semina, dentes?"

and Euripides: (Herc. F. 4, 5:)—

"ενθ' ὁ γηγενης
Σπαρτων σταχυς εβλαστεν."

See also Eur., (Phœn., 953;) and Ovid, (Met., iii., 110:)—

"Crescitque seges clypeata virorum."

Virg., (Georg., ii., 140,) &c.

Who, victor in the Isthmian fray,
Bears the pancratium's palm away;
Conspicuous in triumphant might,
And form pre-eminently bright; 32

While valour with an equal pace
Accompanies corporeal grace.
The dark-hair'd muses crown his fame
Whose triumphs a new grace have shed
On his maternal uncle's name,
Him lately in th' embattled field
The deity with brazen shield
Hath number'd with the dead.
But honour still the brave attends. 36

This let the patriot warrior know
Who drives the cloud of slaughter that impends
O'er his loved native soil, upon the foe.
His fame among the citizens shall bloom,
Growing through life, and living in the tomb.
But thou, Diodotus' brave son,
Rival of Meleager's fame,
Who emulatest Hector's name,
And glories by Amphiaraus won;
Breath'dst forth in war's first ranks thy flower of life,
Where the most brave sustain'd war's hopeless strife.

Then grief ineffable I bore;
But now the god, whose potent might
Girds the firm earth, day's splendour bright
Gives me for winter's gloom that lower'd before.
The victor's praise will I declare,
And fit the chaplet to his hair;
Nor let th' immortal train molest
With vengeful ire my tranquil breast,
Since to the destined term of age
Calm I approach life's closing stage,
And seize the fleeting pleasures of the day;
Though subject to unequal fate,

Death's common stroke we all await·
But he that would the scene beyond survey,
To him will never find it given
To tread the brazen soil of heaven. 63

The winged Pegasus o'erthrew
Bellerophon his lord, who flew
In thought the heavenly seats above
To the bright council hall of Jove;
For still a bitter end alloys
The transport of unlicensed joys.
But, Phœbus, thou whose locks are spread
In golden lustre round thy head,
Grant us to gain the Isthmian crown,
And that which Pytho yields in contests all thine own! 72

THE EIGHTH ISTHMIAN ODE.

TO CLEANDER OF ÆGINA, VICTOR IN THE PANCRATIUM.

ARGUMENT.

THE poet in this ode exhorts the youths liberated from the calamities of the Persian war to apply their minds to the framing of hymns in honour of the victor.—It becomes a Theban to sing the praises of an Æginetan, on account of their common origin.—Thence he digresses to fables of the Æacidæ and the nuptials of Peleus and Thetis; which leads him to panegyrize Achilles.—Returns to the praise of the victor, and his uncle Nicocles, with which he concludes the ode.

To celebrate Cleander's praise,
Oh youths! the hymn of triumph raise,
That ever forms the glorious meed
To crown the blooming hero's deed.
To Telesarchus' splendid halls
Some friend his victor offspring calls
The pomp and revel to convey:
Potent upon the Isthmian plain,
The wreath of conquest to obtain,
And Nemea's guerdon bear away.
For him, though bitter grief control
The wonted ardour of my soul,
To me is given th' unequal task
The golden muses' aid to ask. 12

Now from our mighty sorrows free,
No want of chaplets may we find,
Around the victor's head to bind,
Nor feed again our misery.

Pausing a while, from fruitless wo
Let us direct the patriot mind
Some public blessing to bestow ;
Since a kind god hath turn'd aside
Of threat'ning ills the direful shock
That hung like the Tantalean rock
O'er Græcia's land, unskill'd the storm to bide. 23

But now my fear has pass'd away, 26
And anxious Care relax'd her sway.
To seize each object as it lies
Before his foot becomes the wise.
O'er man impends deceitful age,
Revolving still life's onward stage.
Yet mortals e'en these ills may cure,
While liberty continues sure.
In calm contentment let them rest,
Of favourable hope possess'd.
Me too the happy task awaits,
(Nurtured where Thebes expands her sevenfold gates,)
With the bright muses' wreath to grace
Ægina, nymph of kindred race.
Twin daughters of a common sire,
And youngest of Asopus' line,
Whose beauties could the soul incline
Of Jove himself to fond desire. 41

To her the heavenly lover gave
By Dirce's sweetly flowing wave
O'er that fair city to preside,
Who joys the rapid car to guide.
Thee to Œnopia's isle convey'd,
The thundering sire a parent made
Of Æacus, whose honour'd birth
Raised him above the sons of earth.

24 See the note on Ol., i., 90.

His godlike offspring's latest line
With might from him reflected shine,
Who erst, their skill and prudence to display,
Appeased the brazen din of the celestial fray.

This on the memory dwells impress'd 56
Of the assemblies of the bless'd.
What time for lovely Thetis Jove
And the illustrious Neptune strove;
Each wishing the fair nymph to gain,
Bound in the hymeneal chain:
For mighty love their souls possess'd.
But to complete their nuptial state
The counsels of th' immortal kind,
Soon as they heard the will of fate,
And prudent Themis' voice, declined; 67

Who to the circle of the skies
Pronounced the destinies' decree,
That soon a sovereign progeny
From the sea goddess would arise,
Superior to his potent sire,
Whose hand should wield a dart of fire,
Fiercer than lightning's rapid flame,
Or trident which no force can tame.
Such is the fruit of Jove's embrace,
Or brother's, of immortal race.
Then cease your strife—in battle slain
She who could but a mortal couch obtain
Is doom'd her offspring to behold,
With hands that rivall'd Mars in deed,
And feet which mock'd the lightning's speed.
Should I my mind's intent unfold,
Let the fair prize decreed by heaven
To Peleus, sprung from Æacus, be given;
That pious hero, bred upon Iolcos' plain. 87

76 I. e., Neptune's.

To Chiron's venerable cave
Quick let the messengers repair:
Nor Nereus' daughter give, as once she gave,
To us the records of contention there.
But when at evening's highest noon
Rides in her state the full-orb'd moon,
The hero may untie the zone,
And make the virgin prize his own.
'Twas thus the goddess spoke to the Saturnian train;

When from immortal lids reveal'd
Th' approving nod their purpose seal'd.
Nor fell her words with empty sound,
Like fruitless blossoms on the ground:
For, as 'tis said, high-ruling Jove
Thetis with him to join in wedlock strove.
Hence to th' unskill'd the poet's tongue
Achilles' youthful valour oft has sung;
Who on the Mysian soil, with vines o'erspread,
By Telephus possess'd, black streams of slaughter shed.

Who gave th' Atridæ back to roam
With liberated Helen home,
And sever'd with his spear Troy's nervous strength;
Hector, who in the murderous fray
With Memnon dared a while to stay
His fury o'er the plain's extended length:
And other chiefs to whom Achilles show'd
The path that led to Proserpine's abode.
Guard of th' Æacidæ, whose virtues grace
Ægina and his own illustrious race.
Him the sweet song's melodious breath
Deserted not when cold in death,
But round his tomb and funeral pyre
Stood the fair Heliconian choir,
And gave the sounding notes of wo
In honour of his name to flow;

Since to their hymns it pleased th' immortal train
To render back the valiant hero slain. 132

And now to haste with loud acclaim
The muses' rapid car, agrees
With him who would exalt the fame
Of pugilistic Nicocles,
Whose valour on the Isthmian plain
The Doric parsley could obtain:
Since he as well in days of yore
The palm from neighb'ring rivals bore;
And their presumptuous spirit broke
With his inevitable stroke. 141

Actions like these will ne'er disgrace
His valiant uncle's noble race.
May one of the coeval band
The laurel crown with friendly hand,
For the pancratium's victor twine,
Around Cleander's brow to shine;
Since him before with prosperous fate
Alcathous' game in festal state
Throng'd by the Epidaurian youth, received.
Well may the good resound his praise
Who ne'er the morning of his days
Consumed in idle sloth, by no fair deeds retrieved.

END OF PINDAR.

ANACREON.

TRANSLATED BY

THOMAS BOURNE.

NEW YORK:
HARPER & BROTHERS, PUBLISHERS,
329 & 331 PEARL STREET,
FRANKLIN SQUARE.
1864.

CONTENTS.

BIOGRAPHICAL SKETCH

OF

ANACREON.

Of this delightful author, nothing, beyond what we are already acquainted with, can now be known. Antiquity has long since interposed its impenetrable veil; and however brief and unsatisfactory the accounts which have been handed down to us, with them we must still remain satisfied. Succeeding writers, it is true, may seek to impart an air of novelty to their relations, by a new and ingenious arrangement of the scanty materials they possess; still, however, must they relate facts, substantially the same as others, and present to their readers, if not a tedious, yet certainly a "thrice-told tale." For the only authentic incidents relative to this elegant poet we are indebted to contemporary writers, or to those who flourished shortly after him. and from them we glean the few following particulars.

X

Anacreon was born at Teos, a seaport town of Ionia. Who his parents were is uncertain, though it is conjectured from good authority that his family was noble. The time of his birth, according to Barnes, was in the second year of the fifty-fifth Olympiad, about the beginning of the reign of Cyrus, in the year of Rome 194, and A.C. 554. According to this calculation he was about eighteen years of age when Harpagus, the general of Cyrus, came with an army against the confederate cities of the Ionians and Æolians.

The Teians, finding themselves too weak to make a stand against the enemy, chose rather to abandon their country than to give up their liberty; and accordingly withdrew with their families and effects to the city of Abdera in Thrace; where, however, they had not long been settled before the Thracians, jealous of the new-comers, began to give them disturbance.

From Abdera our poet sailed to Samos, and took refuge at the court of Polycrates; at that time considered the politest and most flourishing of any in Asia; a distinction which it owed in no small degree to the liberality and personal accomplishments of that prince himself.

We may readily suppose that a person of Anacreon's character would meet with a welcome reception wherever wit and gayety were esteemed;

and accordingly we find that Polycrates not only honoured him with his friendship, but even made him the confidant of his most secret counsels. How long he continued at Samos is uncertain; but it seems probable that he resided there the greater part of that prince's reign. This opinion seems also to be confirmed by Herodotus, who assures us that Anacreon of Teos was with that prince in his chamber when he received a message from Orœtes, governor of Sardis, by whose treachery Polycrates was soon after betrayed and inhumanly crucified. Anacreon, it would seem, had left Samos a short time previous to this remarkable event, and had removed to Athens; having been invited thither by Hipparchus, the eldest son of Pisistratus, one of the most learned and virtuous princes of his time; and who, as Plato assures us, sent a vessel with fifty oars to convey him across the Ægean.

Hipparchus being assassinated in the conspiracy of Harmodius and Aristogiton, he returned to his native country Teos; for after the death of Cyrus the Teians had been suffered to reinhabit their country unmolested. Here he remained, as Suidas informs us, till a fresh commotion in the state obliged him once more to fly to Abdera, where he ended his days. There is something so remarkable in the manner of his death, that it seems more in accordance with what might be termed poetical justice than with the sober strain of history, were it not a fact asserted by writers of credit and reputation. He was choked with a grape-stone as he was regaling on some new wine, and expired in the eighty-fifth year of his age.

As to the personal character of this author, he appears to have been a professed despiser of business and the cares of the world, and indeed a lover of pleasure in every shape; though it seems neither just nor generous to form our judgment of him solely from the nature of his writings. The severe and moral Plato condescends to call him the "wise Anacreon;" a title which it is not likely he would have bestowed on him had he possessed no other claim to it than the harmony of his verse or the gayety of his disposition. Independent likewise of this expression of Plato, which must certainly be regarded as no mean evidence in his favour, the grammarian Athenæus distinctly mentions him, as νηφων και αγαθος, *sober and honourable.*

It now remains to speak of his writings, which were long the delight of other days, and are still read and admired by every scholar of taste and learning in our own. His Odes, the only part of his works which have reached us entire, are written in the Ionic dialect, remarkable for its softness and sweetness. The subjects, though often simple and trifling in themselves, are by the master-hand of the poet rendered susceptible of so many beauties, that they deserved to be sung by the Graces to the harp of Apollo.

His language, free and unrestrained, flows on in an uninterrupted strain of melody, like the streamlet so beautifully described in the twenty-second ode as ῥεουσα πειθους, *rolling persuasion;* and the reader is at once charmed with the sweet music of his song, and the beauty and simplicity of his descriptions.

As to their moral tendency, a reflection which now necessarily presents itself, it certainly is my decided opinion, that in this poet far less will be found to offend the reader of taste and delicacy than in almost any other ancient author who has written on the same subjects. His language is everywhere pure and elegant; and his sentiments, however much at variance with our own altered ideas and circumstances, are such as might naturally be expected from one who, ignorant of higher and better hopes, mistook the road to happiness through the flowery paths of pleasure.

In short, while we condemn, and with justice, those licentious thoughts and expressions which occur but too frequently in almost every author of antiquity, and which, in a greater or less degree, debase and disfigure their brightest pages, we should still remember that they are but the erroneous maxims of men who had only the dim light of nature to direct them; and still more thankful ought we to be for those purer precepts of morality which it is our exclusive privilege to enjoy.

From what has been observed respecting the peculiar style of this author's writings, it will easily be supposed that a translation of them into any other language must be attended with many difficulties. To preserve the Ionic elegance of the original, without diverging too far from the text—to imitate its conciseness, without sacrificing its beauties—this indeed is a task much more difficult than might at first be imagined. In fact, I much doubt whether a foreign idiom, confined to the jingling monotony of modern verse, can ever hope to do justice to the sweet warblings of the playful and polished Anacreon. Still more hopeless, I conceive, would be the attempt to render them by a strictly literal version; and in this persuasion, I have endeavoured on every occasion to give what I imagined to be the meaning of my author, without a servile adherence to the letter on the one hand, or a too great license of interpretation on the other. With what success these endeavours have been accomplished, it is the province of others to determine. Perhaps, however, I may here be permitted to observe, that I have never hesitated to sacrifice poetic beauty to purity of language and expression; happy if, by this means, I have rendered accessible to the cabinets of my fair countrywomen a poet whose beauties are many, and whose faults, which were those of his age and country, I have studiously endeavoured to conceal.

T. B.

In the notes will be found no laboured comments on the peculiar force or meaning of a Greek particle, nor any long dissertations on disputed passages.

To the scholar and the critic they would impart no new information, and to those unacquainted with the original must be altogether useless. I have preferred selecting from various writers such extracts as I thought likely to prove interesting to the general reader, and to facilitate his comprehension of the English version, by illustrating those manners and customs, which are still peculiar to the people of the East.

To preceding editors I am indebted for many useful observations, which I have distinguished by the names of their respective authors. In the arrangement of these notes I am happy likewise to acknowledge the judicious advice and assistance of my friend, Mr. T. Gandy, member of the Philomathic Society, and of several other literary institutions.

T. B.

ODES OF ANACREON.

ODE I.—ON HIS LYRE. *

WHILE I sweep the sounding string,
While th' Atridæ's praise I sing,†
Victors on the Trojan plain,
Or to Cadmus raise the strain,
Hark! in soft and whisper'd sighs,
Love's sweet notes the shell replies.
Late I strung my harp anew,‡
Changed the strings—the subject too:
Loud I sung Alcides' toils,
Still the lyre my labour foils;
Still with Love's sweet silver sounds
Every martial theme confounds.§

* As love is the prevailing subject of the poet's muse, this beautiful little ode is with great propriety placed at the commencement of most editions.

† Agamemnon and Menelaus, the sons of Atreus, who were the chief commanders at the siege of Troy. By the Atridæ is meant the Trojan, and by Cadmus, the Theban war.

‡ It was common among the ancient poets to say that "they had new strung their lyre," when about to celebrate any important subject, or extraordinary event.

§ In order to understand this passage clearly, we must imagine Anacreon singing and playing on his lyre, which, instead of returning sounds suitable to the lofty subject of his song, perversely warbles "Love's sweet silver sounds." The original is here beautifully expressive, signifying not merely to send forth a wrong note, but one directly contrary to that intended to

Farewell! heroes, chiefs, and kings,
Naught but love will suit my strings.

ODE II.—ON WOMEN.*

POINTED horns, the dread of foes,
Nature on the bull bestows;
Horny hoofs the horse defend,
Swift-wing'd feet the hare befriend;
Lions' gaping jaws disclose
Dreadful teeth in grinning rows;
Wings to birds her care supplied,
Finny fishes swim the tide;
Nobler gifts to man assign'd,
Courage firm and strength of mind.†
From her then exhausted store
Naught for woman has she more:
How does Nature prove her care?
Beauty's charms is woman's share,

be produced. The lyre is said to have been made of the shell o. the tortoise, and its invention is by some ascribed to Anacreon.

* The sentiment of this little ode is natural and beautiful, and it has been imitated by many succeeding writers. The first of modern poets, Lord Byron, has in the following beautiful passage a similar idea to that contained in the latter part of it:—

"Oh, too convincing, dangerously dear!
In woman's eye the unanswerable tear!
That weapon of her weakness she can wield
To save—subdue—at once her spear and shield."
Corsair, Canto ii., 15.

† The single word in the original thus translated, usually signifies wisdom or prudence; but surely so polite a poet as Anacreon would not have denied these important qualities to the ladies. It may likewise be rendered, as in the text, "Courage, or strength of mind;" but in neither sense may we arrogate to ourselves the title of "the exclusives," so long as the deeds and daring of the softer sex live in the Records of Woman, and are related by such a champion as Mrs. Hemans.

Stronger far than warrior's dress
Is her helpless loveliness.
Safety smiles in beauty's eyes,
She the hostile flame defies:
Fiercest swords submissive fall—
Lovely woman conquers all!

ODE III.—CUPID BENIGHTED.*

'Twas at the solemn midnight hour,
When silence reigns with awful pow'r,
Just when the bright and glittering Bear†
Is yielding to her keeper's care;
When, spent with toil, with cares oppress'd,
Man's busy race has sunk to rest,
Sly Cupid, sent by cruel fate,
Stood loudly knocking at my gate.
" Who's there," I cried, " at this late hour?
Who is it batters thus my door?
Begone! you break my blissful dreams."
But he, on mischief bent, it seems,
With feeble voice and piteous cries
In childish accents thus replies:
" Be not alarm'd, kind sir, 'tis I,
A little, wretched, wandering boy.
Pray ope the door—I've lost my way
This moonless night—alone I stray:
I'm stiff with cold, I'm drench'd all o'er;
For pity's sake pray ope the door."
Touch'd with this simple tale of wo,
And little dreaming of a foe,

* Longuepierre has observed that this is one of the most beautiful odes in the collection; and it is, I think, a good proof of the truth of this remark, that after a lapse of more than two thousand years its spirit and meaning are still preserved, and are to be found imbodied in a pretty little song, which was a few years ago a popular favourite.

† The Bear and Boötes, or the Bearkeeper, are two constellations near the North Pole.

I rose, lit up my lamp, and straight
Undid the fastenings of the gate;
And there indeed a boy I spied,
With bow and quiver by his side.
Wings too he wore—a strange attire!
My guest I seated near the fire,
And while the blazing fagots shine,
I chafed his little hands in mine.
His dank and dripping locks I wrung,
That down his shoulders loosely hung.
Soon as his cheeks began to glow,
"Come now," he cries, "let's try this bow;
For much I fear, this rainy night,
The wet and damp have spoil'd it quite."
That instant twang'd the sounding string,
Loud as the whizzing gadfly's wing:
Too truly aim'd, the fatal dart
My bosom pierced with painful smart.*
Up sprung the boy with laughing eyes,
And, "Wish me joy, mine host," he cries.
"My bow is sound in ev'ry part;
Thou'lt find the arrow in thy heart."

ODE IV.—ON HIMSELF.

On this flowery couch reclining,
  Thick with leaves of myrtle strew'd,†
Every graver care resigning,
  I will drink in joyous mood.

* In the original it is "pierced through the middle of my liver." The ancients, as may be proved by numerous passages, considered the liver to be the seat of the affections; and it is reasonable to suppose that the sympathy existing between this organ and the brain was as well known to them as it is to physicians in the present day.

† Madame Dacier observes that the ancients were fond of reposing on leaves of fragrant herbs and flowers, which afforded them a soft and pleasant couch, and at the same time re-

His tunic shorten'd—standing near me,
His waist with rushy girdle bound,
With rosy wine let Cupid cheer me,
And serve the golden goblet round.

For, ah! with what unwearied pace*
The ceaseless wheel of life runs on!
Just like the chariot's rapid race,
How swift the course, how quickly run!

Yet thus, alas! our moments fly;
Thus pass our fleeting years away;
And soon shall we neglected lie,
A little dust—a lump of clay!

Then why, when life's short scene is o'er,
Anoint a cold unconscious stone?†
Why vainly rich libations pour,
Or call my ghost with useless moan?

galed their senses with their agreeable odours. A passion for perfumes and flowers seems to be common to all oriental nations.

* If, according to the ancient proverb, it is commendable to receive instruction even from an enemy, surely we should not disdain to be made wiser by a heathen. These lines contain a fine moral sentiment; and the Christian reader, excited by higher motives, will seek to improve that time which, ceaseless in its progress, and irrevocable in its flight, is given to him for nobler purposes than to be wasted in trifling pursuits or sensual indulgences.

† The custom among the ancients of pouring sweet unguents on the tombs of their deceased friends, and crowning them with chaplets of flowers, is well known. The eastern nations are still remarkable for the careful and affectionate attention they bestow on their departed relatives.

"The Turkish burying ground stands on the slope of the hill, at a small distance from the town, near that of the Jews and is encircled by a deep grove of cypress trees. No guard or shade around a cemetery can be so suitable as that of this noble tree; with its waveless and mournful foliage, it looks the very emblem of mortality. The Orientals love that everything should be sad and impressive round the abodes of their dead, which

Nay, rather, friends, anoint me now,
While life remains, and fate is kind;
With rosy garlands crown my brow,
And go, my lovely fair one find.

My cares I'll drown in pleasure's tide,
Before my wand'ring spirit go
Where unsubstantial spectres glide,
And dance in dismal shades below.*

ODE V.—ON THE ROSE.†

With sparkling wine sweet roses join,
'Twill make the nectar'd draught divine;
Let mirth and laughter rule the hour,
While roses, pluck'd from Love's own bower,
Around our moisten'd temples twine,
And add fresh fragrance to the wine.

they never approach but with the deepest reverence; and they often sit for hours in their kiosks on the Bosphorus, gazing with mournful pleasure on the shores of Asia, where the ashes of their fathers are laid."—*Carne's Letters from the East*, p. 65.

* It seems not a little remarkable that the ancients, amid all their wild and extravagant fancies, never "affected the skies;" or, in other words, that they contented themselves with an elysium in the infernal regions, assigning the heavens above them to their gods and demigods alone. In this, as in many other respects, Christianity has enlarged our ideas, and exalted our hopes beyond the most daring conceptions of the heathen world.

† Among the ancients, especially the Grecians, the rose was particularly esteemed. It was always introduced at entertainments; and it was customary on such occasions to employ flowers and perfumes, not merely for pleasure, but because they imagined their odours prevented the intoxicating effects of wine. With the Romans they were held in equal estimation, as appears from the following passage:—

"Here pour your wines, your odours shed;
Bring forth the rose's shortlived flower,
While fate yet spins thy mortal thread,
While youth and fortune give th' indulgent hour."
Francis's Horace, b. ii., ode 3.

Oh, lovely rose! to thee I sing,
Thou sweetest, fairest child of spring!
Oh thou art dear to all the gods,
The darling of their bless'd abodes.
Thy breathing buds and blossoms fair
Entwine young Cupid's golden hair,
When gayly dancing, hand in hand,
He joins the Graces' lovely band.
Then bring fresh garlands, crown my brows,
And while thus joyous, I carouse,
Admitted, Bacchus, to thy shrine,
Thy praise I'll sing in hymns divine;
Or, thick with rosy chaplets crown'd,
With Chloe dance a sprightly round,
Whose snowy bosom softly swells,
And tales of tender transport tells.

ODE VI.—THE BANQUET.

With glowing wreaths of roses crown'd.
We'll pass the cheerful goblet round;
But with no squeamish, modest sips,
The cup shall kiss our thirsty lips.
And see, to grace the festive hour,
The maiden seeks our shelter'd bower,*
Whose pretty, slender foot well suits
The music of the soft-toned lutes;
While ivy wreath'd, her thyrsus fair†
She rustles through the yielding air.
And hark! a fair-hair'd youth begins,‡
And as he wakes the warbling strings

* A custom seems to be here alluded to which is still common in Turkey; at the entertainments of persons of consequence dancing girls, called *almas*, are hired to amuse the company by their performances.

† The thyrsus was a spear encircled with ivy, and sometimes with vine leaves, and was carried by those who attended the feasts in honour of Bacchus.

‡ The following extract may perhaps elucidate this pas-

His liquid voice breathes odours round,
And mingles with the melting sound.
With golden locks, young Cupid see,
And Bacchus, young and fair as he;
With these is lovely Venus too,
Who hastes to join the sportive crew;
While we old men can scarce refrain
To live the life we loved again.

ODE VII.—ON CUPID.*

Cupid once, with staff in hand,
(A slender hyacinthine wand,)
Slow walking with a tottering pace,
Defied me to the rapid race.
Away we flew o'er flood and fell,
O'er craggy rock and bushy dell,
Till hastening on with swiftest speed,
A serpent stung me; then indeed†
My heart forgot its wonted play;
I fainted—sunk—and died away.

sage: "The summer is already far advanced in this part of the world; and, for some miles round Adrianople, the whole ground is laid out in gardens, and the banks of the rivers are set with rows of fruit trees, under which all the most considerable Turks divert themselves every evening; not with walking, that is not one of their pleasures; but a set party of them choose out a green spot, where the shade is very thick, and there they spread a carpet, on which they sit drinking their coffee, and are generally attended by some slave with a fine voice, or that plays on some instrument."—*Lady Montague's Letters. Letter to Mr. Pope from Adrianople,* April 1st, 1717.

* As commentators are by no means agreed either as to the text or meaning of this ode, I have given it the turn which I conceived most agreeable to the genius and style of the author. By a pleasing allegory, he seems to intimate, that under whatever disguise love may appear, his power is equally certain and resistless.

† It is observed by Madame Dacier that his being stung by a serpent was a punishment for his insensibility and presumption

The urchin laughed at my disgrace,
And while his pinions fann'd my face,
"My friend," he cried, "you clearly prove
That you are not a match for Love!"

ODE VIII.—ON HIS DREAM.*

Peaceful slumbering through the night,
On a purple couch reclined,
Dreams of joy and visions bright
Bacchus sent to charm my mind.

Methought I join'd in rapid race
With flying nymphs a sportive crew,
And urging on with swiftest pace,
Still kept the lovely game in view.

While youths, as young Lyæus fair,†
With jealous hate, and envy stung,
Who saw my joy, but could not share
Reviled me as I pass'd along.

A kiss I claim'd—my promised prize;
But as on pleasure's brink I seem,
The vision fled my cheated eyes:
I woke, and lo! 'twas all a dream!

Then lonely, sad, and angry too,‡
To find my high-raised hopes were vain,

* For the different metre of this ode, and of some others in the collection, I have only to remark that I have deviated from the usual Anacreontic measure for the sake of variety.

† Lyæus is a name given to Bacchus. It is derived from a Greek verb, signifying to loosen or free, and is, from the circumstance of wine freeing the mind from anxiety, appropriately assigned to him.

‡ There is a similar passage in one of Ovid's epistles; in that from Sappho to Phaon, so beautifully translated by Pope. I

The dear delusion to renew,
  I sigh'd, and sunk to sleep again.

ODE IX.—ON A DOVE.*

Pretty pigeon, tell me, pray,
Whither speeding, whence away?
Breathing balmy odours round,
Where thy fluttering pinions sound?
Who despatch'd thee through the air?
What commission dost thou bear?
"Anacreon, the blithe and gay,
The master dear whom I obey,
Sent me swift from yonder grove
To seek the lady of his love.
I dare not tell the name she bears,
But beauty's sweetest smile she wears:
Possess'd of every pleasing art,
She reigns supreme o'er every heart.
Fair Venus sold me to the bard,
A little hymn the fix'd reward.†

have transcribed it, in order that the reader may have the pleasure of comparing them:—

"Oh, night, more pleasing than the brightest day,
When fancy gives what absence takes away,
And dress'd in all its visionary charms,
Restored my fair deserted to my arms!
But when with day the sweet delusions fly,
And all things wake to life and joy, but I,
As if once more forsaken, I complain,
And close my eyes, to dream of you again."

* To understand this ode properly, we must remember that it was a custom among the ancients, when they undertook long journeys, and were desirous of sending back any news with uncommon expedition, to take tame pigeons along with them. When they thought proper to write to their friends, they let one of these birds loose, with letters fastened to its neck: the bird, once released, would never cease its flight till it arrived at its nest and young ones. The same custom is still common among the Turks and other Eastern nations.

† It is impossible not to admire the address and delicacy of

So now the poet's page am I,
His courier through the pathless sky;
And sometimes, as you see me now,
The bearer of some tender vow.
He thinks, perhaps, he pleases me,
By saying I shall soon be free;
But though I should the boon obtain,
His willing slave I'll still remain.
For, ah! I do not wish to roam,
Or quit my sweet, my happy home,
Far flying over hill and plain
My wretched, rustic food to gain;
Or shivering on some tree to stay,
And coo the cheerless hours away:
For now I feast on dainty bread,
And by the hands I love am fed;
And when the cup has press'd his lip,
His sweet delicious wine I sip;
And when my heart is light and gay,
I sometimes little frolics play;
Upon his shoulder take my place,
And with my wings o'erspread his face.
Or if to sleep my humour suit,
I perch upon his warbling lute,
And by his careful hand caress'd,
By softest sounds am lull'd to rest.
I've told you all—begone! adieu!
And let me now my flight pursue.
Nay, friend, no longer urge my stay,
For I have prated like a jay."

this indirect compliment to his own writings. Venus, the goddess of beauty, and mother of the Graces, is represented as being willing to purchase a little hymn of his composing at the price of one of her favourite doves. This passage is cited by Fawkes as a proof that Anacreon wrote hymns in honour of the gods: but be this as it may, it is certain that few fragments have reached us, and those of doubtful authority.

ODE X.—ON A WAXEN CUPID.

A WAXEN Cupid, nicely wrought,
A rustic youth for sale had brought.
"Say, what's your price, my friend?" I cried,
When thus the silly clown replied,
In Doric phrase,* devoid of skill:
"E'en take him, sir, for what you will:
'Tis cheap, you'll say; but, truth to tell,
No images I make or sell.
But as for this young rogue you see,
He must not—shall not dwell with me."
"If so, my pretty youth," I said,
"Our bargain shall be quickly made:
To you this little coin I'll give,†
And, Cupid, thou with me shalt live.
And do thou now my breast inspire,
There kindle all thy former fire;
Oh let me boast a lover's name,
Or thou thyself shalt melt in flame."‡

ODE XI.—ON HIMSELF.§

"ANACREON," the lasses say,
"Old fellow, you have had your day:

* The Doric dialect was remarkable for its broadness and harshness. It was the most ancient of the four, and was used only by the common people of Greece. It is not therefore without reason, as the commentators have remarked, that Anacreon makes this young rustic speak it, since he was so insensible to the charms of love as to wish to get rid even of his image.

† In the Greek it is a drachm, an Attic coin worth about nine pence English, or, according to some, only seven pence, three farthings, or, eight pence farthing.

‡ Barnes observes that the ancient heathens used to treat the images of their gods in the same manner as they fancied they had been treated by them. The modern Indians, when any calamity befalls them, are accustomed to chastise their idols with scourges.

§ However successfully the spirit and meaning of this author

Consult your mirror, mark with care,*
How scanty now your silver hair;†
Old wintry Time has shed his snows,
And bald and bare your forehead shows."
But faith! I know not where they're gone,
Or if I've any left—or none;
But this I know, that every day
Shall see me sportive, blithe, and gay;
For 'tis our wisdom so to do
The nearer death appears in view.

ODE XII.—ON A SWALLOW.

What punishment shall I decree,
Vexatious, chattering bird, to thee?
Say, shall I clip thy restless wing?
Or, like the cruel Thracian king,‡
Tear out that tongue whose noisy scream
Has roused me from so sweet a dream?

may sometimes be preserved, it is impossible to convey an adequate idea of that facility of thought and easiness of expression which are so peculiarly his own. What would in others justly be considered the perfection of art, in him appears perfectly natural; and one might almost imagine that his numbers flowed spontaneously to the warblings of his lyre. These remarks are particularly applicable to this ode, which, for simplicity and playfulness of expression, is inferior to no one in the collection.

* Before the invention of glass, mirrors were used made of brass or some other metal, and sometimes of stones highly polished.

† It was remarked by an ancient author that Venus herself, if destitute of hair, would not, though surrounded by the Loves and Graces, have had charms sufficient to please her husband Vulcan.

‡ Tereus, king of Thrace, for whose story the reader is referred to the sixth book of Ovid's Metamorphoses. Though Anacreon seems to adopt the less usual acceptation of the fable, that it was Philomela, and not Progne, who was transformed into a swallow.

For oh! methought my love was nigh,
Till, startled by thy twittering cry,
She fled upon the wings of morn,*
And left me joyless and forlorn.

ODE XIII.—ON HIMSELF.

Poor Atys,† as old poets sing,
O'er the wild mountains wandering,
Degraded from his former state,
Cybele's love now turned to hate,
With plaintive cries invoked relief,
Till madness brought an end to grief.
And some who to the waters throng,
Of laurell'd Phœbus, god of song,
At Claros drink the vocal wave,‡
And with prophetic fury rave;
Then shall not I when wine inspires,
And Chloe's eyes dart love's bright fires,
When bathed in sweets, without alloy,
And rapt in wild, delirious joy,
Refuse a while stern reason's sway,
And be as madly wild as they?

* Horace has a similar idea in the first ode of the fourth book which has been thus admirably imitated by Pope:—

"Thee, dress'd in fancy's airy beam,
Absent I follow through th' extended dream;
Now, now I seize, I clasp thy charms,
And now you burst (ah, cruel!) from my arms;
And swiftly shoot along the mall,
Or softly glide by the canal;
Now shorn by Cynthia's silver ray,
And now on rolling waters snatch'd away."

† Atys was a young Phrygian of great beauty, beloved by Cybele, the mother of the gods, who afflicted him with madness for violating his vow of chastity. According to Ovid, he was afterward turned into a pine-tree.

‡ Claros was a city of Ionia, near Colophon, and was famous for a fountain sacred to Apollo. The term vocal alludes to the

ODE XIV.—ON CUPID.*

Cease, cease the combat, I'll obey,
Oh, mighty Love! I own thy sway.
Cupid plann'd a new campaign,
And bade me join his camp again;
But I, grown weary of the trade,
Like a rebel disobey'd.
Straight the monarch, much displeased,
His dreadful bow and quiver seized,
And, wafted on his pinions light,
Defied me to the field of fight.
Then clad for war, like Peleus' son,
A corslet bright I buckled on;
With ample shield and quivering spear,
I waited till the foe drew near.
His bow-string twang'd—then seized with dread,
My courage fail'd—I trembling fled.
He plied his darts till all were spent;
Nor did his anger then relent:
Himself he changed into a dart,
And shot like lightning through my heart.†

property which the waters of this spring were said to have of imparting to those who drank of them the gift of prophecy.

* In this ode Anacreon intends to show the irresistible power of "mighty love;" and he here represents himself as contending with Cupid armed with a spear and shield. The combat is described with much spirit; but in the end the arrows of his antagonist achieve the victory. The poet concludes with an admirable reflection on the uselessness of defending the out posts, when the enemy has already entered.

† "This thought is very beautiful and ingenious. It is taken from an ancient piece of gallantry, which ought not to be passed over in silence. The heroes of antiquity, when in any desperate engagement they found their darts spent, their strength exhausted, and saw no prospect of surviving long, would collect all their spirits and strength, and rush headlong with amazing impetuosity on their enemies, that even in death the weight of their bodies, thus violently agitated, might bear down their adversaries."—*Fawkes.*

Ah me! I felt my life-blood flow;
I sunk beneath my conquering foe
How vainly then a shield I wear!
In vain defensive arms I bear;
For victory who can hope to win
While fiercely burns the war within?

ODE XV.—HAPPY LIFE.

Famed Gyges' treasures I could see,*
From envious thoughts and wishes free.
On golden heaps with scorn I frown;
I would not wear a monarch's crown.
Far other joys and cares are mine,
For which such bawbles I resign.
To bathe my beard with sweet perfumes,†
To crown my brows with spring's fresh blooms;
These—these are things that claim my care.
This day is mine—I'll freely share
The joys it brings; for who can know
If he shall see the next or no?
Then, while thy summer sky is clear,
Nor death nor danger hover near,
The happy hours of life employ
In song, and dance, and festive joy;

* According to Herodotus, Gyges was the favourite of Candaules, king of Lydia, whose queen was remarkably and passionately admired by her husband. In his vanity he extolled her charms above measure to Gyges, and, to convince him of her beauty, determined to give him an opportunity of seeing her undressing. This he effected, but not without the queen's discovering the affront; who next morning sent for Gyges, and resolutely told him he must either suffer immediate death for what he had done, or despatch Candaules, and take her and the kingdom of Lydia for his recompense. The choice was difficult, as he greatly valued his master: however, the love of life prevailed: he stabbed Candaules, married the queen, and took possession of the kingdom.

† The Turks and Persians take a particular pride in this venerable appendage, and consume much time in dressing and perfuming it.

And let the rattling dice assign*
The royal honours of the wine,
Ere surly Death thy garland tear,
Or fell disease with frown severe,
Forbid the nectar'd juice to sip,
And dash the goblet from thy lip.

ODE XVI.—THE CAPTIVE.

Some sing of Thebes, and some prolong†
The battle-shouts of Phrygian wars;
But I must trill a captive's song,‡
Sigh o'er my wounds, and count my scars

Of conq'ring fleets no slave am I,
No armies claim me for their prize;
But all my foes in ambush lie,
And dart their fires from Pyrrha's eyes!

ODE XVII.—ON A SILVER BOWL.

Mulciber, thou skilful wright,
Carve for me this silver bright;
But I do not wish to see
Polish'd arms or panoply.
What are arms or wars to me?

* It was usual among the ancients to appoint a master of the feast by the cast of dice, whose office it was to determine the size and number of the cups, and to decide on the proper ceremonies.

† Anacreon here alludes to the famous war waged by the seven captains against Eteocles, king of Thebes, in order to restore to his brother Polynices his share in the government, according to their agreement on their father's death to reign annually in turn. On this subject Æschylus has written a tragedy, and Statius a noble poem called the Thebaid.

‡ The poet here alludes to the numerous instances in which he had been brought under the dominion of love.

Carve me out a mighty bowl,
That my ever-thirsty soul
In the generous juice may steep.
Make it very—very deep.
On the margin do not trace
Uncouth shape or horrid face:
Grave not there the northern wain,
Stern Orion, god of rain,†
Boötes, or the Pleiades;
What concern have I with these?
Trail thereon the tender vine,
There let purple clusters shine;
Picture too the god of wine.
There let fair-hair'd Cupid be,
And Bathyllus, fair as he:
Make them beautiful and bold,
Burnish'd high like polish'd gold:
Let them in one labour join,
Treading out the gushing wine.

* The author here alludes to the emblazoning of the shield of Achilles as described in the eighteenth book of the Iliad:—

"There shone the image of the master mind;
There earth—there heaven—there ocean he design'd;
Th' unwearied sun, the moon completely round;
The starry lights that heaven's high convex crown'd;
The Pleiads, Hyads, with the northern team;
And great Orion's more refulgent beam,
To which around the axle of the sky
The Bear revolving points his golden eye,
Still shines exalted on th' ethereal plain,
Nor bathes his blazing forehead in the main."

Pope's Homer's Iliad.

† The Greek term signifies "hateful," and is used by the poet, because the constellation Orion was considered the forerunner of tempests, and therefore dreaded by mariners.

ODE XVIII.—ON THE SAME SUBJECT.*

Dear artist, take this silver store,
And try thy skilful hand once more;
Produce a large and handsome bowl
To charm my eyes, and cheer my soul.
Around its polish'd surface bring
The flowery pride of purple spring;
There let the soft and vernal hours
Shed rosy sweets in plenteous showers.
Engrave no foreign mystic rite,
No marv'lous tale that shocks the sight;
But draw the gen'rous god of wine,
Blithe Bacchus, son of Jove divine.
Let Venus, love's sweet smiling queen,
With youthful Hymen deck the scene:
His dread artillery laid aside,
Let Cupid mid the Graces glide,†
As in the sprightly dance they join
Beneath the high-imbowering vine,
Whose glowing clusters peep between
The foliage bright of glossy green.
With these a youthful group display,
As fair as Phœbus, god of day,
Though Phœbus join not in their play.‡

ODE XIX.—REASONS FOR DRINKING.

The earth drinks up the genial rains
Which deluge all her thirsty plains;

* The subject of this ode is the same as that of the preceding.

† "It is not without reason that Anacreon, after having mentioned Venus, introduces Love among the Graces, being sensible that though beauty alone might please, yet, without the aid of other charms, it could not long captivate the heart." *Fawkes.*

‡ This apparently alludes to the fable of Hyacinthus, a youth slain by Apollo while playing with him at quoits.

The lofty trees that pierce the sky*
Drain up the earth and leave her dry;
Th' insatiate sea imbibes, each hour,†
The welcome breeze that brings the show'r;
The sun, whose fires so fiercely burn,
Absorbs the wave; and, in her turn,
The modest moon enjoys, each night,‡
Large draughts of his celestial light.
Then, sapient sirs, pray tell me why,
If all things drink, why may not I?

ODE XX.—TO HIS MISTRESS.

On desert Phrygia's silent sands
Poor Niobe an image stands;§
And Pandion's injured child, we know,‖
Still, twittering, tells her tale of wo.
But would the gods the change allow,
And hear and grant my tender vow,
Dear girl! thy mirror I would be,
That thou might'st always smile on me.

* The poet here refers to the supply of moisture which trees receive by means of their roots and fibres.

† This passage, which seems to have given the commentators some trouble, is by many supposed to be an error in the text. I have followed the usual reading, though I think Fawkes's amendment very judicious. He has it, "the sea drinks up the rivers," certainly a much more natural idea.

‡ The moon is said to drink from the sun, because she borrows her light from that luminary.

§ Niobe was the daughter of Tantalus, king of Phrygia, and wife of Amphion, king of Thebes; by whom, according to Homer, having six sons and six daughters, she became so proud of her offspring and high birth, that she had the vanity to prefer herself to Latona, the mother of Apollo and Diana; who, to revenge the affront offered to their parent, in one day slew all her children: on which Niobe was struck dumb with grief, and remained stupid. For that reason the poets have feigned her to be turned into a stone.—See *Ovid's Met.*, book vi.

‖ The poet here alludes to the fabled transformation of Philomela. See note, p. 25.

Thy vest I'd be, to guard with care
Those heaving breasts, and nestle there.
Oh! would I were a limpid wave,
Thy soft and beauteous limbs to lave;
Thy perfumed oil, that I might share
The glory of thy golden hair!
Or, dearer still, that slender zone,
Which makes thy beauties all its own:
Thy pearly chain, that shines so fair,
But cannot with thy neck compare:
Thy very sandal I would be,*
To kiss the foot that trod on me!

ODE XXI.—SUMMER.

Bring, maidens, bring a well-mix'd bowl,
And let me slake my thirsty soul;
For, scorch'd beneath this sultry sky,
My spirits sink—I faint—I die.
This garland, late so fresh and fair,†
I twined amid my curling hair;
But all its faded flow'rets now
Have wither'd on my burning brow.
Bring fresher wreaths my head to shade;
Bring others still when those shall fade.
But, oh! what ease can wine impart
When love's fierce flame consumes the heart?

* This ode has been imitated by many succeeding writers; and in our immortal bard, who needed no copy but nature, the following passage can only be said to present a remarkable coincidence:—

"See how she leans her cheek upon her hand!
Oh! that I were a glove upon that hand,
That I might touch that cheek!"
Romeo and Juliet, act 2, scene 2.

† The custom of wearing garlands of flowers at entertainments has already been mentioned.

In vain to groves or shades I fly,*
This inward flame will never die!

ODE XXII.—THE BOWER.†

Haste, my love, this shade to seek,
The spreading tree is passing fair,
Like clust'ring curls on Beauty's cheek,
See it waves its wanton hair.

The streamlet murm'ring at our feet
Rolls its music through the grove;‡
'Tis a scene for lovers meet,
Where each object whispers love.

The tree, the stream, the silent hour,
All persuasive, seem to say,

* The reflection here made by the poet is just and natural, and is similar to that at the conclusion of the fourteenth ode. When love has once taken possession of the heart, external defences cease to be useful.

† This elegant little ode seems to be a great favourite with the translators and commentators. It has not been thought unworthy of his genius even by the philosophical Beattie, among whose poems it is to be found translated with singular accuracy and beauty.

‡ In the original it is literally a "fountain rolling or flowing with persuasion;" a beauty of expression which we must be contented to admire with very little hope of imitating, since our language seems to afford few facilities for accommodating sound to sense. Pope, no mean master of melody, has attempted it in that passage in his Art of Poetry intended to represent the whispering breeze and the flowing stream.

"Soft is the strain when Zephyr gently blows,
And the smooth stream in smoother numbers flows."

On this passage Dr. Johnson, in all the pride of acute, but rather ill-natured criticism, remarks, that "the verse intended to represent the whisper of the vernal breeze must be confessed not much to excel in softness or volubility; and the smooth stream runs with a perpetual clash of jarring consonants."—*Rambler* vol. i., No. 92.

"Viewing such a lovely bower,
Can you pass another way?"

ODE XXIII.—THE VANITY OF WEALTH.

Could glittering heaps, or golden store,
Life preserve, or health restore,
Then with ceaseless, anxious pain,
Riches I would strive to gain,*
That should death, unwish'd for, come,
Pointing to the dreary tomb,
I might cry, in sprightly tone,
"Here's my ransom, Death! begone!"
But, alas! since well I know
Life cannot be purchased so,
Why indulge the useless sigh?
Fate decrees that all shall die.
Vainly to our wealth we trust,
Poor or wealthy—die we must.
Present joys then let me share,
Rosy wine to banish care;
Cheerful friends that faithful prove,
Beauty's smiles and blissful love.

ODE XXIV.—LIFE TO BE ENJOYED.†

Born a mortal; doom'd to tread
Life's rough path of pain and wo,

* There is an anecdote in the history of Anacreon, recorded by Stobæus, to which this ode may possibly bear some allusion. He relates that Anacreon, having received a present of five talents of gold from Polycrates, tyrant of Samos, was so embarrassed with cares and solicitudes about his treasure, that he could not sleep for two nights successively: whereon he sent back the present with this apology to his patron, "That however valuable the sum might be, it was not a sufficient price for the trouble and anxiety of keeping it."

† These odes are all nearly similar in subject, and present nothing particularly worthy of remark or illustration.

All the past with ease is read,
  But the future who can know?

Hence! away, distracting cares,
  Make no fellowship with me;
Point not to my silvering hairs,
  You and I shall ne'er agree.

Ere fate forbid all further joy,
  First amid the festive throng,
Bacchus shall my hours employ
  With mirth, and dance, and joyous song.

ODE XXV.—THE CURE FOR CARE.

When with gloomy griefs oppress'd,
Wine can charm those griefs to rest;
Toil and trouble, care and wo,
I'm determined ne'er to know.
Though in care my life were pass'd,
Cruel death would come at last.
Shall I ever anxious grieve?
Shall I thus myself deceive?
No! we'll drain the rosy bowl,
'Tis a cordial for the soul;
'Tis a charm that lulls to rest
Every anxious, aching breast.

ODE XXVI.—IN PRAISE OF WINE.

When the nectar'd bowl I drain
Gloomy cares forego their reign;
Richer than the Lydian king,
Hymns of love and joy I sing;
Ivy wreaths my temples twine,
And, while careless I recline,
While bright scenes my vision greet,
Tread the world beneath my feet.

Fill the cup, my trusty page,
Anacreon, the blithe and sage,
As his maxim, ever said,
Those slain by wine are noble dead.

ODE XXVII.—THE SAME SUBJECT

When the generous god of wine,
Bacchus, son of Jove divine,
Frees my soul from anxious care,
Fills my breast and revels there,
Then I lead the mazy dance,
Rapt in pleasure's giddy trance.
Oh! what transports then I prove—
Sweet the joys of wine and love!
Music breathes its softest strains,
Venus too with Bacchus reigns.
Thus, with wine and beauty bless'd,
Thus I charm my cares to rest,
Ever joyous, blithe, and gay,
Dance the happy hours away.

ODE XXVIII.—ON HIS MISTRESS.*

Best of painters, lend thy aid,
Draw the lines of light and shade;
Master of the Rhodian art,†
Paint the charmer of my heart;

* The version of this ode, first published in the Guardian, is adopted both by Addison and Fawkes; but however beautiful and spirited it may be thought, another translator, Mr. Girdlestone, shrewdly remarks, that no painter could make a beautiful picture from a description which leaves out the nose. In the original not a single feature is omitted; and therefore the version above mentioned must be defective.

† The Rhodians were, according to Pindar, the first people acquainted with the arts of painting and sculpture.

Absent though the maiden be,
Beauties I'll describe to thee,*
Thou, undazzled, ne'er couldst see.
Paint her dark and glossy hair,
Flowing down her neck so fair:
Further yet I must presume,
Let it seem to breathe perfume.
Her iv'ry forehead next thy care,
Shining mid her jet-black hair;
Let thy utmost skill be seen
In the dainty space between,
Where by sable archers cross'd,
Where the less'ning shade is lost.
Let her liquid eye of fire,
Like Minerva's, awe inspire;
With Cytherea's softness too
Temper the celestial blue;

* To give the reader an opportunity of judging whether or not this picture be too highly drawn, I have transcribed the following passage from a work deservedly held in the highest estimation:—

"The women, as I have intimated, are handsome; indeed, you rarely meet with an ugly face among them. The form of the head, the general cast of countenance, are classical; and in their profile I have frequently found that exquisite, gently curving line, we see in ancient Greek statues and medals, (and which we have been accustomed to consider the line of ideal beauty,) identified in 'real flesh and blood.' Their large, black eyes, with long lashes, and their delicately arched eyebrows; the latter, when not denaturalized and spoiled by the too common practice of dying them, are the finest I have ever seen."—*M'Farlane's Constantinople*, vol. i., p. 99. And again, "The Greek village of Panagea, situated on the seashore, to the south of Chesme, is celebrated for the beauty of its women; but throughout these regions the sex is universally handsome and graceful. Poverty, that cruel enemy to the charms of the person as well as of the mind, cannot destroy their attractions: the bright, intelligent, large black eye beams, the clear complexion, the exquisite Grecian nose, mouth, and chin, the classical contour, are there, in spite of its wrongs; and an innate grace of manner and motion develops itself through the covering of rags. I do not seek the recondite causes of this peculi

Paint her lovely cheek and nose,
Blending milk with blush of rose;
Paint her pretty, pouting lips,
Where the bee its honey sips,
Where Persuasion sits and smiles,
With a thousand winning wiles.
Every pleasing grace must deck
Her pretty dimpled chin and neck;
And let nameless beauties dwell
In her bosom's gentle swell.
In a thin and purple dress
Veil this form of loveliness:
Her body hide, her shape express.
Enough! no further proof I seek,
She lives—she breathes—soft! did she speak?

arity; but, be it descent from a superior race, be it the soil and clime, such are the women of Ionia."—*Ibid.*, p. 201.

Perhaps the reader would be pleased to see a portrait of the "fair Ionian" in another light, by a master whose unrivalled pencil has left all competitors at an immeasurable distance:—

"You see, this night
Made warriors of more than me. I paused
To look upon her, and her kindled cheek;
Her large black eyes, that flash'd through her long hair
As it stream'd o'er her; her blue veins, that rose
Along her most transparent brow; her nostril
Dilated from its symmetry; her lips
Apart; her voice that clove through all the din,
As a lute's pierceth through the cymbal's clash,
Jarr'd but not drown'd by the loud brattling; her
Waved arms, more dazzling with their own born whiteness
Than the steel her hand held, which she caught up
From a dead soldier's grasp; all these things made
Her seem unto the troops a prophetess
Of victory, or Victory herself.
Come down to hail us hers."

Lord Byron.—Sardanapalus, act 1, scene 1.

ODE XXX.—CUPID TAKEN PRISONER.*

Cupid, once, was rambling found
On the Muses' hallow'd ground;
Straight they weave a rosy chain,
And the little god detain.
Him to Beauty soon they gave,
Mighty Love is Beauty's slave.
Cytherea ransoms brought,
To release her son she sought;
But no fee, no ransom now,
The happy captive will allow.
Love hath learn'd his art too well,
And with Beauty still will dwell.

ODE XXXI.—PLEASING PHRENSY.

Yes! let me—let me drain the bowl,
And pour its pleasures on my soul;
Let Bacchus now his reign employ,
Till reason reels, oppress'd with joy.
Orestes, by the furies led,†
Barefooted to the mountains fled.
Alcmæon too, in frantic mood,
Like him was stain'd with mother's blood;
But I disclaim such dreadful deeds,
My madness from my joy proceeds.
Then bring the bowl, I cry again,
Who shall that maddening joy restrain?

* "This ode is very fine, and the fiction extremely ingenious I believe Anacreon would inculcate that beauty alone cannot long secure a conquest, but that when wit and beauty meet, it is impossible for a lover to disengage himself."—*Madame Dacier.*

† Alcmæon's father had been put to death by his mother's contrivance, whom on that account he slew. Orestes slew his mother Clytemnestra, to revenge the death of his father Agamemnon, who at his return from the Trojan war had been murdered by her and her lover Ægisth ·

When Hercules went mad of yore,
The Iphitean bow he bore;*
His rattling quiver's dreadful sound
Spread awe and consternation round.
Great Ajax, too, when madness raged,†
Whole hosts of fancied Greeks engaged;
When, grasping fierce his seven-fold shield,
With Hector's sword he sought the field.‡
But though with wine I mad should be,
May no such fury seize on me!
No dreadful bow or sword I bear,
A flowery garland decks my hair.
This brimming bowl shall crown my bliss,
Then welcome madness such as this!

ODE XXXII.—ON THE NUMBER OF HIS MISTRESSES.

If thou canst number o'er to me
Every leaf on every tree,
Or count the ceaseless waves that roar
Against the billow-beaten shore,
Thou sufficient skill hast proved;
Thou shalt count the names I've loved.
At Athens first, Minerva's town,
Full five-and-thirty write me down;
But oh! at Corinth, rich and fair,§
What hosts of loved ones had I there!

* Iphitus was slain by Hercules, who carried off his bow.

† When the armour of Achilles was adjudged to Ulysses, Ajax was so enraged at the affront that he went mad; and falling on a flock of sheep, which he took for Grecians, he first slew them and then himself.

‡ Hector and Ajax made an exchange of presents, which gave birth to a proverb, "that the presents of enemies are generally fatal;" for with this sword Ajax killed himself.

§ Corinth, the metropolis of Achaia, was famous for beautiful women.

For beauteous nymphs it bears the sway,
For none so beauteous sure as they.
Next, my lovely Lesbians tell,
Ionians, Carians, those that dwell
At far-famed Rhodes—you may in all
The trifling sum two thousand call.
What! think'st thou that I yet have done?
Resume thy tablets—one by one,*
I'll count thee o'er my Syrian fair,
And Egypt too must claim a share;
And fertile Creta yet remains,†
Where Love his empire still maintains.
The dark-eyed nymphs that shared my flame,
At Spain and Afric, shall I name?
To sultry India's farthest pole,
Whose dusky charms have fired my soul!

ODE XXXIII.—ON A SWALLOW.

Pretty, twittering, fickle guest,
Here you build your summer nest;
But, ere storms deface the sky,
Back to warmer worlds you fly;‡

* The page to whom Anacreon is here making this extravagant enumeration, may well be supposed to drop his tablets in astonishment, as the original expression is, "add still to the wax." The ancients wrote on tablets made of this material with a pointed instrument called a stylus or style, the upper end of which was flat and blunt, for the purpose of making erasures. Hence arose the term "an author's style," as applied to his peculiar mode of expression.

† Anacreon, to denote its fertility, calls it Crete abounding in all things. It is mentioned by the ancient poets as having a hundred cities.

‡ "Since the days of Anacreon to our own, this is a problem in natural history which has never been solved. Among the ancients it was a generally received opinion that swallows and other birds, on the approach of winter, crossed the sea in search of warmer climates; but more accurate observers have taught us to doubt the truth of this opinion. Pecklinius, in his book

To Memphis, or the banks of Nile,
Where bright suns for ever smile.
But, alas! nor peace nor rest
Dwells within my hapless breast:
Love still builds and hatches there,
Full-fledged loves for flight prepare;
Some, unhatch'd, yet quiet dwell,
Some just struggling through the shell,
While their ceaseless chirping noise
Every hope of peace destroys.
Some usurp the parent's care,
And the younger nestlings rear;
These, when grown, will young ones breed;
Others still to them succeed.
Thus, alas! what hope remains—
What can ease my bosom's pains,
Since within its secret cell
Loves innumerable dwell?

ODE XXXIV.—TO HIS MISTRESS.

Fly me not, thou scornful fair,
  Why reject me so?
Is it that my scanty hair
  Is whiter than the snow?

'De Aëris et Elementi defectu, et Vita sub Aquis,' assures us that swallows retire to the bottom of the water during the winter; and that it is common for the fishermen on the coasts of the Baltic to take them in their nets in large knots, clinging together by their bills and claws; and that on their being brought into a warm room, they will separate, and begin to flutter about as in spring. Kircher, in his book 'De Mundus Subterraneus,' affirms the same, and that in the northern countries they hide themselves under ground in the winter, whence they are often dug out."—*Longuepierre.*

If the reader be desirous of further information on this point he may consult Buffon's Natural History, or Goldsmith's Animated Nature.

Beauty's blooming flower is thine,
And on thy cheek it glows;
But do not lilies brighter shine
When blended with the rose?

ODE XXXV.—ON A PICTURE REPRESENTING EUROPA.*

This bull, my boy, is surely meant
The mighty Jove to represent,
Since on his back he seems to bear
Through pathless seas a Tyrian fair.
With steady strength he stems the tide,
His hoofs the billows dash aside;
For sure no other bull but he
Would from his lovely heifers flee,
And tempt the dangers of the sea.

ODE XXXVI.—LIFE TO BE ENJOYED.

Why prate to me of critic rules,
And jargon of the jangling schools?
Your learned dogmas, prithee, spare,
They're useless all—not worth my care.
I'll hear thee gladly, canst thou tell
The happy art of living well;
How best to mix the sparkling wine,
To make the mellow draught divine;

* We must here imagine that we have before us a picture or medal representing the fable of Europa. According to the poets, it was from this princess that our quarter of the globe derives its name.

"Yet sigh no more, but think of love,
For know thou art the wife of Jove;
Then learn to bear thy future fame
When earth's wide continent shall boast thy name."
Francis's Horace, book iii., ode 27

How best to please the lovely fair,
For this indeed is worth my care.
Alas! each day, each hour I know,
My hoary locks still whiter grow:
Then bring the goblet—let me drink,
'Twill only make me sad to think
How near, how very near the day*
When, mix'd with earth and kindred clay,
My soul no more shall taste of joy,
Nor schemes of bliss my mind employ.

ODE XXXVII.—ON THE SPRING.

The newborn Spring awakes the flowers,
And bathes their buds in dewy showers:
The roses bloom, the Graces wear
Fresh flowery garlands in their hair.
How sleeps the sea in placid rest!
No storms disturb its peaceful breast;
But oft upon its surface green
The diving duck is sporting seen.
From distant skies now comes the crane†
To seek her well-known haunts again;

* What can present a stronger picture of the deplorable state of those who only in this life have hope, than this desponding reflection? The prospect of death, considered merely as a termination of the pleasures of life, was too dreadful to be entertained, and therefore he resolves to banish all thoughts of such an event in scenes of mirth and festivity. Is it not to be feared that he has too many imitators, even among those who, enlightened by Revelation, know that this life is but a probationary state, and yet not only neglect its duties, but, judging from their conduct, seldom bestow a single thought on them?

† The migratory habits of the crane are thus described by Goldsmith in his History of Animated Nature: "The crane changes place like a wanderer; he spends the autumn in Europe; he then flies off, probably to some more southern climate, to enjoy a part of the winter; returns to Europe in the spring; crosses up to the north in summer; visits those lakes that are never dry; and then comes down again to make depredations on our cultivated grounds in autumn."

The smiling sun resumes his sway,
And drives the dismal clouds away;
The teeming earth is big with fruits,
Forth into day the olive shoots;
Rich, juicy clusters deck the vine,
Which soon shall ripen into wine:
The charming sight with joy I see,
To Bacchus welcome—and to me.

ODE XXXVIII.—ON HIMSELF.

True, ah! true, I'm growing old;
Why should not the truth be told?
Still, from youths I never shrink
When the business is to drink.
When the joyous troop advance,
Still I join the merry dance:
I no useless sceptre bear;*
But on high my bottle rear.
Should the grape some hero fire,
Should he wars and fights desire,
Let him fight then, if he please,
I prefer my peaceful ease.
Bring me, then, my gentle page,
Wine that glows with strength and age.†

* Among the ancients, the leader in the Bacchanalian dances bore a rod or sceptre.

† However degenerated in other respects, the modern Greeks still know "where the best Chian, and what it may cost them;" at least if we may judge from the following extract:—

"The red wine is the most esteemed in the island: a small part only is exported, the Greeks making too good a use of it themselves. It cannot greatly sooth or propitiate a Turk's feelings towards the despised and infidel Greeks to see them quaffing with keen delight the rich juice of the grape, and giving loose in the moment to unbounded gayety; while he, poor forbidden follower of Islam! must solace himself gravely with the pure fountain, his meager sherbet, or at most a cup of the coffee of Mocha."—*Carne's Letters from the East*, vol. i., p. 63.

True, I'm old; but you shall see
Old Silenus, full of glee,*
Acted to the life by me.

ODE XXXIX.—ON HIMSELF.

When the rosy wine inspires,
Every muse my bosom fires,
All the joys of love and song
Cheer my heart and tune my tongue.

When the joys of wine I share,
Farewell every anxious care;
Sportive winds my sorrows sweep
To the restless, roaring deep.

When I drain the spacious bowl,
Bacchus charms my ravish'd soul;
Perfumed gales from beds of flowers
Bathe in bliss the happy hours.

When with rosy garlands crown'd,
The social cup I pass around;
Rapt in fancy's airy dream,
Peaceful pleasures are my theme.

When I quaff the grape's rich juice,
Bathed in liquid sweets profuse,
Venus claims my votive strain,
Chloe fills my arms again.

* Silenus was the foster-father and tutor of Bacchus, represented as a little, flat-nosed, bald, fat, tun-bellied, old, drunken fellow, riding on an ass. His picture is thus drawn by Ovid:—

"Around the Bacchæ and the Satyrs' throng,
Behind, Silenus drunk lags slow along;
On his dull ass he nods from side to side,
Forbears to fall, yet half forgets to ride."—*Eusden.*

When the joy-inspiring draught
Frees my soul from anxious thought,
Graver thoughts I fling away,
Sporting with the young and gay.

When I glow with generous wine,
Life's real blessings all are mine,
Joys beyond the reach of fate—
Death is sure in every state.

ODE XL.—CUPID WOUNDED.*

YOUNG Cupid, once, in luckless hour,
Saw and pluck'd his favourite flower,
A blooming rose—whose leaves among
A bee that slept his finger stung.
Loud he scream'd with sudden pain,
Stamp'd and sobb'd—then scream'd again.
He runs—he flies through mead and grove,
To seek the beauteous Queen of Love.
"Ah me! mamma, I'm kill'd," he cries,
"Thy child, thy own dear Cupid dies!
For, as I play'd on yonder plain,
A winged serpent†—ah! what pain!
A thing the ploughmen call a bee,
With dart of poison wounded me."
Fair Venus, smiling, thus replies:
"Oh dry those pretty pearly eyes;

* The ideas contained in this ode have been made the subject of a song, which was a great favourite, and is still frequently heard. It is however very doubtful whether many who sing it know that they are warbling the strains of a poet who flourished more than two thousand years ago; or, in other words, that they are singing a new version of one of the odes of Anacreon.

† In order to make Cupid express his pain and alarm more strongly, Anacreon has made him persist in calling the bee a serpent. Theocritus has imitated this beautiful ode in his nineteenth idyllium.

Think if a little insect's sting
Such painful smart to Cupid bring,
Oh, what must their keen anguish be
Who're wounded to the heart by thee!"

ODE XLI.—THE BANQUET OF WINE.

Come, let the mantling cups be crown'd,
And let the jovial song go round.
To Bacchus still the strain prolong,
Who taught the dance, and loves the song.
Companion blithe with Cupid seen,
Beloved alike by beauty's queen;
The father, he, of joy and mirth,
To him the Graces owe their birth.*
He heals the wounds of pain and grief,
In him the wretched find relief.
When blooming youths present the bowl
Sweet joys alone possess the soul;
And, borne aloft, our sorrows fly
On swift-wing'd storms that sweep the sky.
Then let us anxious thoughts dismiss,
And pledge the cup to scenes of bliss;
For what avails heart-rending care,
Since mortal man is sorrow's heir.
How short his life's uncertain date!†
Unknown and dark his future state.
But when the brimming bowl I drain
I love to dance along the plain,

* Madame Dacier supposes this to be the passage on which was founded the opinion that the Graces were the daughters of Venus and Bacchus.

† The ancient poets all agree in enforcing the necessity of enjoying life, on account of its brevity and uncertainty. Martial says,

"I'll live to-morrow, none but fools will say:
To-morrow is too late—live then to day."

If this be true in the sense in which they meant it, how much

With sweet perfumes to bathe my hair
And frolic with the young and fair.
Let anxious idiots still despise
The joys which wiser men will prize.
Then, while the jovial cup goes round,
To Bacchus let the song resound.

ODE XLII.—ON HIMSELF.

A FRIEND to mirth and harmless sport,
I love the dance which Bacchus taught.
I dearly love to wake the lyre
When wine or love my lays inspire;
But dearer, sweeter joys I prove,
When with gay smiling maids I rove;
While hyacinths sweet odours breathe,
And round my brows their blossoms wreath,
My heart from envious thoughts is free,*
And even Envy still spares me:
From Slander's venom'd tongue I fly,
And shun the shafts of calumny.
Fierce quarrels o'er the festive board
My honest heart has e'er abhorr'd:
But, dancing to the lute's soft strain,
I love to join the blooming train.
Oh! let us banish barb'rous strife,
And lead a happy, peaceful life.†

ODE XLIII.—ON THE GRASSHOPPER.‡

HAPPY insect! all agree
None can be more bless'd than thee;

more forcibly will it apply to our own altered views and circum stances!

* Such sentiments as these do honour to the poet, and establish his claim to the title of "the wise Anacreon."

† Anacreon seems to have esteemed tranquillity the greatest blessing of life: thus, ode 39, "Peaceful pleasures are my theme.'

‡ This insect, though called a grasshopper, is certainly of a

Thou, for joy and pleasure born,
Sipp'st the honey'd dew of morn.
Happier than the sceptred king,
Mid the boughs we hear thee sing.
All the season's varied store,
All thy little eyes explore,
Fruits that tempt, and flowers that shine,
Happy insect! all are thine.
Injuring nothing, blamed by none,
Farmers love thee—pretty one!
All rejoice thy voice to hear
Singing blithe when summer's near.
Thee the tuneful Muses love,
Sweetly chirping in the grove;
Thee the great Apollo bless'd
With a voice above the rest.
Thou from wasting age art free,
Time has naught to do with thee.
Skilful creature, child of song,
Though to earth thou dost belong,*
Free from Nature's woes and pains,
Free from flesh, or blood-fill'd veins,†
Happy thing! thou seem'st to me
Almost a little god to be!

very different species of locust from that so common in our fields and meadows. Indeed, its habit of settling on trees is of itself a sufficient distinction. I am not aware that it has any proper English name, though by some writers it is called the cicada, or cicala.

* The ancient Athenians compared themselves to these insects, either on account of their skill in music, or because, like them, they were descended from the earth. They likewise wore golden ornaments in their hair, resembling grasshoppers. The Chinese ladies still wear fastened to their heads by springs small golden figures of a bird, the wings of which flutter with the slightest motion.

† Homer represents the gods as being free from blood; and, speaking of Venus being wounded, he says,

"From the clear vein a stream immortal flow'd,
Such stream as issues from a wounded god;

ODE XLIV.—THE DREAM.*

I DREAM'D, that over earth and sky,
Possess'd with wings, I seem'd to fly;
While Love pursued with swiftest pace,
And soon o'ertook me in the chase;
Though at his little feet were hung
Large leaden weights, that loosely swung.
"What can this vision mean?" I cried;
"It surely may be thus applied,—
That I, who once could freely rove
Through all the flowery paths of love,
Who laugh'd at lovers and their pains,
Am fetter'd now with stronger chains."

ODE XLV.—CUPID'S DARTS.

THE rugged mate of love's soft queen
Was at the Lemnian forges seen;†

Pure emanation! uncorrupted flood!
Unlike our gross, diseased, terrestrial blood.
(For not the bread of man their life sustains,
Nor wine's inflaming juice supplies their veins.)"
Pope's Homer, book v.

* Madame Dacier says that this is one of the finest and most gallant odes of antiquity, and if she for whom it was composed was as beautiful, all Greece could produce nothing more charming. Its meaning seems to be simply this: that passion suddenly conceived is generally transient and fleeting; but love founded on esteem and regulated by reason, though slow in its approaches, and imperceptible in its growth, makes an impression on the heart at once permanent and indelible.

† Lemnos was an island in the Ægean Sea, sacred to Vulcan, who, in the first book of the Iliad, gives an account of Jupiter's throwing him from heaven, and his fall on that island:—

"Once in your cause I felt his matchless might,
Hurl'd headlong downward from th' ethereal height;
Toss'd all the day in rapid circles round;
Nor till the sun descended touch'd the ground;

And while their fires intensely glow,
Was forging darts for Cupid's bow;
Sharp-pointed shafts of polish'd steel,
Which human hearts so keenly feel.
The gentle Venus, for her part,
In honey dipp'd each finish'd dart;
But cruel Cupid took them all,
And steep'd their barbed points in gall.
Returning from the battle rude,
The mighty Mars their business view'd;
And, leaning on his massy spear.*
"What use," he cried, with scornful sneer
"These puny darts—these trifling toys—
Mere playthings—only fit for boys?"
"Hold!" Cupid cries, "here's one—try this,
You'll find it not so much amiss;
'Tis strongly made; and, for its size,
Its weight will cause you much surprise."
The god received it. Venus tried
To check her laugh, and turn'd aside;
But Mars, with sudden grief possess'd,†
Cried, groaning from his inmost breast,
"This little shaft gives wondrous pain;
Here—take it—take it back again."
"Nay, Mars, I give it with good will;
Pray keep the pretty plaything still."

Breathless I fell, in giddy motion lost;
The Sinthians raised me on the Lemnian coast.'
Pope's Homer.

* The proportions of the spear and arrow are finely contrasted. The tiny weapon makes the deeper wound.

† This sentiment is extremely beautiful; intimating that one cannot even touch the darts of Cupid with safety. Moschus concludes his first idyllium with a similar thought:—

"Perhaps he'll say, 'Alas! no harm I know,
Here, take my darts, my arrows, and my bow.'
Ah! touch them not, fallacious is his aim,
His darts, his arrows, all are tipp'd with flame."
Fawkes.

ODE XLVI.—THE POWER OF GOLD.

A THOUSAND pains we lovers prove,*
Still what were life devoid of love?
But ah! what wo, when doom'd to mourn
The love that never meets return!
In vain we boast of noble birth,
And vain is wisdom, wit, or worth,
Since sordid wealth alone is sought,
And even love with gold is bought.
Oh may he sleep in endless night,
Who brought the shining plague to light;
Who first gave worth to useless ore,
And taught mankind to sigh for more!
Gold breaks through every sacred tie,
And bids a friend or brother die;
The fruitful source of kindred strife,†
Gold would not spare a parent's life.
Long wars and murders, crimes untold,
All spring from cursed thirst of gold;

* "Oh, love! what is it in this world of ours
Which makes it fatal to be loved? Ah! why
With cypress branches hast thou wreath'd thy bowers,
And made thy best interpreter a sigh?
As those who dote on odours pluck the flowers,
And place them on their breast—but place to die.
Thus the frail beings we would fondly cherish
Are laid within our bosoms but to perish."

Thus sings the bard; the magic of whose verse, in spite of reason, leads the fancy captive; the efforts of whose mighty genius will be regarded by future ages with sentiments of admiration, pleasure, and regret. For him the muses wove their brightest wreaths: why did he perversely mingle weeds, rank, poisonous weeds, with their sweet perennial flowers?

† The ancient poets are loud in their invectives against the "auri sacra fames." Ovid says,

"This is the golden age; all worship gold:
Honours are purchased, love and beauty sold.
Our iron age is grown an age of gold,
'Tis who bids most, for all men would be sold."

And I by sad experience know
'Tis gold that works the lover's wo!

ODE XLVII.—YOUNG OLD AGE.

I love the cheerful, blithesome sage,
Whose temper ne'er betrays his age.
I love the youth that dances well,
To music of the sounding shell.
But when an aged youth like me
Can join the dance with sportive glee,
Though age in hoary locks appears,
His heart is young, despite his years.

ODE XLVIII.—HAPPY LIFE.

Oh! for the harp, the harp of fire,
That godlike Homer strung:
But ah! on such a blood-stain'd lyre
Could love's soft notes be sung?

No! let the measured cups be brought,*
And from this scroll divine
I'll read the laws which Bacchus taught
To votaries of the wine.

Then warm in heart, but wisely gay,†
I'll join the sportive throng;

* The custom of appointing a master of the revels by the cast of a die has already been alluded to.—See ode xiv.

† I find but few commentators who have noticed the very singular expression of the original in this passage. It means literally, "preserving the mind;" and is intended to express that degree of pleasurable excitement which exhilarates the spirits without overpowering the senses; or, as Cowper says,

"Cups which cheer but not inebriate:"

though the remark is certainly applied to a beverage of a very different nature

With joy the merry harp I'll play,
  And thrill the jovial song.

ODE XLIX.—TO A PAINTER.

Dear artist, while I wake the string,
Paint thou the lovely scenes I sing:
First, let my fix'd, delighted eyes,
Behold a well-built city rise;
And with inventive skill portray
Its people happy, blithe, and gay.
Describe the Bacchanalian throng,
Engaged in festive dance and song;
Where, while the shrill-voiced pipe is mute,
Is heard the softly-breathing flute.
And if the crowded space permit,*
To make the blissful scene complete,
Let happy pairs be seen to rove,
Intent on life's best bus'ness—love.

ODE L.—ON BACCHUS.

See! the youthful god descends;
Bacchus, who the youth befriends,

* Allusion is here again made to the famous shield of Achilles, thus described by Homer:—

"Two cities radiant on the shield appear,
The image one of peace, and one of war;
Here sacred pomp and genial feast delight,
And solemn dance and hymeneal rite;
Along the streets the new-made brides are led,
With torches flaming, to the nuptial bed:
The youthful dancers in a circle bound
To the soft flute and cittern's silver sound;
Through the fair streets the matrons in a row
Stand in the porches, and enjoy the show."
Pope's Homer's Iliad.

Strings his nerves, strong toil to bear,
Courage gives to win the fair;
Graceful ease and skill bestows.
When the vigorous dancer glows.
In his hand behold he bears
An antidote for human cares;
Bless'd with which poor mortals gain
Pleasure's draught unmix'd with pain.
He preserves the future wine,
While the crimson clusters shine,
Ere the juice is taught to flow,
Sweet assuager of our wo.
Wine, the cure of every ill,*
Proves the best physician still;
All its happy patients find
Health of body, ease of mind.
Sound in mind—in body sound,
While the rolling year goes round,
Till the grapes again appear,
Med'cine for another year.

ODE LI.—ON A MEDAL REPRESENTING VENUS.

What matchless skill! what art divine
On this bright silver medal shine!
On every side; above, below,
The floods of ocean seem to flow;

* A similar passage occurs in the Odyssey, book iv., in which the princess Helen is introduced mixing this sovereign cordial:

"Meantime with genial joy to warm the soul,
Bright Helen mix'd a mirth-inspiring bowl;
Temper'd with drugs of sovereign use, t' assuage
The boiling bosom of tumultuous rage;
To clear the cloudy front of wrinkled care,
And dry the tearful sluices of despair.
Charm'd with that virtuous draught, th' exalted mind
All sense of wo delivers to the wind."

Fenton.

While softly gliding, calm and clear,
The undulating waves appear.
Some heav'n-taught genius, in its flight,
Has dared attempt the wondrous sight*
Of Venus, love's soft deity,
Emerging from the silver sea.
What bright and dazzling beauties rise
To charm the gazer's ravish'd eyes!
And those the jealous waves conceal,
Sure none but impious hands reveal.
She, like some sea-flower, fresh and gay,
Shines glittering on her watery way.
Where'er the lovely goddess swims,
Obsequious billows kiss her limbs;
Now rise above, now sink below
Her rose-bud breasts and neck of snow.
As virgin lilies brighter show
Amid the dark-leaved violet's glow,
So through the dark-blue wave is seen
The beauteous form of love's dear queen.
See, gayly sporting at her side,
Young laughing Loves on dolphins ride,
And o'er the silvery surface glide.
The crooked natives of the deep,
With wanton curve and bounding leap,
Attend the goddess in her train,
Where'er she smiling skims the main.

* Many a poet has dared attempt the description. Ticke., in his "Prospect of Peace," has the following lines :—

"As when sweet Venus, so the fable sings,
Awaked by Nereids, from the ocean springs;
With smiles she sees the threat'ning billows rise,
Spreads smooth the surge, and clears the low'ring skies:
Light o'er the deep, with fluttering Cupids crown'd,
The pearly conch and silver turtles bound;
Her tresses shed ambrosial odours round."

ODE LII.—ON THE VINTAGE.

Now ripen'd by the genial sun,
The grapes are glean'd; the sports begun
See youths and smiling virgins bear*
The purple produce of the year;
In vats the luscious burden lies,
And home the modest maiden hies:
For joyous youths alone remain,
With blood-red juice their limbs to stain,†
To crush the cluster's bloomy pride,
And revel in the crimson tide.
Then loud they raise the vintage hymn,
When foaming o'er the vessel's brim
They view the joy-inspiring juice,
Which Bacchus sends them for their use.
Should hoary age inhale the draught,
His youth renew'd, at least in thought,
His tott'ring, trembling limbs advance,
And try the long-forgotten dance.
But when the youth its influence feels,
When wine prevails, and reason reels;
When wandering through the lonely grove
His heart beats high with hopes of love;
If there, beneath the secret shade,
He chance to spy some lovely maid,
Who, press'd by sleep's invading pow'r,

* "Fair maids and blooming youths, that smiling bear
The purple product of th' autumnal year."
Pope.

† We are informed by travellers that the ancient custom of treading the grapes is still practised in many of the wine countries. Matthews, in his "Diary of an Invalid," has given us a full description of this disgusting process, which he witnessed in Portugal. After the juice is crushed out it is put into vats to ferment itself fine, during which process all impurities are carefully removed. It may however be proper to mention, that of late years wine-presses have come into more general use

Lies slumb'ring mid the leafy bower,
Herself the fairest, frailest flower,—
Before the startled maid can rouse
He breathes his hasty, burning vows,
And while his breast with Bacchus glows,
His lawless love he dares propose.
In vain the angry fair denies,
He better reads her telltale eyes ;
And sure of victory ere 'tis won,
His eager suit he urges on;
And when his soft persuasion fails,
Rude, boisterous Bacchus oft prevails.
And thus the wanton god decoys
The youth to wild intemperate joys.

ODE LIII.—ON THE ROSE.*

Thou, my friend, shalt sweep the string,
I, in softest strains will sing,
While its fragrance round us flows,
The queen of flowers—the lovely rose.
Its perfumed breath ascends the skies
On every gentle gale that sighs:
Its sweets descend to earth again
Alike beloved by gods and men.
When Spring awakes the slumbering flowers,
And music breathes amid the bowers,
Thee, darling gem, the Graces wear
Intwined amid their flowing hair;
And rosy wreaths alone may dress
The queen of love and loveliness.
In every song and fable known†
The Muses claim thee as their own.

* This ode will be understood by supposing that Anacreon, while celebrating a rose, requests a lyrist to accompany his voice.

† The editor of an ingenious little edition of this author observes: "Did Anacreon anticipate the beautiful fable of the

Thou bidd'st thy blooming sweetness blow
In thorny paths of pain and wo.
But, oh! what joy, when bless'd we rove
Through rosy bowers, and dream of love;
While bliss on every breeze is borne,
To pluck the rose without the thorn;
With gentlest touch its leaves to press,
And raise it to our soft caress!
Oh! thou art still the poet's theme,
And thee a welcome guest we deem,
To grace our feasts and deck our hair,
When Bacchus bids us banish care.
E'en Nature does thy beauties prize,
She steals thy teints to paint the skies;
For rosy-finger'd is the morn
With which the crimson veil is drawn
The lovely nymphs we always deck
With rosy arms and rosy neck,

rose 'Sultana of the Nightingale,' so justly a favourite with later eastern poets?

"All the country is now full of nightingales, whose amours with roses is an Arabian fable, as well known here as any part of Ovid among us."—*Lady Montague's Letters.*

"For well may maids of Helle deem
That this can be no earthly flower,
Which mocks the tempest's withering hour,
And buds unshelter'd by a bower;
Nor droops, though Spring refuse her shower
Nor woos the summer beam:
To it the livelong night there sings
A bird unseen, but not remote:
Invisible his airy wings,
But soft as harp that Houri strings
His long, entrancing note!
It were the bulbul; but his throat,
Though mournful, pours not such a strain:
For they who listen cannot leave
The spot, but linger there and grieve
As if they loved in vain!"—*Bride of Abydos*

The reader will, I trust, pardon the length of this extract, on account of its enchanting beauty.

And roseate teints are ever seen
To bloom the cheeks of beauty's queen.
Its power to sooth the pangs of pain*
Physicians try, nor try in vain;
And e'en when life and hope are fled
Its deathless scent embalms the dead:
For, though its withering charms decay,
And, one by one, all fade away,
Its grateful smell the rose retains,
And redolent of youth remains.†
But, lyrist, let it next be sung
From whence this precious treasure sprung—
When first from ocean's dewy spray
Fair Venus rose to upper day;
When, fearful to the powers above,
The armed Pallas sprung from Jove;
'Twas then they say the jealous earth
First gave the lovely stranger birth.
A drop of pure nectareous dew
From heaven the bless'd immortals threw;
A while it trembled on the thorn,
And then the lovely rose was born.
To Bacchus they the flower assign,
And roses still his brows intwine.

ODE LIV.—ON HIMSELF.

While I view the youthful throng
Fancy whispers I am young!
To the merry dance I fly,
Who so gay, so brisk as I?
Haste, Cybele, bring me flowers,
Bring sweet roses from the bowers;

* In Anacreon's time roses were frequently used medicinally.

† "And redolent of joy and youth
To breathe a second spring."
Gray's Ode to Eton College.

Quick a graceful garland twine,
Youthful vigour still is mine.
Hateful, hoary age, away!
Let me sport with striplings gay;
Bring the bright autumnal bowl—
Age can ne'er subdue the soul.
Still I raise the cheerful strain,
Still the brimming bowl I drain;
Still with native humour gay,
Sport the happy hours away!

ODE LV.—THE LOVER'S MARK.

The courser bears a brand of fire,
To mark his owner, or his sire;
The turban, twisted round his brows,*
The fiery foreign Parthian shows;
And I by instinct sure can tell
The lover's mark—I know it well:
For love in vain concealment tries,
The soul peeps through the telltale eyes.†

* The tiara worn by the ancient Parthians resembled the modern turban. Addison has translated from Dionysius the following description of the situation and manners of this ancient people:—

"Beyond the Caspian straits those realms extend,
Where circling bows the martial Parthians bend.
Versed only in the rougher arts of war,
No fields they wound, nor urge the shining share;
No ships they boast to stem the rolling tide,
Nor lowing herds o'er flow'ry meadows guide:
But infants wing the feather'd shaft for flight,
And rein the fiery steed with fond delight.
On every plain the whistling spear alarms,
The neighing courser, and the clang of arms;
For there no food the little heroes taste
Till warlike sweat has earn'd the short repast."

† The eyes, the windows of the soul, are notorious telltales of what is passing within.

ODE LVI.—ON HIS OLD AGE.*

Alas! my youth, my joys have fled,
The snows of age have bleach'd my head.
Tedious, toothless, trembling age,
Must now alone my thoughts engage!
Adieu, ye joys which once I knew—
To life, to love, to all, adieu!
Henceforth, unhappy! doom'd to know
Tormenting fears of future wo!
Oh! how my soul with horror shrinks†
Whene'er my startled fancy thinks
Of Pluto's dark and dreary cave,
The chill, the cheerless, gaping grave!
When death's cold hand has closed these eyes
And stifled life's last struggling sighs,
In darkness and in dust must I,
Alas! for ever—ever lie!

ODE LVII.—THAT MODERATION ENHANCES ENJOYMENT.

Haste! haste thee, boy, and bring the bowl,
To quench this fever of the soul;
The copious stream with skill combine,
Add ten parts water, five of wine;‡

* It is supposed by many that the five following odes were not written by Anacreon; but, as Barnes admits them into his edition, and they are given in most other translations, it was thought proper to insert them here.

† Let the reader contrast this exclamation of the despairing heathen philosopher, with the exulting language of "Paul the aged"—when ready to be offered, and the time of his departure at hand.

‡ Hesiod, with all the minuteness of "narrative old age," gives many directions to be observed in the summer season. Among the rest, in book ii., he thus advises us:—

"With Byblian wine the rural feast be crown'd,
Three parts of water, let the bowl go round."—*Cooke.*

The cooling draught will thirst assuage,
Nor in the breast too fiercely rage.
Oh cease, my friends, for shame, give o'er
These clamorous shouts, this deaf'ning roar:
This Scythian scene all peace destroys ;*
Turns joy to madness, mirth to noise.
Let cheerful temperance rule the soul,
The best ingredient in the bowl.

ODE LVIII.—LOVE IN THE HEART.†

As once, amid the rosy bowers,
I wove a crown of fairest flowers,
Love, little urchin, lurking sly
Beneath the leaves I chanced to spy ;
Around his wings the wreath I twine,
And plunge him in a cup of wine :
Then love, in each delicious draught,
I from the foaming goblet quaff'd.
Oh! still he moves his fluttering wings,
Still to my heart strange transport brings

ODE LIX.—ON HIMSELF.‡

Methought, in sleep's delightful trance,
I saw Anacreon advance ;

* The Scythians were particularly remarkable for their intemperance in drinking, and for quarrelling in their cups.

† This ode is by some ascribed to Julian, a king of Egypt, who wrote several other elegant little pieces. Being supposed to possess much beauty, it is given in most translations of Anacreon, and is consequently inserted here.

‡ In the Vatican copy this is placed as the first of Anacreon's odes. By many it is thought that he was not the author, because he himself is the subject of it. Barnes endeavours to prove that he was, by a reference to the ninth ode, in which Anacreon makes mention of himself, and to similar instances of poets introducing their names in their works.

The tuneful Teian, skill'd to sing
The lays of love on warbling string.
I hasten'd to his kind embrace,
And kiss'd his sweetly smiling face.
Though somewhat old, he seemed to wage
Successful war with spiteful age:
For love still beam'd in each bright eye,
And from his lips there seem'd to fly
Sweet gales of rich and rosy wine,
Which shed a fragrance quite divine.
His slow and staggering steps were stay'd
By laughing Cupid's kindly aid.
The garland that intwined his hair
The bard unbound and bade me wear.
Anacreon's burning soul it breathed,
And I with it my brows enwreathed.
E'er since my heart is doom'd to prove
The pleasing pains of lasting love.

ODE LX.—ON THE SPRING.

How sweet through sunny meads to stray,
With Flora's rich profusion gay,
While Zephyr breathes its softest sighs,
And mingled perfumes round us rise!
How sweet beneath the secret shade,
By the vine's broad foliage made,*
With some loved fair to pass the day,
And talk th' unheeded hours away!

* "The country from hence to Adrianople is the finest in the world. Vines grow wild on all the hills, and the perpetual spring they enjoy makes everything gay and flourishing."—*Lady Montague's Letters.*

THE END.

www.ingramcontent.com/pod-product-compliance
Lightning Source LLC
LaVergne TN
LVHW020219110826
845151LV00003B/758